Dear _____,

Thank you for being such a very
good friend to me and my
family for a long, long time.

Carol O'Connell

A BUSINESS IN RISK

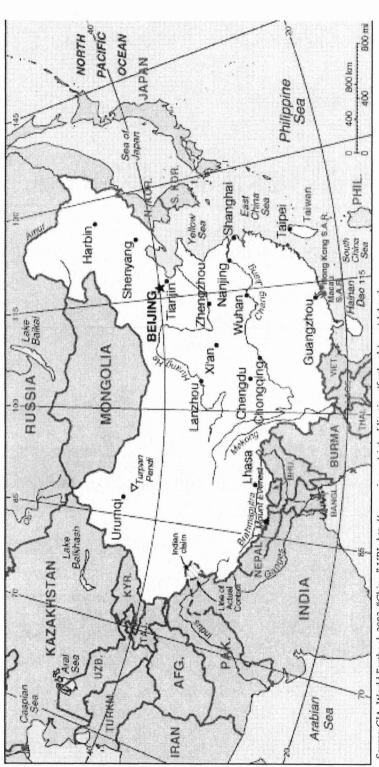

Source: CIA. World Factbook 2003. "China." URL: http//www.cia.gov/cia/publications/factbook/geos/ch.html

A BUSINESS IN RISK

JARDINE MATHESON AND THE HONG KONG TRADING INDUSTRY

Carol Matheson Connell

PRAEGER

Westport, Connecticut
London

Library of Congress Cataloging-in-Publication Data

Connell, Carol Matheson, 1948–
    A business in risk : Jardine Matheson and the Hong Kong trading industry / Carol
    Matheson Connell.
        p.   cm.
    Includes bibliographical references and index.
    ISBN 0–275–98035–9 (alk. paper)
    1. Jardine, Matheson & Co.—History.   2. Corporations, British—China—Hong
Kong—History   3. Trading companies—China—Hong Kong—History.   4. Consolidation
and merger of corporations—China—Hong Kong—History.   5. Hong Kong
(China)—Commerce—History.   6.   Risk management—China—Hong Kong.   7.
Globalization—Economic aspects—China—Hong Kong.   8. Competition, International.   I.
Title.
HF486.J372C66   2004
382′.095125—dc22   2003057978

British Library Cataloguing in Publication Data is available.

Library of Congress Catalog Card Number: 2003057978
ISBN: 0–275–98035–9

First published in 2004

Praeger Publishers, 88 Post Road West, Westport, CT 06881
An imprint of Greenwood Publishing Group, Inc.
www.praeger.com

Printed in the United States of America

The paper used in this book complies with the
Permanent Paper Standard issued by the National
Information Standards Organization (Z39.48–1984).

10 9 8 7 6 5 4 3 2 1

To Marion Frances and David Matheson Connell
whose passion for solutions inspired this work

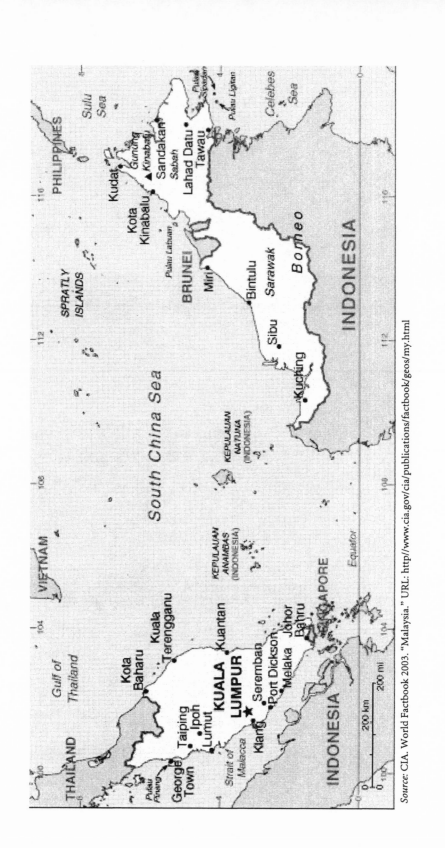

Source: CIA. World Factbook 2003. "Malaysia." URL: http//www.cia.gov/cia/publications/factbook/geos/my.html

CONTENTS

INTRODUCTION:
THE HONG KONG TRADING INDUSTRY
IN ECONOMIC HISTORY

Demand volatility, government policy shifts, shocks—unpredictable elements in the life of any business—are familiar to the Hong Kong trading companies. They have learned to survive, even excel, in the face of uncertainty. Some, like Jardine Matheson & Company, Hutchison Whampoa, Wheelock, and Swire Pacific, are descendants of the old agency houses and share the opprobrium of a colonial—or, worse, an opium—past.

Emerging in Hong Kong and on the mainland, new business enterprises or new configurations led by Chinese businessmen—like Cheung Kong's Li Kashing—are challenging the old houses for investor dollars because they afford leading-edge development prospects without the corporate center, asset baggage, and history. This chapter introduces the Hong Kong trading industry and its major participants. It explains the choice of Jardine Matheson as the touchstone firm in this study. The chapter includes an exploration of the significant themes that emerged in the course of this study and concludes with an investigation of the major theorists and their theories.

THE HONG KONG TRADING INDUSTRY AS A STUDY SUBJECT

The Hong Kong trading company is an example of success, survival, and transformation in a highly uncertain social and political environment. Any search for characteristics and practices responsible for their sustainability must include collaboration, capabilities, learning, and interdependent multifirm networks that protect the core business and diffuse risk. Because their business lines, customers, or markets have evolved in different directions depending on their capabilities, the Hong Kong trading companies infrequently compete with each other brand against brand; they compete more often for investment capital, coalition participation, and influence in the region.

Six of today's largest Hong Kong-headquartered trading companies are diversified conglomerates, with trading and distribution only a fraction of their business. These six contribute significantly to the gross domestic product (GDP) of Hong Kong, currently estimated at US $180 billion. Swire Pacific is considered a property company, with 75% of its earnings coming from local property holdings, but with other interests including airline services, aircraft engineering, hotels, industries, trading, marine services, and insurance. Swire's industrial operations include bottling facilities and a contract for Coca-Cola production in China. First Pacific is a banking company and is much more geographically diversified, with 46% of sales coming from Europe and the Middle East. Founded in 1981 as a small consumer savings bank, First Pacific has expanded rapidly through organic growth and acquisitions and has evolved into a conglomerate with four major core business activities: marketing and distribution, telecommunications, property, and banking. Telecommunications, marketing, and distribution represent 94% of First Pacific's revenues. Hutchison Whampoa is a conglomerate within a still larger conglomerate, the Cheung Kong Group. Its areas of business include (1) property development and real estate brokerage, (2) container terminals and shipping-related services; (3) telecommunications; (4) retail manufacturing; (5) power; and (6) media. Nearly 70% of its revenues come from Hong Kong and China, and 54% from ports and terminals. The China International Trust & Investment Corporation (CITIC) Pacific has major business interests that include motors, trading, and China Industrial & Power and growing sectors like rentals, property sales, tunnels, and China Water Plant. Its associated companies include Cathay Pacific, Dragonair, Hong Kong Telecom, CTM Power Plant, Manhattan Card, Envirospace, SE NT Land Fill, Discovery Bay Property, Eastern Harbour Tunnel, and others. A full 88% of its revenues are generated in Hong Kong and China. The revenue spread is 50% motors, and 35% retailing and distribution. Wheelock has five core business areas: property, telecommunications, container terminals, investment banking, and trading and services. Approximately 75% of Wheelock's profits are derived from its property holdings. Jardine Matheson & Company is the oldest of the firms and the focus of this study. Its current business lines include retail and distribution (Jardine Pacific, Dairy Farm, Jardine International Motors, Cycle & Carriage); Financial Services (Jardine Fleming, Jardine Insurance Brokers); Property (Hong Kong Land); and Hotels (Mandarin Oriental chain). Hong Kong and China account for 61% of Jardine's earnings. Jardine's income is derived from retailing and distribution, 40%; property, 30%; and finance, 19%.

Outside Hong Kong, additional members of the extended Hong Kong trading industry include the UK-headquartered Inchcape and the Japanese general trading companies. Inchcape began as a shipping and export company during the golden age of the British Empire. Inchcape is a global company focusing on automotive distribution, retail, and financing operations. Operating mainly in Greece, Belgium, Australia, Hong Kong, and Singapore as well as the UK, the group distributes Toyota, Subaru, Ferrari, Jaguar, and Land Rover vehicles. The firm also owns Autobytel UK, which sells cars online in the UK under license from the U.S.-based Autobytel. Inchcape has sold its nonauto businesses, and it is now moving away from new auto sales to focus more on automotive services, including fleet management and leasing. Mitsubishi, Mitsui, and others. are Japanese general trading companies, members of *keiretsu*, a network of Japanese companies organized around a major bank and associated with a range of businesses that include finance, insurance, shipping, distribution, and marketing as well as trading.

While a few of these companies were among the original members of the strategic group of Hong Kong trading companies—notably Jardine Matheson and Swire Pacific—this study of the Hong Kong trading industry reveals how significantly the industry has changed, how the prevailing business models have changed, and how much "turnover" there has been among the major participants. This study also identifies the characteristics of the market that have remained the same and to which the distinctive capabilities of the trading companies have remained valuable. Figure 1.1 depicts the progressive change from trade to investment.

At the outset of the story, the largest trading company was Palmer & Company, but the firm went bankrupt in a currency crisis in 1830. Another early competitor of Jardine Matheson & Company, Dent & Company, was bankrupted in another currency crisis in 1867. An important aspect of trading was the provision of insurance and trading credits to firms with low working capital. While the practice was

Figure 1.1

Changes in Major Trading Company Participants 1870–2002, Top Five Ranked by Group Capital Available for Investment

1870	1919	1939	1960	1977	1996	2002
E.D. Sassoon& Co.	Dodwell & Co.	Harrisons & Crosfield	Dodwell &Co.	Jardine Matheson & Co.	CITIC	Swire Pacific
Butterfield & Swire	Wilson & Co.	Booker McConnell	Guthrie & Co.	Sime Darby	Jardine Matheson & Co.	Jardine Matheson & Co.
Finlay & Co.	Borneo Co.	Finlay & Co.	Harrisons & Crosfield	Finlay & Co.	Swire Pacific	Hutchison Whampoa
Jardine Matheson & Co.	Finlay & Co.	Swire & Co.	Jardine Matheson & Co.	Inchcape	First Pacific	CITIC
	Swire & Co.			Harrisons & Crosfield	Harrisons & Crosfield	

novel and important to bringing would-be buyers and sellers into interaction, it was risky and required superior foreign exchange and financial management. Speculating in commodities or currencies was a frequent root cause of business failure.

An early survivor was Jardine Matheson & Company. The firm was formally constituted in 1832 but had evolved from an unbroken line of partnerships and was the inheritor of extensive trading relationships. Another survivor was Finlay & Company, founded in Bombay in 1862. Like Jardine Matheson & Company, Finlay was focused on trading, shipping, banking, and insurance—the core cluster of "agency services"—and cotton textiles (again, emulating Jardine Matheson and other trading houses plying Lancashire cottons to balance the trade). Finlay focused on the development and management of tea estates, supplying the increasing demand for tea in Britain with Assam, Darjeeling, and other Indian alternatives to counter the Chinese monopoly. Another member of this early group of trading companies was Butterfield & Swire, founded in Shanghai in 1867 and, like Jardine Matheson and Finlay, engaged in trading, shipping, and banking. Seeing head-to-head competition for shipping lanes, Butterfield & Swire founder John Swire established the Shipping Conferences, which regulated shipping lanes and required the pooling of shipping profits. A fourth company, E. D. Sassoon, was founded in Bombay in 1867 and, like Jardine Matheson, Finlay, and Butterfield & Swire, was engaged in core "agency services," with a significant difference. Sassoon offered production credits to growers—first to opium growers, then to Indian cotton textile producers. Indian suppliers gravitated toward Sassoon, permitting a firm that had gotten a relatively late start in the markets for opium and cotton to soon lead them, hence, the comparative strength of Sassoon's group capital in Figure 1.1

By 1895, leading firms reflected the increasingly global economy. Wilson, Sons & Company was founded in Bahia, Brazil in 1837, and established a London head office in 1845. The firm concentrated on coal importing and related shipping services, supplying coal to shipping companies. After losses in the 1880s from its diversification into railroads and dockyards, Wilson returned to coal imports and shipping services, including stevedoring, lighterage, towage, ship repair, and related engineering. The firm's decision to concentrate on coal imports led to the development of the River Platte and to the emergence of Argentina as the firm's major market. Wilson merged with Ocean Coal in 1908.

The Niger Company originated in 1879, at the height of the race to establish first-mover advantage in Africa. The Niger Company focused on exports and imports, buying local produce from peasant cultivators—palm oil, tin, hide, groundnuts, rubber, ivory—and importing whatever the market wanted. The advent of steamships and growth of the petroleum industry changed the competitive landscape and encouraged the African trading companies to work together as a consortium of trading firms, first as the African Association, later as the Niger Pool, a contractual profit pooling scheme similar to Butterfield & Swire's Shipping Conferences.

The Borneo Company was founded in 1856 in Singapore by a group of Glasgow merchants and expanded rapidly in Southeast Asia, focusing on jute and sugar mills. The Borneo Company enjoyed an exclusive contract in Sarawak, Borneo, and was one of the first firms to trade in Thailand, opening a representative office there in 1856. The firm was an early adopter of a new organizational model for sharing business risk, the public liability company. By 1895 Swire had terminated its partnership with Butterfield and taken total control of Butterfield & Swire, expanding the Far East business to include a variety of shipping interests, sugar refining, dockyards, and petroleum interests. Swires became a public limited company in 1914.

In 1919, Wilson, Swire, Borneo, and Finlay were still leading the industry, but a new firm had joined them, Dodwell & Company, a trading and shipping agency founded in Shanghai in 1858 and growing to prominence in 1887, when the firm secured the agency for chartering and managing ships on behalf of the Canadian Pacific Railway between Hong Kong and Vancouver, Canada. In 1912, Dodwell developed as a trading firm with branches in China; Japan; Sri Lanka; Vancouver; Tacoma and Seattle, Washington; and New York. By 1919, Dodwell could claim to be the largest shipping firm on the Pacific Coast. The firm was a large exporter of China and Japanese teas, which they sold to Britain, the United States, and Russia. When demand began to shift to Indian teas, Dodwell opened a branch in Sri Lanka to purchase and sell Ceylon teas and later coconuts. The Vancouver branch invested in salmon canneries. The Tacoma and Seattle branches of Dodwell in the United States were focused on developing flour-milling interests.

A pattern was emerging—a pattern of trading activity followed by diversified investment, often the result of exclusivity contracts or first-mover advantage, leading to capital growth and further investment. The pattern, with changes in leading participants, played out fairly consistently until the 1970s, when extensive horizontal investments in manufacturing and natural resources led some of the trading companies into high debt or bankruptcy and others into a new role as consolidator or vertical integrator of whole trading company acquisitions. For example, Inchcape, at one time an amalgamation of shipping and trading companies focused on India, became a public limited company in 1958 and by 1977 had absorbed previous trading company leaders Borneo Company, Dodwell and Anglo-Thai, as well as Gibb Livingston, Gilman and Binny & Company. John Swire & Sons had acquired Finlay. Sime Darby and Guthrie & Company were acquired by local Malaysian interests, in a government effort to bring the country's tin and rubber industries under local control.

By 1996, further consolidation, the emergence of financial conglomerates and Chinese-led multinationals, again changed the character of the trading industry. For the first time appear the Beijing-owned CITIC group and Hutchison Whampoa, led by the Harvard-educated Li Kashing. First Pacific, a multinational banking group with trade and industrial investments, also joined the group of leaders in 1996.

All of the companies in the industry today succeed in their chosen product/services niche because of the ability to finance, insure, distribute, and market. The accelerated globalization of economic activities that began in the late 1950s and continued into the 1990s made it impossible for firms like these to rely only on their own resources to survive the tyranny of global competition, reinvent themselves, and grow. They were forced to pull together other firms, both competitors and collaborators, to help ride out unpredictable storms in the global economy, share knowledge, and reduce business risk. This "pulling together" has taken several forms, including vertical integration, external corporate networks based on both equity and nonequity arrangements, and virtual trading networks based on access to lowest-cost sources anywhere in the world.

The diversification of the Hong Kong trading companies in the mid-1970s into broadly horizontal and vertical business interests, which leveraged the company's existing capabilities in finance, insurance, trading and shipping, marketing, and distribution, was a special case of merger and acquisition behavior, very similar to the Japanese general trading company or *sogo shosha*, in which internal and external corporate networks represent different stages of the same production chain as well as different production chains altogether that share some key linkages.

Not at all a new phenomenon for the Hong Kong trading companies, the concept of intra- and interfirm networks to reduce risk began as early as the 19th century with the Canton Insurance company, headed in alternate years by Jardine Matheson and by Dent & Company, which set insurance rates for shippers; the Shipping Conferences, established by John Samuel Swire, to which Butterfield & Swire and Jardine Matheson (among others) were parties, which established guaranteed routes and rates for shippers; and the British and Chinese Corporation, headed by Jardine Matheson and Butterfield & Swire to raise and manage Chinese railroad funds. Relationships and network building are embedded in the social and economic relations of Association of Southeast Asian Nations (ASEAN) firms, where culture, cooperation, and trust are essential to business operations under uncertainty. In fact, the quality and distinctiveness of these intrafirm and interfirm contracts and relationships create competitive advantage for the firm within its market.

JARDINE MATHESON & COMPANY AS THE TOUCHSTONE OF THIS STUDY

From 1832 and for 100 years, Jardine Matheson's business was risk-broking for buyers and sellers of goods from/to Europe and Asia—and based entirely on commissions. The firm extracted commissions—as much as 45 cents on every dollar—for services that included sales, returns, cost and freight, guarantees of bills, ship's disbursement, insurance, arranging insurance, chartering ships, receiving inbound freight, obtaining outbound freight, settling insurance losses, negotiating bills of exchange, arbitration of debts, debt settlement, managing estates, executors of estates, and transshipping goods. Jardine Matheson could charge a commission on 16 separate "agency" services because the business was very risky and the participants in the business—not knowledgeable enough themselves and lacking the clout of a big operator like Jardine Matheson—preferred to have that risk managed by a firm with market knowledge, reputation, influence, and strong financial management skills.

The early Jardine Matheson & Company was the direct descendant of the first private trading company with a history and experience in the Far East that spanned 200 years. Figure 1.2 depicts the evolution of Jardine Matheson & Company from the first private trading company. The firm was the inheritor of administrative routines and a network of trading relationships that grew out of the very special business, social, and political environment in China during the early 19th century. The opportunity—as well as the uncertainty—of the China trade made profitable a

Figure 1.2
Evolution of Jardine Matheson & Company

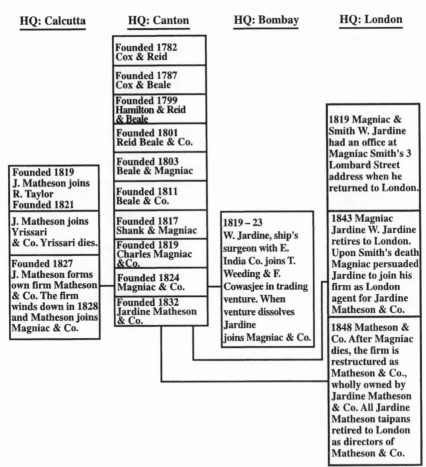

HQ: Calcutta	HQ: Canton	HQ: Bombay	HQ: London
	Founded 1782 Cox & Reid		
	Founded 1787 Cox & Beale		
	Founded 1799 Hamilton & Reid & Beale		
	Founded 1801 Reid Beale & Co.		1819 Magniac & Smith W. Jardine had an office at Magniac Smith's 3 Lombard Street address when he returned to London.
	Founded 1803 Beale & Magniac		
Founded 1819 J. Matheson joins R. Taylor Founded 1821	Founded 1811 Beale & Co.		
J. Matheson joins Yrissari & Co. Yrissari dies.	Founded 1817 Shank & Magniac	1819 – 23 W. Jardine, ship's surgeon with E. India Co. joins T. Weeding & F. Cowasjee in trading venture. When venture dissolves Jardine joins Magniac & Co.	1843 Magniac Jardine W. Jardine retires to London. Upon Smith's death Magniac persuaded Jardine to join his firm as London agent for Jardine Matheson & Co.
	Founded 1819 Charles Magniac &Co.		
Founded 1827 J. Matheson forms own firm Matheson & Co. The firm winds down in 1828 and Matheson joins Magniac & Co.	Founded 1824 Magniac & Co.		
	Founded 1832 Jardine Matheson & Co.		1848 Matheson & Co. After Magniac dies, the firm is restructured as Matheson & Co., wholly owned by Jardine Matheson & Co. All Jardine Matheson taipans retired to London as directors of Matheson & Co.

range of services to businesses and individuals that protected their investments and shipments, while Jardine Matheson & Company absorbed the risk. The firm was in a position to do this so long as it did not invest in the commodities in which it traded or which it insured. Fundamental to Jardine Matheson's success and the reputation it built for financial probity was the fundamental strategic decision to eschew speculation and to concentrate on building a pattern of relationships within and outside the business that would foster the flow of information, the knowledge with which to interpret it, the ability to influence others, and the reputation to attract and retain trading partners.

The decisions made by the early firm frame the resource and services choices made by Jardine Matheson & Company after World War II, the near destruction of the firm and its assets, and the imprisonment or exile of many of the firm's managers. There was little left after the war beyond the ambition of the Keswicks—the descendents of William Jardine, a cofounder of the trading company—to rebuild in an uncertain environment they believed they knew far better than the Europeans and Americans who saw advantage in marketing their products in China. The pace of growth, the sometimes-speculative decision making, made some degree of failure inevitable. Just as inevitable, given the firm's inexperience with strategic failure, was a trial-and-error approach to climbing out of failure. Part of the firm's escalating fear of failure was the level of debt financing incurred to fund growth.

Today, Jardine Matheson is a multinational company with a range of activities encompassing financial services, supermarkets, consumer marketing, engineering and construction, motor trading, property, and hotels. Jardine's insurance, motors, supermarket, and hotel businesses are market leaders across Asia.

MAJOR THEMES

This study of the Hong Kong trading industry shows how capabilities, organization, relationships, and innovation were developed and consciously used to sustain the enterprise, generate high performance, and compete successfully whatever the environment and nature of the industry. Several themes emerge:

The First Period of Globalization

- The Hong Kong trading companies and their investment houses were responsible for the growth of a truly global economy in what is often described as the "first period of globalization." The free flow of capital, talent, and goods was essential to this model.

- The Hong Kong trading companies made up for lackluster economies by providing credit terms and insurance to encourage would-be participants to enter the global economy at low cost.

- Unlike government intervention in the interwar period, this private sector support stimulated production, consumption, investment, and innovation.

The Retreat of Globalization in the Interwar Period

• Government intervention and market restrictions in the interwar period elevated business risk. The Hong Kong trading companies curtailed product/market expansion and concentrated on their local investments during this period.

Investment Intensity and Industry Clusters around Entrepôt Centers

• After World War II, when trade restrictions were removed, the Hong Kong trading companies were important financiers of the growth of Hong Kong, Singapore, and Australia as entrepôt centers, especially the growth of financial services, transportation, electronics, and business services sectors.

The Value of Outsourcing

• While there was a period after the opening of China in 1971 when corporations around the world felt little need for the intermediary services of the Hong Kong trading companies, pursuit of supply chain efficiencies from the late 1980s onward made the use of local trade and logistics outsource companies more cost-effective than internalization.

• The Hong Kong trading company's strategy of sharing business risk with their customers has become a model for consultants/outsourcers in all industries. There is much to be learned from the Hong Kong trading company about the way this worked.

The External Organization as a Substitute for Markets and Hierarchies

• The Hong Kong trading company's network of relationships with associated firms, like that of the Japanese *sogo shosha*, provides another learning example for managing risk and achieving supply chain coverage at low cost and with higher returns and greater reliability than might be available via market transactions. The advantages of an "external organization" with dispersed and redundant resources might prove even more compelling to companies coping with today's uncertain world. The network was often built through minority investments in smaller firms at various stages of the value chain.

THEORY AND THEORISTS

The current study draws heavily on the work of Edith Penrose, including her 1959 Theory of the Growth of the Firm and 1960 case study of the Hercules Powder Company.[1] In the early Jardine Matheson & Company, with its external network of suppliers, buyers, agents, ship's captains, British and Chinese government emissaries, competitors, and partners, one finds the creative and dynamic interaction between the firm's unused productive resources and its perceived market opportunities that governs the growth and the direction of the growth of the Penrosean firm.

Penrose's firm with a view to expansion is both an administrative organization and a pool of productive resources including its own previously acquired or inherited resources and those it must obtain from the market in order to carry out its expansion program. In the case of the early Jardine Matheson & Company, the firm had inherited a relationship with the largest supplier of Indian opium, Jamsetjee Jeejeebhoy from the firm's previous incarnation as the partnership of Magniac & Jardine, and a group of some 50 agents in Bombay, Madras, and Calcutta. When Magniac & Jardine brought the young James Matheson into the firm as partner, the firm inherited a European and South American client list from Matheson's earlier partnerships. Just as important to the firm's growth plans as inherited managerial resources were the growing contact list and information sources of James Matheson's biweekly publication, the *Canton Register*, which he began in 1827 and continued to produce through 1843. The first English-language newspaper in China, the *Canton Register* provided complete information on commodity prices and expected deliveries, as well as information from its broad trading network on social and political events in the Americas, Europe and Asia.

This study of the evolution of a Hong Kong trading firm demonstrates a close relationship between the various kinds of resources with which the firm worked and the development of the ideas, experience, and knowledge of its founders. Over time, the changing experience and knowledge of James Matheson, William Jardine, and their successors affected not only the productive services available from banking and financial services, marine insurance, and shipping but also the "demand" that the firm considered relevant for its activities, leading the firm into capital and risk management, reinsurance, and shipping services in the Pacific and investment broking in London.

The story of Jardine Matheson's growth from Hong Kong trading company to Asian multinational supports a Penrosean view in which expansion must draw the productive services, including entrepreneurial services, of the firm's existing management. Consequently, the services available from such management set a fundamental limit to the amount of expansion that can be either planned or executed even if all other resources are obtainable in the market. This is as true for growth by acquisition as for internal growth, although growth by acquisition is faster and often facilitates diversification.[2] Essential to Penrose's theory of the growth of the firm is the view that at all times there exist within every firm pools of unused productive services and that these, together with the changing knowledge of management, create a productive opportunity that is unique for each firm. Unused productive services are, for the enterprising firm, at the same time a challenge to innovate, an incentive to expand, and a source of competitive advantage. In a sense, the final products being produced by a firm at any given time merely represent one of several ways in which the firm could be using its resources.[3]

Not only is the actual expansion of a firm related to its resources, experience, and knowledge, but a firm's productive opportunity is shaped and limited by its ability to use what it already has and the kinds of opportunities it investigates when it considers expansion. Once a firm has made its choice and has embarked on an expansion program, its expectations may not be confirmed by events. The reactions of the firm to disappointment—the alteration it makes in its plans and activities and the way in which it adapts (or fails to adapt)—are again to be explained with reference to its resources.[4]

Uncertainty and incomplete knowledge underlie managerial decision making. Managers make fallible conjectures and, knowing that they may not have complete information, must make the best decisions they can.[5] Uncertainty limits expansion only to the extent that managerial resources are limited. Each new activity undertaken by the firm requires an increased input of managerial services, not only to obtain sufficient information but to develop sufficiently well worked-out plans to reduce risk. The greater the risk or uncertainty, the greater the managerial task. Hence, the expansion plans of a firm are necessarily restricted by the capacity of management. The continuous, but limited, growth of the firm is based on entrepreneurial vision or "image." In order to focus attention on the crucial role of a firm's inherited resources, the environment is treated as an "image" in the entrepreneur's mind of the possibilities and restrictions with which he or she is confronted. Such an "image" determines a person's behavior; whether experience confirms expectations is another story.[6]

Penrose illustrated her theory of the growth of the firm in a case study of the Hercules Powder Company, a spin-off of Dupont and predecessor of Alliant Powder, a subsidiary of Alliant Techsystems. For Penrose, Hercules' creation of consumer demand was a consequence of the entrepreneurial desire to find a use for available productive resources.[7] Hercules' new product development and moves to create new markets came from "the extensive knowledge of cellulose chemistry possessed by Hercules [which] . . . has provided a continuous inducement to the firm to search for new ways of using it."[8] Hercules' technically trained salesmen were "expected to take an active interest in the production and market problems of their customers. This permits them to acquire an intimate knowledge of the customers' businesses and not only to demonstrate the uses of their own products and to suggest new ways of doing things, but also to adapt their products to customers' requirements and learn what kind of new products can be used."[9]

Hercules Powder was able to develop new products on the basis of its "extensive knowledge" of cellulose technology as manifest in nitrocellulose (originally used in the production of explosives) derived lacquers for the rapidly growing automobile industry. Its technological base enabled Hercules to enter new markets, which, in turn, led the company to refine and leverage its knowledge of cellulose technology in a strategy of moving into, and developing, promising markets. The company was so effective in meeting customer requirements quickly that competitors acknowledged Hercules' superior business model and withdrew, rather than engage in a fight to the finish that they would lose.

The evolving story of Jardine Matheson & Company from agency house to investment house to multinational, building out from a core group of "agency services," provides an interesting example of Penrose's concepts of the receding managerial limit, the evolutionary growth of knowledge, the importance of enterprise and entrepreneurial vision, the respective importance of the firm and the environment, the possibility of failure, and the persistence of uncertainty and risk.

Edith Penrose left a rich legacy that her admirers, including Brian Loasby and George Richardson, William Lazonick, and other contributors to Christos Pitelis' recent volume, have amply and some more recently acknowledged.[10] While recognizing the inventiveness of Penrose, it would be thoughtless not to credit the foresight of her influences and the extensions to theory of her followers, specifically in the areas of capabilities, the role of the environment, architecture, and learning, and the explanation and role of failure in innovation and knowledge.

Capabilities

The Penrosean idea of capabilities as the basis of deliberate strategic product/market choice can be traced to Adam Smith's belief that economic progress was fundamentally the result of the division of labor, which resulted in progressive improvements in skill, dexterity, judgment, and productive capabilities of all kinds as well as increased specialization.[11] George Richardson, inspired by Penrose, replaced her "resources" and "services" terminology with capabilities and produced an analytical framework to explain which activities are likely to be collected within a single organization, which are coordinated by market transactions, and which are coordinated by businesses otherwise independent. According to Richardson, what sets cooperative relationships apart from market transactions is that the parties to them accept some degree of obligation—and therefore give some degree of assurance—with respect to their future conduct. Coordination is accomplished through cooperation when two or more independent organizations agree to match their related plans in advance.[12] The institutional counterparts of this form of coordination are the complex patterns of cooperation and affiliation that characterize the 19th Century trading firm's external organization of suppliers, buyers, agents, and associated financiers to meet the requirements of a three-way trade and complicated balance-of-payments situation between Great Britain, China, and India.

Alfred Chandler emphasized creation, maintenance, and expansion of resources and organizational capabilities as keys to competitive advantage and the continued growth of the enterprise. Highly product–specific and process–specific, these organizational capabilities affected and often determined the direction and pace of small numbers of first–movers and challengers, as well as the direction and pace of the industries and national economies in which they operated.[13]

Just as an important theme in Penrose is the interrelatedness of resources and mental models as two sources of firm distinctiveness, Chandler illustrated how resources and mental models of managers interact.[14] The accumulation of resources and the need for change demand new mental models for coping with diversification. The accumulation of resources, therefore, creates a base for organizational learning.

More recently, William Lazonick cited the Penrosean firm as an example of an innovative enterprise:

Each move into a new product market not only enables the firm to utilize unused productive services but also requires investments in the creation of new productive services that are the basis for the continuing growth of the firm. These unused productive services can enable a firm to grow not only through diversification of its products but also through the acquisition and absorption of other firms that have developed complementary productive services. Key to the determination of which product opportunities the firm pursues and, in the case of merger and acquisition, which firm absorbs which, is the possession of what Penrose calls "entrepreneurial services" by the growing firm.[15]

Lazonick argued that, in a growing enterprise, entrepreneurial services do not yield success if the productive resources under the firm's control are not administered in an integrated way by the firm's managers. Hence, administrative integration is critical to growth and to embedding innovative capability into the ongoing operations of the firm. Over time, the firm uses its unique pool of resources to generate new products for competitive advantage and, even more importantly, new unique capabilities for continued innovation.[16]

The Role of the Environment

In the Penrosean firm, the choice of resources and services for development and growth would be explained by managers' perception of the opportunities resident in the business, social, and political environment of the firm. While Penrose acknowledged the firm's conjectural ability to shape its "image" of the environment, she added:

There can be no question that for any particular firm the environment "determines" its opportunities, for it must take its resources as given . . . and must look to the opportunities it can find for using them for the source of its power to grow. Whether we should treat the resources of the firm or its environment as the more important factor explaining growth, depends on the question we ask: if we want to explain why some firms see the environment differently, why some grow and some do not . . . or why the environment is different for every firm, we must take the "resources" approach; if we want to explain why a particular firm or group of firms with specified resources grows in the way it does, we must examine the opportunities for the use of those resources.[17]

Alfred Marshall and, later, George Richardson provided insights into how a firm might simultaneously build a pattern of relationships and shape its environment by coordinating its activities with other firms through an external organization, that is, a network of social, technical, and commercial arrangements that link a business with its customers, suppliers, and rivals.[18] According to Brian Loasby, "In developing its own organization and its particular market, each business draws on the institutions of the society within which it operates, and then develops, through a mixture of deliberate decisions and the consequences of day-to-day interactions, rules and conventions which serve to coordinate its activities and to align them with the activities of its suppliers and customers."[19]

Lazonick acknowledged that, while "the main theoretical strength of Penrose's work is that she placed organizational learning at the center of the analysis," "the main weakness of the Penrosean 'theory of the growth of the firm' for building a theory of innovative enterprise is its implicit assumption that, in all times and places, all organizational learning is managerial learning."[20] Penrose's theory lacks a theory for integrating a learning role for the administrative, technical, and professional personnel into the managerial structure of the corporation.[21]

Architecture and Organizational Learning

The Penrosean firm creates an "architecture" or "administrative framework" for learning and collaboration. This framework includes both interorganizational linkages and internal processes for learning, for the development of capabilities, the exploitation of productive opportunities, and the development of consistent routines important for trustworthiness, consistent patterns of behavior, and effective forms of governance.

Again, the ideas central to the "architecture" of the firm derive from Adam Smith. Reinterpreted by Penrose in *The Theory of the Growth of the Firm*, the division of labor both within and between firms leads to the development of skills and the perception of possibilities, while firms within a similar line of business develop somewhat different skills and perceptions. Firms are learning organizations, continually changing their organization to align their increasing knowledge with their productive opportunity.

George Richardson extended the internal growth dynamic of the firm as Penrose described it to account for interfirm relations. Firms specialize in activities that use a similar capability and affiliate with other enterprises that specialize in complementary activities. Hence, economic activities are no longer coordinated either by hierarchy within the vertically integrated enterprise or by price, spontaneously in the market; economic activities can be coordinated by affiliated or networked groups of cooperating firms. Instead of isolated islands of firms, Richardson's image of industry is a "dense network of cooperation and affiliation by which firms are interrelated."[22]

Using the network as an example of administrative coordination, Penrose credited D'Cruz and Rugman for their view of a network as a "governance structure for organizing exchange through cooperative, non-equity relationships among firms and non-business institutions"[23] and Benjamin Gomes-Casseres for his understanding of a network as "groups of companies joined together in a larger overarching relationship . . . each company fulfilling a specific role within the group."[24]

Speaking of the network as a vehicle for knowledge creation, Ikojiro Nonaka wrote of the spiral of knowledge creation, whereby individuals, then groups, then organizations as a whole, convert tacit knowledge into explicit knowledge.[25] Loasby characterized such knowledge as coping strategies, the strict observance of routines and decision rules, the building of reserves, and the generation of alternative institutions, record keeping, among other artifacts, on which future decision making will be based.[26]

Ranjay Gulati, Nitin Nohria, and Akbar Zaheer extended firm knowledge and learning to the networks of relationships in which firms are embedded that provide the firm with access to information, resources, markets, and technologies; with advantages from learning, scale, and scope economies, while sharing risks and outsourcing value-chain stages and organizational functions. In their strategic network model, industries, strategic groups and value-chain partners can be seen as embedded networks of resources and capabilities extending well beyond the formal boundaries of the firm. Gulati et al. argued that the knowledge embedded in relationships can serve as a source of sustainable competitive advantage, providing valuable information that, in turn, provides strategic advantage by allowing the firm to act more quickly than rivals.[27]

The Explanation of Failure

Like capabilities, the concept of failure owes much to Adam Smith's account of the growth of knowledge through the invention and application of fallible connecting principles. Thus, according to Loasby, "a theory of economic development that respects both human abilities and the historical record must rest on conjecture and exposure to refutation rather than rational expectations."[28]

In a Penrosean firm, failure can be attributed to the firm's misunderstanding of its own capabilities or the capabilities required in a new market. Loasby argues that "Penrose's most significant analytical innovation," that is, the distinction between resources and the inputs into production, which she called productive services, "inserts fallible conjecture into the firm's understanding of its capabilities, its environment, and its opportunities."[29]

Knowledge and learning often come at the expense of failure, one of the outcomes of uncertainty. Elaborating on the uncertainty that underlies business decisions, Frank Knight writes: "The business man himself not merely forms the best estimate he can of the outcome of his actions but he is likely to estimate the probability that his estimate is correct."[30] In a world of change and uncertainty, "[t]he essence of the situation is action according to opinion, of greater or less foundation and value, neither entire ignorance nor complete and perfect information, but partial knowledge."[31]

Competitive advantage aside, the knowledge of the individual and that of the firm serve a supremely practical purpose: they are the best defense individuals and firms have against uncertainty. The current study is based on the notion that auditing the past can provide insight and lead to a better understanding of current knowledge. Knight provides support for this approach when he says that "in order to live intelligently in our world . . . we must use the principle that things similar in some respects will behave similarly in certain other respects even when they are very different in still other respects."[32]

As referenced earlier, Lazonick, too, would appear to provide support for such an undertaking:

To make use of history to understand the process of economic development, it is not enough to say, as have proponents of "path dependency," that "history matters." Depending on the configuration of industrial, organizational, and institutional conditions, path dependency can either promote or constrain the innovation process, and for the analysis of economic development, it is of central importance to identify what social conditions have which impact. For a particular business enterprise or national industry, a set of social conditions that yielded innovation and economic development in the past may now become obstacles to change.[33]

This study makes its contribution to the Penrosean literature as an empirical analysis of early services firms that grew to become investment houses and later multinational conglomerates by offering a core set of "agency services" to up-stream and downstream value-chain partners in a dozen or more industries. Jardine Matheson sat in a maritime version of the Marshallian industrial district, specifically the deepwater ports of the Pacific, Indian, and South Atlantic Oceans, related to other horizontal and vertical industries through minority investments. Such a definition of an industrial district reflects Jardine Matheson's "image" of its trading environment and potential productive opportunity, for, without a land-based trading district in its early history, the firm's innovative and visionary founders thought in terms of oceans and ports, rather than in terms of bricks and mortar. It is interesting to reflect on the fact that James Matheson ran the business for three years on board the ship *Hercules*, after Jardine Matheson was expelled from China during the First Opium War.

The dense network of Richardsonian affiliative and cooperative relationships by Jardine Matheson exerted administrative coordination over a vast trading empire and was seamed together through 200 years of correspondence delivered from principal to agent by slaver, by clipper and by steamship, as Jardine Matheson sought faster vessels for communication. By the mid 20th century, these relation-ships were seamed by minority investments that provided a balance of administrative control and autonomy for associated firms.

APPROACH AND STRUCTURE

This interpretation of strategic management in the Hong Kong trading industry uses a Penrosean or resource-based view as its principal theoretic framework to answer some critical questions:

- How and why did the firm's founders and managers develop particular resources and services of resources?

- What internal factors (including the firm and its agents) and external factors (including governments, social policy, competition, new entrants, buyers and suppliers) were responsible for their choices?
- How is failure explained and what was learned from failure?
- What role did the firm play in the development of markets and market institutions?
- What was the organizational structure of the firm, including internal governance and external organization?
- How did the firm promote managerial initiative while curbing opportunism?
- How did the firm raise funds for growth?

In this interpretation, a firm's strategic choices are aimed at developing and applying profitably its distinctive capabilities, an idea that derives from Adam Smith's belief that economic progress was fundamentally the result of a division of labor that resulted in the progressive improvement in skills. Resources and services are chosen for development and growth in response to internal and external factors. Failure is inevitable, in a Knightian sense, and can be attributed to a misunderstanding by the firm of its own capabilities or the capabilities needed in a new market. Of particular interest is the firm's role in creating markets or market institutions, that is, the development of routines for the functioning of the various markets the firm was trying to develop. In a resource-based interpretation, the founders and subsequent managers develop an internal and external architecture (or organization) to learn, collaborate, address opportunities, and reduce risk. Initiative is primary and encouraged; only reasonable routines are established to curb opportunism, in marked contrast with a transaction cost economics approach. Finally, raising funds, when necessary, is part of the managerial or entrepreneurial task.

The theory literature identified in this chapter provides a seamless interpretative framework for analysis. Beyond that literature, other examinations of diversification (e.g., Chatterjee and Wernerfelt; Hoskisson, Johnson and Moesel; Moshe Farjoun and many others) are used for the tools they bring to bear on analysis, rather than for their contribution to theory. Similarly, John Kay's frameworks for auditing industry and firm strategy are used to compare historical "break points," points that mark a change in business environment, in customers, and therefore in capabilities and business design. Authors and their tools are referenced in the chapters in which the tools are used.

PURPOSE AND CONTRIBUTION

A Business in Risk is fundamentally the history of a Hong Kong company in its environmental and industry context. The main focus of this study is on the process of external organization building, through repeated acquisitions and divestitures along the company's history.

This alone would be insufficient because what is of theoretical interest is how capabilities are accumulated through an external organization.

Acquisitions and divestitures cannot lead to sustained capabilities in and of themselves, since critical resources are accumulated rather than acquired in strategic factor markets.[34] They are just the methods to build an external organization.

Important to the purpose and ultimate contribution of this study are the firm's early resource decisions and capabilities, and the way these capabilities were institutionalized through years of usage and experience, the way they evolved through business design and industry influence, as well as acquisition and divestiture from 1832 to the present.

Chapter 2 addresses the early years of the private trade. The chapter deals with the early resources and services choices made by the Hong Kong trading industry and Jardine Matheson in particular, including the very special business, social, and political environment into which the firm entered, the development of markets and the firm's establishment of mechanisms to raise funds for investment.

Chapter 2 takes a historical-transformation approach to depict the evolution of the industry and the firm from 1832 to 1885. In this approach, the two periods are compared in terms of demand, markets, market institutions, customers, value proposition, and so on.

Chapter 3 carries the story of the Hong Kong trading industry from 1885 through the interwar years, including the reasons for decline, the increasing strength of the Japanese *sogo shosha* in Southeast Asia, and the survival strategies of the Hong Kong trading companies.

Chapter 4 covers the economic history of Jardine Matheson from World War II to 2002, a period characterized by international growth and expansion, debt, and recovery. The chapter focuses on Jardine Matheson's growth strategy. The firm's first serious experience with failure is considered, as are the mechanisms used by the firm to raise funds for further growth.

Chapter 5 analyzes Jardine Matheson's investments across industries and geographies and the skills required by the firm's historical and acquired businesses, to demonstrate how the firm accumulated competencies in areas of historical strength, deepening and broadening their application through vertical and horizontal acquisitions.

Chapter 6 examines the internal governance of the firm and its relationship with acquired firms.

Chapter 7 takes a historical-transformation approach to change and learning in the Hong Kong trading industry, with specific consideration to Jardine Matheson & Company. Three break points are considered: 1977, at the height of the period of internal expansion and integration; 1996, after the sell-offs and consolidations of the 1980s and before the Asian financial crisis; and 2002, after the crisis and during the economic downturn.

Chapter 8 summarizes the findings of this study and reexamines the applicability of a Penrosean interpretation of the growth of Jardine Matheson and the Hong Kong trading industry.

ACKNOWLEDGMENTS

I wish to thank Jeremy Brown, formerly managing director of Jardine Matheson & Company, who provided access to the company's archives at Cambridge University and early annual reports at Matheson & Company, London.

I am grateful to William Lazonick and William J. Hausman, editor of Enterprise & Society, for their interest and faith in my work. The literature section in chapter 1 and chapter 2 first appeared in Enterprise & Society in April 2002; they appear here with permission.

I am also appreciative of the constructive criticisms of John McGee, associate editor of Strategic Management Journal.

Throughout the process of readying this manuscript, Ellen Donohoe has been a careful project manager. I am thankful for her efforts and for the efforts of Deborah Whitford, production editor, and Catherine Lyons, senior editor, Greenwood Publishing Group.

NOTES

1. Originally published in 1959, *The Theory of the Growth of the Firm* (1959; 3rd ed., New York: John Wiley & Co, 1995) includes an introductory essay by Edith Penrose in which the author acknowledges some of her major influences and a few theorists who have continued to evolve her thinking about the growth of firms. Penrose's 1960 article, "The Growth of the Firm—a Case Study: The Hercules Powder Company," *Business History Review* 34 (Spring 1960): 1–24 was originally to be included in *The Theory of the Growth of the Firm* but was excluded by the publisher because of space constraints.

2. Penrose, "Growth of the Firm—a Case Study," p. 3. Hereinafter referred to as "Hercules."

3. Ibid.

4. Ibid.

5. Penrose, *The Theory of the Growth of the Firm*, (1995), 59. Hereinafter referred to as *Theory*.

6. Penrose, *Theory*, 5.

7. Penrose, "Hercules," 9.

8. Ibid., 8.

9. Ibid., 13.

10. Christos Pitelis, *The Growth of the Firm: The Legacy of Edith Penrose* (UK: Oxford University Press, 2002).

11. Brian J. Loasby, "Edith T. Penrose's Place in the Filiation of Economic Ideas," *Oeconomia* 29 (1999a): 104.

12. George B. Richardson, "The Organization of Industry," *Economic Journal* 82 (1972): 891.

13. Alfred D. Chandler, *Scale and Scope: The Dynamics of Industrial Capitalism* (Cambridge: Belknap Press, 1990), 496.

14. Ibid., 186.

15. William Lazonick, "Innovative Enterprise in Historical Transformation," *Enterprise & Society* 3 (2002): 22.

16. Ibid., 22–23.

17. Penrose, *Theory*, 217 referring to Boulding's "Image" of the firm.

18. Alfred Marshall, *Principles of Economics* (London: Macmillan, 1920), 266. See also Brian J. Loasby, "Marshall's Economics of Progress," *Journal of Economic Studies* 13 (5): 10. Richardson, "The Organization of Industry," 891.

19. Brian J. Loasby, "Market Institutions and Economic Evolution," *Journal of Evolutionary Economics* 10 (2000b): 302.

20. Lazonick, "Innovative Enterprise," 25.

21. Ibid.

22. Richardson, "The Organization of Industry," 883.

23. Joseph D'Cruz and Alan Rugman, "A Theory of Business Networks," in L. Eden, ed. *Multinationals in North America* (Calgary: University of Calgary Press, 1994), 276.

24. Benjamin Gomes-Casseres, "Group versus Group: How Alliance Networks Compete," *Harvard Business Review* 72 (July–August 1994): 4.

25. Ikojiro Nonaka, "A Dynamic Theory of Organizational Knowledge Creation," *Organization Science* 5 (1): 14–37.

26. Brian J. Loasby, "The Evolution of Knowledge: Beyond the Biological Model," *Research Policy* 31 (2002): 1229.

27. Ranjay Gulati, Nitin Nohria, and Akbar Zaheer, "Strategic Networks," *Strategic Management Journal* 21 (2000): 203–215.

28. Brian J. Loasby, "The Significance of Penrose's Theory for the Development of Economics," *Contributions to Political Economy* 18 (1999b), 38.

29. Brian J. Loasby, "Organizations as Interpretive Systems," *Revue d' Economie Industrielle* 97 (4th Quarter, 2001): 17–34.

30. Frank H. Knight, *Risk, Uncertainty, and Profit.* (Boston: Houghton Mifflin, 1921), 230.

31. Ibid., 188.

32. Ibid., 206.

33. Lazonick, "The Theory of Innovative Enterprise," 39.

34. Jay Barney, "Strategic Factor Markets: Expectation, Luck and Business Strategy," *Management Science* 32 (1986): 1231–1241.

MANAGING RISK:
THE CHINA TRADE TO 1885

Chapter 2 examines the industry environment and Jardine Matheson's perception of productive opportunities between 1832, the year the firm was formally constituted, and 1885, the year the firm's accounts begin to show significant investments in manufacturing, mines, and railroads. Each of the chosen years finds the firm in a different industry, with different competitors. The chapter draws on John Kay's framework for auditing industry and firm strategy.[1] A close comparison reveals the extent to which business models were changing, geographic boundaries were changing or disappearing, new competitors were emerging, and new relationships were changing competitors into collaborators for survival and advantage in Hong Kong and the ASEAN.

ENVIRONMENT AND INDUSTRY, 1832–1885

Industry Background

The industry in 1832 was trading in commodities, largely carried on by the British East India Company, which had for two centuries dominated trade, raised armies, and minted money. It was the operational arm of Britain in China, Australia, India, the American colonies, and the West Indies. While the East India Company's monopoly on the India trade ended in 1813, the company continued to operate through 1858.[2] Trade between India, the Eastern Archipelago, and China was known from the end of the 17th century until the middle of the 19th century as "the Country trade." While such trade was originally carried on by the British East India Company, increasingly it was left to private merchants, hence, the term "private trade." The relationship between the British East India Company and the private trade was symbiotic: a portion of the cash raised by the private trade financed the East India Company's China tea purchases.[3]

There were two strategic groups at the outset of this study—the East India Company and the growing private trade. This early private trade was characterized by independent merchants who, for low working capital, could earn commissions on up to 45% of every transaction by absorbing the risks of their customers. The wealthier of these merchants, through investment or partnerships, would integrate forward into shipping, finance, and insurance to appropriate more of the value of the transaction. In 1832, the largest of the private traders in the Canton trading district, with large teams of agents working on their behalf, were Jardine Matheson & Company and Dent & Company.[4] Palmer & Company had been the leading competitor until 1830, when the firm was bankrupted in a speculation crisis.

The principal trends in the industry in 1832 were the emergence of the agency house with many associated private merchants and the institutionalization of the group of services that became known as "agency services." While the agency house was primarily a trading firm, through its "agency services," it also acted as banker, bill-broker, shipowner, freighter, insurance agent, and purveyor, maintaining a growing network of branch houses and agents. The agency house reduced the entry barriers for would-be traders with low working capital: they could become associated agents. The agency house reduced as well the risks for buyers and sellers—offering credit or insurance at each stage of a transaction for a commission. The environment for trade in 1832 was volatile because Chinese government pursuit of private traders intermittently suspended business activities and because piracy was an everyday threat.

By 1885, the strategic groups had changed: the trading firm with associated investment house was now in competition with banks and investment houses, located not in the Far East but in London. The major members of the strategic group were Jardine Matheson & Company and Butterfield & Swire—still competing in Far East with 100 other agency houses—and the London investment offices of Matheson & Company, John Swire & Sons, and the Hongkong & Shanghai Bank.

The principal trends in the industry of 1885 were the development of the "free standing companies"[5] associated with a Pacific or otherwise distant trading firm and the investment in infrastructure (railroads) and manufactures, raw materials, and mines in the Far East, South Africa, and even parts of Southern Europe. Knowledge of investment opportunities and operational management of the mining, manufacturing or railroad project were the roles that fell to the Far East trading company. The associated investment house lined up the investors and offered an "independent" evaluation of the merits of the investment. The Treaty Port System opened markets to direct and dependable trade at fixed tariffs, reducing trading risk and encouraging commerce and investment.

Demand and Markets

In 1832, the long list of commodities offered for sale could be reduced to four staples, tea and silk from China, sold to Great Britain and Europe; cotton textiles from Great Britain and India, sold to China; and opium from India, sold to China. The legitimate trading frontier was limited to a thin sliver of Canton. The merchants could not venture further inside and were allowed to trade only indirectly with the Chinese through Chinese Co-Hong merchants, who intermediated the trade. The opium trade was conducted offshore, along the China coast. Hong Kong did not become available to trade until after the First Opium War, when it was ceded to Britain. The first trading firm to buy a plot of land in Hong Kong and move its head office there was Jardine Matheson & Company in 1844.

Demand was affected by product quality in the case of tea, silk, and cotton. Local weather and transport could affect tea quality. Some higher grades were not always available. Tea had to be kept dry and suffered if it was at sea too long. Quality degradation resulted in lower prices paid by London tea buyers. Silk culture was impacted by weather and disease, and high-quality varieties of silk were not always available. Lesser-quality silk did not sell. British cottons were of very limited appeal in China but were required to offload excess manufactures. The private traders had more success selling Madras cotton to the Chinese. Opium was illegal, and its sale suffered when the Opium commissioner enforced antismoking laws. In 1832, buyers and sellers learned about prices, quantities, and commodity shipments from trade papers like the *Canton Register* and the *Straits Times* and from communications between the private traders and their suppliers and major customers. The Co-Hong merchants in China communicated to their native clientele.

By 1885, the Treaty Port System guaranteed a minimum purchase of British cotton, although the rich agency houses formed joint ventures for textile manufacture in China, as well as cotton and silk factories in Japan. By this time, the agency houses brokered all of the tea and silk sales; the East India Company was long out of the picture.

Costs and Value

The value chain of the Hong Kong trading firm in 1832 began with suppliers in India, loading goods onto a receiving ship bound for Canton. Payment was made via letter of credit from the merchant's bank. Goods were sold to Co-Hong merchants in Canton (on financing terms). In return, teas, and silks were purchased on behalf of merchants in London, Glasgow, and the West Indies (for finance, credit, and insurance). Goods were transported via ship to the West Indies, London, and Manchester, where they were sold and where tin, steel, textiles, and so on were picked up for sale on consignment. Each stage of the value chain had associated risks: from India to Canton, price volatility, risk of piracy or shipwreck; at Canton, loan default on the part of Co-Hong merchants and Chinese government restrictions on trade; from Canton to London, weather that could slow arrival or damage goods and price volatility. In 1832 firms with a reputation for strong financial management as well as architecture (a long-lasting network of local relationships) achieved competitive advantage and appropriated more value than their peers.

The value chain looked different in 1885 because the treaty ports had created new markets for supply and demand. Suppliers in India, Japan, Singapore, and Malaysia boarded their goods onto merchant steamers bound for one of 15 treaty ports in China. Payment was made via letter of credit from the merchant's bank. Goods were sold to merchants in the treaty ports (on financing terms); tea and silks were purchased for resale in London (for finance credit and insurance). In London, steel and textiles were purchased for resale at the treaty ports (on consignment). The transaction opportunities (and credit financing opportunities) increased as the number of supplier and purchaser markets increased.

In 1885 the supply insufficiency from India and Japan was a major influence on value, resulting in higher prices. At the treaty ports, tariff regulation was an issue. In London, angry merchants pushed the agency houses to sell more textiles for China. Four firms established before 1885 were thriving and adding value, as evidenced in their ability to undertake investments[6]: Jardine Matheson & Company, established in Canton in 1832, with £1.72M (1891)—trading, banking, shipping, insurance, cotton, mines, and railways; Finlay & Company, established in Bombay 1862, with £4.36M (1898)—trading, banking, shipping, cotton mills, and tea estates; Butterfield & Swire, established in Shanghai in 1867, with £5.14M (1900)—trading, banking, harbors and docks, shipping, railways, and petroleum; E. D. Sassoon & Company, established in Bombay, with £6.7M(1920)—trading, shipping, banking, breweries, cotton mills, and tramways. Jardine Matheson's group capital figure is understated, reflecting the tradition of partners to remove their contribution to total capital upon retirement.[7]

Distinctive Capabilities and Strategic Assets

In 1832, only the British East India Company enjoyed strategic assets; that is, advantages external to the capabilities of the firm. Innovations—in speed, in routes, in financing and in communications—were important to competitive advantage. Architecture was essential to what was essentially an interfirm market, and strong architecture provided the information flow that communicated information about supply, demand, and risk conditions. A trading firm's ability to broker risks depended on a reputation for sound financial judgment. A very few firms in the industry could charge higher prices because of this reputation.

By 1885, the business model had changed, from pure trading house to trading house with associated investment house. Innovation was critical to respond to new opportunities to benefit from investment in fixed assets, from license and contract arrangements. Trading firms put their architecture to work identifying investment opportunities in the supply-and-demand markets. The reputation of a trading house and that of an investment house were separate, hence, the move by trading firms to establish independent "freestanding companies" with veto power over investment proposals. Investment houses were headed by members of the trading firm who had gone home to London and had constituencies there—in both the metaphorical and literal sense. Relationships with the Chinese government as an investment partner were critical.

By 1885 it is evident that firms were looking for a fixed, external advantage, evidenced in the Treaty Port System, in railway contracts, in licensed shipping routes, and in fixed assets like gold and tin mines. Reliable returns through rule of law were the common, underlying motivation for this search for strategic assets: treaties guaranteed trade and line-of-sight duties; railway contracts were supported by the Chinese government; and what became known as the Far East Shipping Conferences literally amounted to industry self-regulation. It is obvious from the behavior of firms in 1885 that the acquisition of strategic assets was seen by participants as a guarantee of sustainability and appropriability beyond that afforded by distinctive capabilities alone.

Sources of Competitive Advantage

In 1832, competitive advantage depended on architecture, reputation, and innovation. Firms strong in these distinctive capabilities attracted more agents and more business-to-business trade as participants in the trade sought to reduce their own risk. The advantage provided by architecture and reputation was sustainable, because it was built on self-selected business behavior that was also very important to the China market, where long-term relationships were favored over spot contracts.

In 1832, the marginal firm—an individual merchant or private partnership—could appropriate 35% of earnings, with 10% for meager office, warehouse, and staff and 55% for cost of goods sold. Competitive advantage was not necessarily reflected in added value. It was the practice of many early firms for partners to remove all of their accumulated capital when they retired from the business. So, available financials would give an incomplete view of the money available to the business.

By 1885, architecture, innovation, and reputation remained as important as they had been in 1832, but reputation had become far more important as a capability and as a drawing card to attract strategic assets, including government contracts, licenses, and concessions among other distinctions, as well as London investors for raw materials and mining projects. The advantage derived from distinctive capabilities was sustainable, so long as firms continued to grow and evolve those capabilities to address changes in the business model.

JARDINE MATHESON & COMPANY, FIRM RESPONSE AND STRATEGY 1832–1885

Business to Business on Commission

From 1832 and for 100 years thereafter, Jardine Matheson's business was risk broking for buyers and sellers of goods from/to Europe and Asia and was based entirely on commissions. The firm extracted commissions on 16 separate agency services, including sales, returns, cost and freight, guarantees of bills, ship's disbursement, insurance, arranging insurance, chartering ships, receiving inbound freight, obtaining outbound freight, settling insurance losses, negotiating bills of exchange, arbitration of debts, debt settlement, managing estates, executors of estates, and transshipping goods. Jardine Matheson could charge for these "agency" services because the China trade was very risky and participants in the business (usually smaller businesses with low working capital and operating at a distance from the trade, for example, from Latin America or from Europe) were less knowledgeable and lacked the clout of a big operator like Jardine Matheson. Hence, they preferred to have business risk managed by a firm with market knowledge, with reputation, influence, and strong financial management skills.

The competitive environment was highly unstable: speculation and reliance on credit meant that firms were only as a strong as their decisions were sound. Access to information was critical and an important differentiator. Stability could have been increased, but only with the intervention of the British government. Market segmentation was very rudimentary. In China, the trading frontier was limited to Canton.

Reputation as Capability

In 1832, the firm's reputation was a distinctive capability. If the environment had not been unstable, Jardine Matheson might have begun extending its capability into Europe and the Americas, because the Canton trading environment was already filled with Spanish, Portuguese, and North American traders who had come to know and trust Jardine Matheson. In fact, Jardine Matheson had already extended its capability to London, where partners served as members of Parliament (MPS) and sat on the Select Committee for Trade. In many respects, the firm's reputation was a lightning rod for suppliers, agents, customers—as well as for private individuals who used the trading firm as a deposit bank, earning returns of 8% or more. Jardine Matheson's practice of resorting to American bills on London limited the firm's exposure during what became known as the "Calcutta Credit Crisis" of 1829–1834, when peer trading firms, which exchanged each other's bills, were bankrupted, including Palmer & Co., the richest merchant of them all, Alexander & Co., Mackintosh & Co., Colvin & Co., Fairlie & Co., and Richard Mackintosh & Co., London, among others. The argument for a Marshallian or Richardsonian external organization with Penrosean administrative coordination is made by comparing Jardine Matheson's focus on abjuring speculation, admonishing its agents to adhere to a strict commission basis only, and constant regard of its reputation.

Jardine Matheson's bills of credit were trustworthy, and banks in London and the United States backed them. The Jardine Matheson archives confirm the firm's use of its agents to keep an eye on the creditworthiness of the banks with which it did business. Hence, Jardine Matheson enjoyed an advantage over firms that did not have its superior reputation or its routines for effective financial management.

From Canton in 1832 James Matheson wrote about Jardine Matheson's financial policy to his nephew Hugh, then a partner in Lyall Matheson & Company, Calcutta:

Of the bills which we endorse, those on Baring Brothers & Co. are always drawn under credits either from themselves or their attorney at New York, Mr. T.W. Ward, who has authority for the purpose. Other bills are drawn under credits from a known capitalist John Jacob Astor of New York, who owns lands almost equal to a principality in the United States. Bills on Gledstone [sic], Drysdale & Co. are either drawn under credits from them or on the security of bills of lading for goods.... Mr. Thomas Weeding on whom we draw is a merchant possessed of at least a lack of pounds sterling. Thomas Wyatt on whom we also pass bills is a still greater capitalist 'tho only an oilman. ... On the whole, we feel that we are now committing ourselves with people of far greater solidity than those whose bills are vaunted forth at 7/10–1/2 at Calcutta. And if any disappointment should occur to us, divided as our risk is among various parties, it cannot but prove comparatively insignificant.[8]

In 1835, Hollingworth Magniac established with John Abel Smith, MP, and Oswald Smith the firm of Magniac Smith & Co., of 3 Lombard Street. William Jardine, who claimed to be "fully aware of the wealth, respectability and high character of the parties," agreed to make them London agents with this reservation: "At no time shall it be expedient that we should give up the option of carrying on transactions with other London houses. ... The principal advantage we look to from our house connection is the certainty of our Bills being protected to whatever extent we may have occasion to draw in the course of any one season, without reference to immediately available assets to meet them."[9]

On the strength of its reputation and relationships, Jardine Matheson & Co. was thus able to build a banking business, finance shipments, open credit, and offer general merchant banking facilities. Time and again, the Jardine Matheson correspondence inveighs against speculation and advises its agents and affiliates to adhere to a strict commission basis. Operating on a commission basis, competitive advantage was fully appropriable to the trading firm. Given the importance of reputation, a time and location-based capability, Jardine Matheson could expect to sustain its advantage, until the requirements of the market changed.

Building Market Institutions to Insure Rich Cargo against High Risk

In addition to banking, another major aspect of the agency business that sprang from the China trade was marine insurance, indispensable in a trade of rich cargo and high risk. In 1801, there was no public insurance office of any kind in Canton, but several individuals would combine in temporary associations to underwrite a ship and its cargo. In 1805, the Canton Insurance Society was founded. This institution lasted 30 years and was managed alternately, every 5 years, by the Davidson-Dent house and that of Beale-Magniac-Jardine.. In 1832 Jardine Matheson & Company as managers of the 10th Canton Insurance Company bestowed the Calcutta agency on their protégé, Lyall Matheson & Company. A list published in the *Canton Register* of February 1829 shows Magniac & Co. as agents of six Insurance companies, including the 8th Canton Insurance Company, and Dent & Co. as agents of four. In 1829 Jardine started a private underwriting account "J. M. and Friends," with the firm holding 20 of the 36 shares, with each share worth $1,000 per annum. As the volume of the China trade increased, the insurance revenue increased. In 1835, when the 10th Canton office came to a close, Dent decided to set up its own China Insurance Company, leaving Canton in the hands of Jardine Matheson & Company. The Canton Insurance Company laid the foundation for Jardine Matheson's large interest in many forms of insurance services. The increased cash flow from insurance services enabled the firm to invest in new businesses—particularly in shipping.

Building Dominance in Shipping: Jardine Matheson as Owner, Investor, and Innovator

The firm's shipping business was inseparable from trading. For Jardine Matheson's London agents—Magniac Smith, Magniac Jardine, and later Matheson & Company—canvassing for ship consignments was important to maximizing capacity on incoming and outgoing ships. This led to close relationships with shipowners and extended to outward cargoes such as coal with the introduction of steamships in the Far East. Investment in technology for rapid transport and communication was important to competitive advantage, particularly in tea sales.

Jardine Matheson was also an investor in the shipping interests of other firms. The firm invested in Russell & Company's shipping operations on the Yangtze River in 1860 and in the China Coast Steam Navigation Company in 1872. The China Coast Company was the precursor to Jardine Matheson's Indo China Steam Navigation Company, formed in London in 1881, which brought together all the ships and operations on the Yangtze. From an initial 12 ships, the Indo China Steam Navigation Company expanded its ships to 20 at 100,000 tons by 1905. From 1864 to 1912 the bulk of the coasting trade was in the hands of the Indo-China Steamship Company (Jardine Matheson's subsidiary) and the China Navigation Company (owned by Butterfield & Swire).

Jardine Matheson's External Organization for Administrative Coordination at a Distance

Its inherited network of agents from past partnerships (the inherited managerial resources important to growth in the Penrosean firm) allowed Jardine Matheson to build on a firm foundation of known routines and trusted business behaviors, avoiding both the learning curve and expense of building a business organization from scratch. This network provided regular information on the prices and availability of commodities that informed James Matheson's biweekly *Canton Register*, published from 1827 to1843, and the regular dispatches Jardine Matheson sent to its agents, suppliers, and buyers by ship.

Letter writing was the principal means of setting rules, sharing market information and building relationships with suppliers and agents, communicating strategy to partners, training and disciplining agents, organizing industry support, and communicating with, and influencing, the British government. The firm's major markets in 1832—and those in which its distinctive capabilities were most valuable—were Canton/Macau, for the purchase of tea and silk, financed by cash and opium; India, where opium was purchased and paid for with bills of credit; and Great Britain, from which the firm bought cotton, paid for with bills of credit, and sold tea and silk. Spain, Portugal, and the Americas sought trade opportunities in Canton/Macau, and access to those nationals in fact extended Jardine Matheson's market and information reach well beyond the Far East. The Jardine Matheson archive also indicate a rich correspondence between the firm and its contacts in markets linked to the firm's major markets by scale and scope economies, namely, the East Indies, a source of many commodities; Ceylon, which was beginning, with Chinese labor, to be built into a tea-producing nation; and Australia, also being built with Chinese labor, a source of wool and other commodities.

Simple Decision Rules for Managing Uncertainty

With competitors seesawing from stability to near bankruptcy, Jardine Matheson offered a safe haven to customers and suppliers who banked, borrowed, insured, and shipped with the firm. It was important to Jardine's reputation and to the firm's own stability that associated agents and staff follow closely the firm's prohibition against speculation on their own account, particularly speculation in commodities and especially speculation in indigo. As James Matheson explained to Charles Thomas of Singapore, who was urging on Matheson a coffee investment:

While you speculate in the face of a high exchange and at your own risk, your neighbors do so at the risk of their constituents and often for the sake of effecting sales at anything likely to pay an indifferent exchange. Hence, it generally happens that those who are first in the market on these occasions, whether from priority of information or superior discernment in foreseeing a use, make handsome profits, while those who follow experience a very different fate. It is not, however, on account of these views that we feel an insuperable objection to incur the risk of such speculation. They are foreign to the line of our business, and we have neither the time nor inclination for acquiring the requisite information to give us a fair chance of avoiding the most serious errors.[10]

Inculcating sound financial management in its agents was the most pressing management issue faced by Jardine Matheson & Company in the firm's early years. Advances and speculation were the most common concerns. James Matheson chides the firm's Bombay agent De Vitre & Company: "Excuse my mentioning to you that it would be some satisfaction to me if you could manage to square up your account with us about once a year, if not putting you to much inconvenience. Your balance would thus be really what it ought to be, say, a series of temporary advances in anticipation of your remittances and not a permanent loan forming a part of your trading capital."[11]

The firm of E. de Otadui, a Portuguese agent working in Manila, and his American partner, John Shillaber, were reprimanded sharply for "the injudiciousness of the speculative views, which you have allowed yourselves to be led away by, as much to the injury of your friends. You will probably accuse your bad fortune, but if this has been the case during a large portion of your life, is it not high time, at length to avoid exposing yourself to a choice which has proved so uniformly ruinous?"[12] Again, to Otadui,

Sincerely desirous as we are of the prosperity of your house, and of contributing to it by every means in our power, it is a service of great regret to us that our wishes should to all appearance have been hitherto thwarted in this respect. And we are anxious that a better system should, if possible, be adopted to insure you enjoying the full advantage of the extensive agency business which you have the means of commanding. I have written strongly to Mr. Shillaber my opinion of the injudicious magnitude and seemingly wild character of his speculative views.[13]

Speculation led to the request for advances and loans, anathema to the firm. In a letter of May 1, 1838, to John Purvis in London, James Matheson wrote: "We must confess however it is with some reluctance we agree to this, experiences here show that such advances in place of benefiting the receivers are too apt to accumulate with a still larger debt. It will be a source of much satisfaction to us, should you care to prove to be an exception to the general rule."[14]

Discipline at a distance was not limited to correspondence. Jardine Matheson would send one of its agents to oversee the finances of a fractious firm, as in the case of Otadui & Company. In the early 20th century, Jardine Matheson would shut down a representative office if the agents engaged in speculation on their own account.[15]

Building a Reputation for Regular and Candid Information

A network of correspondents in East Asia, Europe, South America, and Africa, including the commanders of Jardine Matheson's vessels, supplied to the early firm information on prices, markets, exchange rates, and political events, some of which was communicated to a larger audience via the *Canton Register* from 1827 to 1846 and some withheld for Jardine Matheson's own benefit. Beginning in 1848 through 1870, the commander of each Jardine vessel submitted this information in a formal monthly report. Jardine Matheson & Company depended on Jamsetjee Jeejeebhoy and others for their knowledge of the Malwa crop and Bombay market trends to prepare instructions for commanders on the coast. Jardine, Skinner in

Calcutta also informed Jardine Matheson about the monthly auctions, watched market trends, and forwarded the official reports of the opium agencies.

Developing a Relationship with the Government in China

While the East India Company had acted on the authority of the Crown as an arm of the British government with a militia of its own, the private trade in China found itself with no authority and no protection. The object of its on-again, off-again relationship with government, whether British parliamentary or Chinese, was trade. The relationship went through three phases during the period covered in this chapter: the first, a campaign to engage all British traders and suppliers in China and India to support the British government's intervention in trade whether by guns or diplomacy; the second, a campaign to engage all foreign traders in pursuit of the establishment of free trade at negotiated treaty ports; the third, a campaign to provide loans to the Chinese government for armaments and infrastructure, often involving the collaboration of peer companies and competitors.

In 1832, the firm held no strategic assets but tried successfully to build influence by entertaining Her Majesty's superintendent of trade in Canton and London and by seeking election to Parliament. In the General Election of 1841, William Jardine was elected as the Liberal member at Ashburton; James Matheson succeeded Jardine after Jardine's death in 1843. The firm's parliamentary interest continued until the seat was disfranchised in 1868.

James Matheson campaigned for British government protection of the right of free trade where a precedent of such trade had been established. In 1828, he delivered an address to Parliament, which was subsequently published by Smith, Elder in 1836. James Matheson's *Present Position and Prospects of the British Trade with China* was directed to the House of Commons, where its purpose was to argue from Emmerich De Vattel, the Swiss natural law jurist, that the historical precedent of trade between China and Great Britain having been established "for a couple of centuries," the merchants of Canton now "deny their [China's] right to expel us from China; or equally effectually to attain that object, by imposing ruinous exactions, and inflicting such insults and degradations as would render it impossible for us, with a due regard either to individual or national honour, to continue our intercourse. It is a sound and settled principle of law, applicable equally to nations and individuals that no one shall be permitted to do that indirectly, which it would be unlawful to do directly."[16]

Upon joining Magniac & Company, James Matheson solicited the Bombay and Canton merchants to sign a petition to Parliament supporting his treatise. The following excerpt from a letter to Jamsetjee Jeejeebhoy is typical of many of the period: "As you must feel interested in whatever tends to the improvement of our commercial relations with China, I take this opportunity of enclosing a copy of a Petition calling the attention of the House of Commons to the subject signed by every British subject here, out of the Company's employ, except Mr. L. Dent and Capt. Glover. Much good has already been done by the energetic measures adopted."[17]

In 1841, the firm persuaded the British foreign secretary, Lord Palmerston, to send warships to China to arrange for reparations to be made for 20,000 chests of opium that had been seized by the Chinese authorities. The hostilities that ensued became known as the First Opium War. The Chinese lost and were forced to sign a treaty in 1842 awarding the British traders reparations. The treaty opened the ports of Canton, Amoy, Foochow, Ningpo, and Shanghai and ceded the island of Hong Kong to Britain. The second phase of the relationship with the Chinese government had begun.

After continued hostilities, a Second Opium War broke out in 1860. As victors, the British won virtually unrestricted commercial rights to conduct business in China, but so did the other trading nations, France, Germany, and the United States, among others. The firm was substantively involved in the establishment of the Treaty Port System, which established a system of customs duties at the ports to replace the old tribute system under which gifts and respect were paid to the Imperial throne for the privilege of conducting trade. The firm developed and maintained close relations with both Chinese and British leaders, attempting to find the right, timely, mutually beneficial instrument of influence.

After many years of seeking parliamentary assistance on behalf of the merchants of Canton (and after many years of making minor loans at interest to officials and Chinese merchants), Jardine Matheson was involved in the first sizable loan to the Imperial government—a loan at 15% in the amount of £400,000 guaranteed by the customs revenue in April 1867—for China's campaign against the Muslim rebels. Jardine Matheson was asked for £200,000. Peking did not authorize further provincial loans until 1874, when £600,000 was needed again to finance military operations. The firm declined the whole amount but offered £150,000, if customs security were again provided.[18]

The opening of the Yangtze River, the third phase of the firm's relationship with the Chinese government, raised Jardine Matheson & Company's confidence in a Chinese government-directed program of economic development for China. Nevertheless, the participation of foreigners in China's external trade, as owners or agents in the exchange of goods, was still restricted at all open ports, except Shanghai and Hong Kong. Hence, the auxiliary services of trade were vital to the prosperity of foreigners in China. Jardine Matheson & Company reacted to these developments by an increased emphasis on agency services—finance, insurance, and shipping—as well as facilitation of Chinese government loans and industrial projects and the pursuit of cooperation and joint investment with the emerging Chinese merchant community.

From 1885, Jardine Matheson was primarily interested in railway contracts. Loans, however large and profitable, were regarded as a means of obtaining leverage with Chinese officials responsible for the award of railway contracts. China was not alone; Japan, Thailand, Singapore, and other ASEAN nations welcomed foreign investment. This was the beginning of significant foreign direct investment by British entrepreneurs.

Jardine Matheson had the financial strength, and the firm's sustainability in the Far East depended on its ability to lend funds and generate investment capital. Jardine Matheson was increasingly in competition with banks as well as other trading firms for the privilege. The acquisition of strategic assets—railway contracts, for example—involved a formidable capital investment and was often pursued with a partner. In the case of the railroads, the Jardine's partner was former shipping competitor, Butterfield & Swire.

By 1885, Jardine Matheson's relevant markets were the 15 treaty ports of China and the new treaty port in Japan. Through Matheson & Company, London, the firm was engaged in joint ventures in treaty territories like Singapore, Straits, Malaysia, Siam, and Borneo for tin, rubber, petroleum, and gold.

The Evolving External Organization—From Trading House to Investment House, 1885

The three major functions derived from trading, earlier described as agency services—namely, banking, shipping, and insurance—dominated the Hong Kong investment market and reflected the commercial character of the Treaty Port System. From the 1870s forward, Jardine Matheson and its competitors made substantial investments in joint-stock enterprises in the service of trade.

By 1885, Jardine Matheson had made investments in wharf property, piers and godowns, the expansion of insurance services, shipping, and sugar refining. Funded with the retained earnings of trading profits, Jardine Matheson & Company opened Ewo Silk Filature in 1895 and Ewo Cotton Spinning and Weaving Company, Ltd. in 1897 to meet the incipient Japanese competition and internalize the supply chain.[19]

After a period of opposition, during which Jardine Matheson and its founders perceived the Hongkong & Shanghai Bank as a direct competitor for banking services, Jardine Matheson taipan William Keswick, a great-nephew of William Jardine, joined the bank's Board of Directors in 1877 and later became its Chairman. While the firm had early reservations about membership on the bank's board because of the bank's direct access to member firm finances, as a member of the board, Jardine Matheson was joined by collaborator/competitors like Butterfield & Swire and Sassoon.

The advantages of board membership were access to investment and shared financing opportunities not only in China and Hong Kong but also in the bank's branch markets. Early in 1898 the British and Chinese Corporation was created jointly by the Hongkong and Shanghai Banking Corporation and Jardine Matheson & Company to construct railways linking the Yangtze River to the interior for product inflow and outflow. There were intense competition with, and eventual collaboration by, German, American, and French interests in the construction of railways. The combined contribution of Jardine Matheson and the Hongkong and Shanghai Bank—operating as the British and Chinese Corporation—to railway development was £26 million.[20]

Opportunity for Exploration in Japan and Southeast Asia

Jardine Matheson's shipping business and management communications brought the existence of new investment opportunities to the attention of the firm and its network. Because the cash contribution necessary to fund massive infrastructure or mining projects was beyond the means of a single firm, collaboration was necessary for participation and eventual gain from the investment.

There was dramatic development of natural resources throughout Asia from the 1860s through 1914, made more opportune to nominally British, Asia-based investors and their investment groups in London because of the relationship between Britain and countries under treaty or protection. These countries included the Crown Colony of the Straits Settlements (comprising Singapore, Penang, Malacca, Province Wellesley, and the Dindings); the four Malay States of Perak, Selangor, Negri, Sembilan, and Pahang; and the five Federated States of Johore, Trengganu, Kelantan, Kedah, and Perlis.

Singapore refined not only the tin of Malaya but also from Siam, Indochina, Burma, Australia, China, andCentral and South Africa. Railways, necessary for transporting tin from the mining center of Larut to Singapore's Port Weld—8 miles distant on a deepwater inlet of the Larut River—were constructed in 1884. In the same year a railway, 22 miles long, was built from Kuala Lumpur to Klang. In 1895, a railway was completed from the port of Teluk Anson to Ipoh. The West Coast Railway was completed and Singapore was linked with Bangkok through Kedah. There were 1,909 miles of road and 805 of railways by 1914.[21]

Drilling for oil in Burma began in 1887. North Borneo began petroleum production in 1910, when the first well was sunk in Sarawak. To transport the oil, railways were built to link Rangoon to Prome in 1877; Rangoon to Mandalay in 1889; a branch line from Thazi to Myingyan was completed in November 1899.[22]

Trade with Japan, initiated after the first treaty ports were opened in 1854, involved exportation of raw materials—raw cotton from India; rubber, iron ore, tin, and spices from Malaya and the Netherlands East Indies, Siam, Indochina, Burma, and Borneo—largely through Singapore, which had become a great entrepôt for Western Pacific trade—as well as wool from Australia and timber and pulp from Canada. Like China and the markets previously described, Japan needed foreign capital. The first foreign loan, which was for railway construction, was floated in London in 1870 and secured on customs duties and railway earnings.[23]

After 1870, Jardine Matheson & Company placed emphasis on Japan and also began to explore new business opportunities in Southeast Asia, including tin mines at Selangor, Malaya, railways and mines in northwest Korea, and copper ore in the Yangtze.[24] The company began selling small amounts of Russian oil, carried via Suez, at Shanghai in the early 1870's and by 1884, imports had risen to 839,000 gallons. Jardine Matheson began to import American oil in 1881 and handled smaller consignments of Sumatran oil from 1883. Jardine Matheson also acted as agent for Tide Water Oil Company, a Standard Oil associate.[25]

Early Contribution to Foreign Direct Investment

Companies like Jardine Matheson (or Matheson & Company, its investment arm) made substantial direct foreign investments in Asian development. The firm actively sought other investment opportunities in Europe, the United States, and Latin America. Matheson & Company would have provided stock or investment promotion and legal services, but even more importantly, the existence of a British company traded on British markets, with securities denominated in sterling, encouraged the investment of British individuals and financial intermediaries. Matheson & Company connected the overseas project to potential investors. The skill acquired in doing this for one venture enabled the promoter to repeat it many times and develop a reputation for experience and access to resources.

Jardine Matheson was increasingly an investment company, in search of strategic assets on which to build sustainable advantage and added value. The firm's Far East trade had changed dramatically from 1832 to 1885. Interfirm credits were a continuing fact of merchant life, but they now began to be offered by E. D.Sassoon & Company to the opium producers, at the far upstream end of the value chain, an innovation that gained the Bombay firm advantage over former opium leader, Jardine Matheson & Company. One of Jardine Matheson's competitors, Butterfield & Swire, established in Shanghai in 1848, bought American shipbuilders Russsell & Company and became the largest shipper in the region. Jardine Matheson sought to establish its advantage in investment, through joint ventures in sugar, silk, textiles, cold storage, warehousing, and docks in Hong Kong and Japan. Through Matheson & Company, its London investment house, by 1885 it was well spread out in mining, manufacturing, and railway investments.

Dynamics of the Growth of Jardine Matheson and the Theory of the Growth of the Firm

These research findings support a Penrosean interpretation in which the growth of Jardine Matheson & Company is based on the firm's initial resources and capabilities and strategy evolves to take advantage of manager-perceived opportunities to capture value. The resource and services choices made by Jardine Matheson were necessitated by the trading environment, including the distance, the risk, and the cultural divide between Chinese and Indian and private English participants, as well as the piratical practices that prevailed on the high seas and coastal waters. The demand for security was of paramount concern to participants in the burgeoning private trade. Trading credits loans and insurance on every facet of the trade reduced risk for buyers and sellers; hence, financial management, insurance, banking, shipping, and trading became the cluster of capabilities known as "agency services." Security of buyers and sellers depended largely on the financial probity of the agency house, an intangible factor ascertainable largely through reputation, if not actual experience. Realizing how business continuity depended on favorable word of mouth, Jardine Matheson jealously guarded its financial reputation and the reputation of firms on which its activities depended.

Jardine Matheson's External Organization

A central theme of this study is the Richardsonian view that Jardine Matheson's development of a pattern of external relationships would foster the flow of information, the knowledge with which to interpret it, the ability to influence others, and the reputation to attract and retain trading partners. Long before the establishment of Hong Kong and the treaty ports made trade more consistent and reliable, a volatile trading environment and the distance between buyers and sellers made partnerships and alliances both necessary and attractive to Jardine Matheson and peer firms. Clearly, an early inherited asset to the firm was the 50 agents inherited from the previous partnership of Magniac & Jardine. Jardine Matheson went on to build a network of some 150 agents in the Pacific.

In the absence of a market, Jardine Matheson & Company and the early private traders created the market institutions necessary to regularize trade and reduce risk, putting buyers and sellers in such free interaction that the prices of the same goods tended toward equality easily and quickly. Among the first steps the firm took to create an informed community among the European traders, their suppliers, and their customers was the publication of the *Canton Register*, which included commodity prices, market conditions, and social and political developments, as well as routine news of impending shipments. When Jardine Matheson needed support for its appeal to Parliament to protect the trade, the trading community signed a petition that James Matheson read in the House of Commons.

Although working capital requirements were generally low for private traders, the more prosperous trading firms like Jardine Matheson sought to own their own ships. Given the capital-intensive nature of shipping, it was a costly endeavor for a single firm to attempt to expand market penetration. Jardine Matheson's range and flexibility increased dramatically when partnerships were created that linked Hong Kong and Calcutta, Hong Kong and Singapore, and Hong Kong and London. Relationships with American and British manufacturers increased the firm's access to capital and investments. Even when the Chinese government forced British traders out of Canton, Jardine Matheson & Company continued its trade using competitive American firms as intermediaries. The captains or supercargoes of foreign merchant ships were useful partners, strengthening shipping interests, increasing international contracts, and introducing into the firm associates who knew another aspect of the import-export trade. Collaboration with competitors was also a means of survival in the insurance business. Jardine Matheson and Dent & Company shared management responsibility for the Canton Insurance Company and pooled their resources to manage the risks of piracy, storms at sea, and spoilage, among other potential hazards to which they and their customers were exposed.

The Evolving External Organization—From Trading House to Investment House

A Richardsonian interpretation would argue that the external or networked organization of Jardine Matheson & Company created an environment in which information was shared and new opportunities uncovered, allowing the firm and its network to learn and adapt based on their perception and response to productive opportunity. But preemption and ownership would have been inadequate responses to new opportunity. Between 1832 and 1885, value was beginning to migrate from trading activities to investment, as new opportunities to build infrastructure, extract natural resources, or develop agricultural and forest resources in the treaty ports offered shared risk and protection from seesawing demand for British manufactures. While China and the treaty countries had opened major projects for private investment and comanagement by foreign firms, it was excess trading profit that made cash available for investment in railways, mines, and manufacturers. The lure of wealth with limited risk appealed to London and European investors.

By 1885 Jardine Matheson had responded to changes in the competitive environment by setting up its own investment house, Matheson & Company, soliciting investments in mines, railways, shipping, manufactures, and finance and insurance businesses; by joining its potential competitor, the Hongkong & Shanghai Bank as a member of the bank board and as an investment partner in Chinese railway projects; and by partnering with competitor Butterfield & Swire on a number of joint-venture projects in China.

Impact of Stasis on the Growth of the Firm

Some things did not change. Between 1832 and 1885 the customer for Jardine Matheson's products and services was more often a business than a private individual and at a significant distance from the market for supply or demand. For example, the customer in 1832 was Chinese merchants buying opium for distribution and London merchants buying silk, tea, and other commodities. By 1885, Asian and London merchants were transporting, financing and insuring goods carried by third-party ships. The investment in manufacturing plants, railways, and mines was infrequently through the contribution of a wealthy individual and far more often the contribution of a firm. In 1832 and 1885, business customers had a single goal: to grow rich through trade. But by 1885, the emphasis had moved to growing rich with less effort—through investment.

Another thing did not change between 1832 and 1885: at both points it was of highest value to the business customer to achieve wealth while lowering risk through the agency services of a trusted partner, like Jardine Matheson. The basis of trust remained reputation, built on financial probity and the ability of the firm to absorb trading risk while profiting from the experience. To absorb the risk of others, Jardine Matheson itself continued to require long-term internal and external relationships built on high trust and the avoidance of speculation in commodities (like indigo in the early period)—or in other business interests (like Hongkong Land)—about which information (in this case about individual investments and commitments) was incomplete. While environmental change brought on by competition, globalization, change in the regulatory environment—and other aspects of the external environment—make it unlikely that any capability will continue to remain valuable independent of the scenario in which a firm is operating, there has been great stability in the value of Jardine Matheson's capabilities and the resources underlying them, the firm's trading relationships, market knowledge, and investment capital. Risk brokerage, supply chain expertise, and financial and capital management were the early capabilities or competencies of the firm on which it continued to build as the period covered by this study comes to an end.

Figure 2.1
Jardine Matheson & Company Framework for Growth, 1832–1885

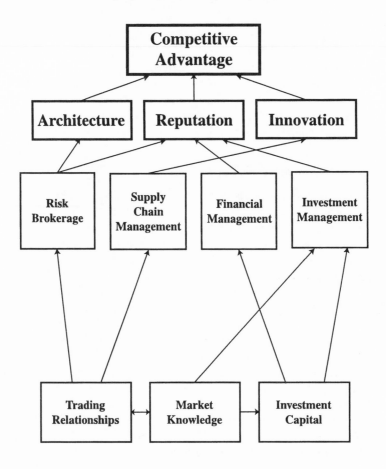

The Evolution of Resources and Capabilities

Figure 2.1 depicts the evolving relationship between resources, the use and development of capabilities, and their contribution to the growth of Jardine Matheson & Company. In Figure 2.1, the firm's trading relationships are a source of market knowledge, and vice versa. In 1832, the firm leveraged these intangible resources to become a risk broker and supply chain expert, the basis for its strategic position in 1832. Through risk brokerage, a source of strategic control, the firm came to own the relationship between customers, agents, and suppliers (i.e., the architecture or external organization of interfirm relationships) and to develop a reputation for financing and capital management. Managing risk and stretching capital required innovation, which further increased the firm's financial returns and freed up some of the company's financial capacity for further investments. By 1885, Jardine Matheson had applied its trading relationships, market knowledge, and financial investment to the creation of a freestanding investment house, Matheson & Company. In 1885, while still engaged in the Pacific trade, the firm leveraged these resources to become an investment manager and financier. The firm earned a reputation for financial management, risk management, capital management, and deal structuring, competencies that are transferable across many markets and businesses. The firm's reputation was a source of added value for continued growth.

NOTES

1. John Kay, *The Foundations of Corporate Success* (London: Oxford University Press, 1993), 283–319. A capabilities-based scholar, Kay suggests a set of questions for examining industry and firm strategies. I have adopted his frameworks for comparison of historical periods.

2. The Charter Act of 1813 documents the end of the East India Company's monopoly on the India trade—or "Country trade." The East India Company continued to hold a partial monopoly on the China trade through 1842. Remnants of the East India Company continued to operate through 1950. The company's letters are preserved in the British Library Oriental and India Office Collections, A/2/24, London.

3. Michael C. Greenberg, *British Trade and the Opening of China 1800–42* (Cambridge: Cambridge University Press, 1951), 10–17.

4. Geoffrey Jones, *Merchants to Multinationals* (Oxford, UK: Oxford University Press, 2002), 33. Jones confirms, "Jardine Matheson and Dent's were by far the largest of the British traders of the period." Dent & Company went bankrupt in 1867.

5. Mira Wilkins, "The Free-standing Company, 1870–1914: An Important Type of British Foreign Direct Investment," *Economic History Review* 2nd ser. 41 (1988): 263.

6. Stanley D. Chapman, *Merchant Enterprise in Britain* (Cambridge: Cambridge University Press, 1992), 313.

7. Note also that Matheson & Company income was not included in the group capital figure until 1910.

8. James Matheson, Canton, 25 April 1832, to Hugh Matheson, Calcutta, Jardine Matheson Archive Private Letter Books (hereinafter JMA PLB) C5/1.

9. William Jardine, Canton, 9 February 1835, to Hollingworth Magniac, London; JMA PLB C5/3.

10. James Matheson, Canton, 30 September 1832, to Charles Thomas, Singapore: JMA PLB C4/2.

11. James Matheson, Canton, 24 July 1832, to M. DeVitre, Bombay, JMA PLB C4/1.

12. James Matheson, Canton, 26 April 1838, to E. de Otadui, Manila, JMA PLB C5/3.

13. James Matheson, Canton, 30 April 1838, to E. de Otadui, Manila, JMA PLB C5/3.

14. James Matheson, Canton, 1 May 1838, to John Purvis, London, JMA PLB C5/3.

15. Jones, *Merchants to Multinationals*, 217.

16. James Matheson, *Present Position and Prospects of the British Trade with China* (London: Smith, Elder, 1836), 39–40.

17. James Matheson, Canton, 31 January 1831, to Jamsetjee Jeejeebhoy, Bombay, JMA PLB C4/1.

18. Edward LeFevour, *Western Enterprise in Late Ch'ing China* (Cambridge: Harvard University Press, 1968), 65–66.

19. By 1885, the firm—through Matheson & Company, its investment house—invested £7,514,790 in Hong Kong and China, not including railway loans of £26 million with investment partners Hongkong and Shanghai Bank.

	Taels (Ounces of Silver, Chinese)
Hunt's Wharf Property	213,846
Jardine's Piers and Godowns	331,000
Canton Insurance Office	36,000
Hong Kong Fire Insurance Company	44,100
Hong Kong and Whampoa Dock Company	81,568
Hong Kong, Canton and Macao SS Company	36,672
Indo-China Steam Navigation Company	817,560
Hong Kong and Shanghai Bank	463,968
China Sugar Refining	109,858
Luzon Sugar Refining	119,850

Source: JM Archives, Account Books, 1885.

20. Frank H. H. King, *The History of the Hongkong & Shanghai Banking Corporation: The Hongkong Bank in Late Imperial China, 1864–1902* (Cambridge: Cambridge University Press, 1988). The figure includes:

Shanghai-Woosung	£100,000 (Jardine Matheson)
Taku-Tientsin	£50,000 (Jardine Matheson)
Canton-Hankow	£10,000,000 (Investor: Jardine Matheson)
Shanhaikuan-Newchwang	£2,300,000 (British and Chinese Corporation (Jardine Matheson and the Hongkong & Shanghai Bank)
Shanghai-Nanking	£3,250,000 (British and Chinese Corporation as above)
Canton-Kowloon	£1,500,000 (British and Chinese Corporation as above)
Tientsin-Pukow	£7,400,000 (British and Chinese Corporation with Deutsche Asiatische Bank)
Shanghai-Hangchow-Ningpo	£1,500,000 (British and Chinese Corporation)

21. E. M. Gull, *British Economic Interests in the Far East* (New York: Institute of Pacific Relations, 1943), 89–90.

22. Ibid., 92.

23. Ibid., 88.

24. Edward Lefevour, 141.

25. Ibid., 144–145.

3

BETWEEN THE WARS:
DIMINISHED GLOBALIZATION,
GOVERNMENT PROTECTIONISM, AND
TRADING COMPANY RESPONSE

The nature of war and role of government, impact on spending, investment, GDP, and future growth are of special relevance to the history of the Hong Kong trading industry and to all services firms, not less because the developed world of 2003 entered a stage of economic development in which government assumed a far greater role as consumer and investor, a world of profound geopolitical uncertainties, intensification of regional tensions, and threat to globalization and its achievements.

One might argue that the late-20th-century world economy, the "second global economy," differs significantly from the first. It is broader in terms of the number of national markets included and deeper in terms of the density of interaction, including flows of both trade and investment. The governance of international economic transactions has changed significantly from market transactions to hierarchy as the preferred organizational model. A significant proportion of what appears to be trade is actually cross-border intrafirm transfers.

Until 2001, there was, as Stephen Kobrin suggests,[1] general agreement that major and positive changes were taking place in the scope and organization of international economic activities—some, like Eric Hobshawm[2] in 1979 claiming that what has ended is "the age of extremes," specifically the economic dislocation and mass destruction, real or threatened, that characterized the period 1914 to the end of the Cold War; and others, like Jean-Marie Guehenno,[3] linking emerging global networks with the death of nation-states and the state structure. However, in 2003, it remained to be seen whether the return to a larger role for government in trade and markets represents either the death of "the age of extremes" or something entirely different, possibly the institutionalization of the global economy through international security initiatives and international trade law. Something entirely different did come to prominence in the interwar period—the Japanese *sogo shosha*.

Chapter 3 reviews the impact of the Hong Kong trading industry on globaliza-tion and growth through World War II, and focuses on the decline of globalization during the interwar years. The chapter also deals with the increasing importance of the Japanese *sogo shosha* in Southeast Asia—and the survival strategies of the Hong Kong trading companies.

THE CONTRIBUTION OF THE TRADING COMPANIES TO GLOBALIZATION AND TRADE GROWTH

The Hong Kong trading industry contributed substantially to the global move-ment of goods, services, capital and income payments. Alan Taylor's work reveals several uneven periods of trade growth, including the most rapid from the early 1840s to 1873, when trade volume growth rose to 6% annually, five times faster than population and three times faster than output. There was some slowdown in the following two decades, but in the years 1893–1913, growth picked up again to 4.5% per annum. Growth of trade averaged 3% per annum for the period, a rate similar to that seen in the whole 20th century.[4]

The role played by the trading companies as bankers and insurers, dependent on an active and reputable London (or New York) bond market, substantially pro-moted the growth of trade, increased the number of economic players, and intro-duced new nations into the world trading network, while lowering overall risk. The trading community was in frequent interaction through ship-borne correspon-dence that made commodity prices transparent to all buyers and sellers alike. Table 3.1 provides valuable detail on the frequency of the Jardine Matheson & Com-pany's correspondence with buyers and suppliers in key markets for over 100 years.

The three-way correspondence between China, India, and Britain predomi-nated through 1870— not unreasonably, because of the prevailing triangular pay-ments system that reduced the extent of international gold and silver flows. After the 1870s, the picture began to change. The closing down of the opium trade in the 1880s, the economic penetration of China by European powers other than Britain (through the treaty ports), and the rise of Japan as the first Asian industrial power significantly altered the pattern of trade in the Far East. As Japan industrialized, the structure of its foreign trade changed from one in which raw materials were ex-ported and finished manufactures imported to one in which manufactures were exported and raw materials imported. The direction of Japan trade changed in sympathy with these developments. Asia replaced Europe and the United States as the main source of Japanese imports, supplying almost one-half of these needs by 1913. By that date Asia had also become Japan's leading regional export market.

Despite the growing importance of Japan and the United States, Europe contin-ued to dominate world trade in the period before World War I, especially in its de-mand for food and raw materials. As Kenwood and Lougheed suggest, trade among non-European countries accounted for less than one-quarter of world trade in merchandise in 1913.[5]

The distribution of world trade changed dramatically from 1913 to 1937, with non-European imports and exports representing 49% of total trade. The strongest growing region was Asia, with 11% of total trade in 1913 and 16% of total trade in 1937. While the volume of trade of the trading companies' European customers declined from 62% in 1913 to 51.4% in 1937, the total trading volume of Latin America, Asia, Africa, and Oceania, largely brokered by the trading companies, increased from 23.4% in 1913 to 32% in 1937.[6] While, overall, the percent of trade brokered by trading companies grew between 1913 and 1939, the loss of European customers directly affected the Hong Kong trading companies. How much of that advantage was now captured by the Japanese general trading companies is covered in a later section.

A RETREAT FROM GLOBAL ECONOMY

The period between World Wars I and II saw a retreat from the notion of an integrated international economy that had characterized the period from 1870 to the outbreak of World War I.[7]

The phrase "global economy" derives from H. J. Mackinder's paper of 1904, published in the *Geographic Journal*. From the 1820s through 1913 world trade grew at 46% per decade; from 1874 to 1913 capital invested grew between 25 and 40% of gross domestic savings.[8]

John Dunning acknowledges that although complete economic interdependence has never existed in practice, "it came near to it in the second and third quarters of the nineteenth century."[9] In contrast, the period between the two world wars was characterized by recession, deflation, high unemployment, and trade restrictions. The end of the war was followed by a deep depression in 1920; a period of recovery was followed by the Great Depression beginning in 1929. By the early 1930s, the global economy had been shattered and replaced by one of trading blocs, exchange controls, and protectionism. How the trading companies fared is discussed later.

The rate of growth of total trade per decade declined from an average of almost 40% between 1881 and 1913 to 14% between 1913 and 1937. Figure 3.1 depicts world trade volume from the first era of globalization to the interwar decline, including the impact of transportation costs, which had held steady or declined because of advances in transportation technology through World War I, and which rose disproportionately high because of government trade control schemes leading up to and after the war. The figure also depicts the rise in tariffs from 1920 to 1939.

A. J. Arnold calls the interwar period "one of the most important in British economic history, covering the years of active hostility, in which the state spent more, taxed more and organized a greater part of the economy than ever before, the 1919–20 boom, in which there were more mergers and acquisitions than at any time until the 1950s, the sudden and very severe slump of 1920–21, and the period of deflation that preceded the return to sterling, and to the gold standard in 1925."[10] Britain imposed the McKenna duties (up to 33% on foreign manufactured

Table 3.1
Frequency and Distribution of Correspondence, 1801–1906

Market	Subtotal	Dates: From–To
Africa	193	1825–1881
America	5,176	1821–1898
Amoy	4,402	1833–1901
Australia	5,961	1824–1898
Bombay	16,674	1822–1881
Calcutta	8,950	1818–1893
Canton	18,249	1815–1904
Chefoo	819	1842–1901
Chinchew	600	1833–1863
Chinhai	14	1853–1871
Chiukiang	1,155	1863–1901
Chuenpee	13	1835–1841
Chusan	87	1840–1860
Coast	1,226	1825–1893
East India	11,354	1821–1898
Europe	6,975	1820–1891
Foochow& River	4,083	1846–1881
Formosa	209	1865–1881
Hankow	1,948	1861–1901
Hoihow	49	1876–1881
Honam	352	1858–1869
Great Britain	8,363	1822–1891
India	1,755	1819–1898
Ichang	1	1883
Japan	3,878	1859–1892
Kahing	3	1869–1878
Kapsingmum	39	1830–1891
Kienning	10	1861–1864
Kienyang	3	1863–1864
Korea	190	1883–1884
Kowloon	9	1837–1900
Kumsingmum	1,389	1835–1856
Lintin	171	1823–1898

Table 3.1 continued

Market	Subtotal	Dates: From–To
London	21,017	1814–1898
Lookong	74	1847–1854
Madras	2,164	1823–1881
Macao	11,638	1823–1891
Namoa	27	1844–1883
Newchang	470	1861–1901
Pakhoi	52	1877–1880
Pekin	29	1860–1901
Pingtu	1	1886
Port Arthur	3	1888–1901
Shanghai	12,231	1824–1891
Suiching	4	1857–1863
Suyeada	1	1869
Suykut	1	1861
Swatow	2,910	1853–1880
Taitau	5	1851–1856
Taku	5	1860–1871
Tientsin	1,166	1860–1901
Tonkoo	109	1839–1840
Tsingsan	3	1864–1901
Tamsui	941	1860–1898
Tungshaw	1	1861
Twatutia	2	1872–1879
Wei-hai-wei	4	1859
Wenchow	2	1877–1879
Whampoa	1,253	1825–1885
Woosung	646	1854–1871
Wuhu	121	1883–1884
Other	5,690	1813–100
Total	183,018	

Source: Based on Jardine Matheson Archives, Cambridge University.

Figure 3.1
World Trade, Transportation Costs and Tariffs, 1870–1939

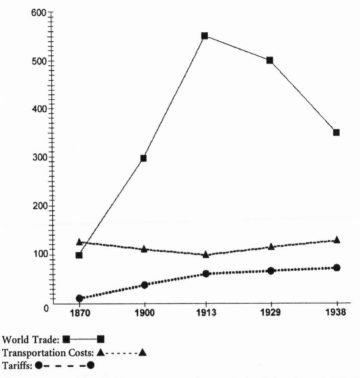

World Trade: ■——————■
Transportation Costs: ▲- - - - - -▲
Tariffs: ●- - - - -●

Source: Antoni Estevadeordal, Brian Frantz, Alan M. Taylor, "The Rise and Fall of World Trade, 1870–1939," National Bureau of Economic Research, February 2002.

goods) in 1915 and discriminated in trade in favor of countries and locales that were part of the British Empire. France raised the minimum tariff from 5% to 20% by 1918 and the maximum tariff from 10% to 40% and introduced quotas in 1919. The Germans were forced to give five years of most-favored-nation status to the Allies, but when the period ended on 10 January 1925, there was an immediate return to protectionism.[11]

Italy, Spain, Belgium, and the Netherlands all imposed or raised tariffs in the 1920s. "Antidumping" tariff legislation was enacted in Japan in 1920 and in Australia, Britain, New Zealand, and the United States in 1921. In the United States, the Fordney-McCumber Tariff Act of 1922 contained the highest rates in American tariff history until the passage of the Smoot-Hawley tariff in 1930. Canada's 1904 legislation was amended and extended to 1921. Up to 1930, Britain retained the option to impose an additional 33% tariffs on any devaluing country. The war of escalating tariffs was exacerbated as the depression worsened.

The free-trading Netherlands and Scandinavia formed a bloc and reacted to sterling devaluation. Quotas expanded in France to encompass most goods. Germany built bilateral trade channels and exchange controls. Protection was heavy, increasing after 1930 with quotas, controls, and regional or bilateral arrangements that restricted international trade as a way to improve internal economic position.

The working relationship between government and business during the interwar years changed considerably, affecting industrial profitability. During the war, the government abandoned business as usual, mediating interest, explicitly bargaining profit controls and taxes in exchange for cooperation with the war effort by organized labor. In the postwar period, the state largely withdrew from collective bargaining and removed the economic controls of the war years, although higher taxes on business profits were continued through the postwar boom.

While World War I undoubtedly stimulated some technological developments and encouraged greater standardization of industrial processes, it also helped to extend capacity in a number of traditional industries, including shipbuilding, iron and steel, and general engineering. The war had intensified the problem of industrial overcommitment and increased home competition in industries such as textiles, iron, steel, and shipbuilding, while postwar protectionism saw a loss of overseas markets for the output of these industries. In the developed world, government's role was redefined as a consequence of the war and carried into the interwar period. Government expenditures on goods and services quadrupled, squeezing out consumer expenditure and flattening GDP formation.[12]

The war badly disturbed the complex, existing framework of international economic and financial arrangements, sharply reducing the volume of exports. Broadberry has argued that the collapse of British exports explains the overall low level of activity in interwar Britain, falling to 50% of 1913 levels in 1921. Unemployment in Britain (30% in shipbuilding, 22% in iron and steel in 1924) reached levels very different from those prevailing in the new industries, reflecting the particular decline in the exports of staple goods, in comparison with 1911–1913, when coal, iron, steel, machinery, vehicles, ships, and textiles jointly contributed two-thirds of British total imports.

In Britain, there were also important reductions in working hours—about 13% in 1919–1920, which caused a rapid rise in real wages relative to GDP between 1913 and 1924. The slump of 1920–1921 was very severe given wage costs and high dividend payouts. During the 1920s, rising output of many products led to weakening prices, especially for raw materials, sugar, and wheat.

While Europe's share in world trade declined during the interwar period, Japan's rising share of world trade led to commodity control schemes and collaborative arrangements to restrict output in sugar and rubber, coffee, petroleum, tin, and most of the world's primary products. The trade in minerals—such as petroleum, copper, bauxite and iron ore—as well as trade in cocoa, coffee, and bananas grew rapidly in the interwar years. However, the trade in nontropical foodstuffs stagnated, and agricultural raw materials, including cotton, silk, and hides and skins experienced falling trade volumes.[13] By the early 1930s the volume of Japan's textile exports had overtaken those of Lancashire.

RISE OF JAPAN IN SOUTHEAST ASIA

The outbreak of World War I provided favorable circumstances for Japan's southward expansion into Southeast Asia. While the war curtained trade between the Western countries and Southeast Asian markets, an opportunity was available to Japan to move in and fill the vacuum by selling food, textiles, and other products. As a result, full-scale economic relations began between Japan and Southeast Asia. Between 1914 and 1925, exports from Japan to Southeast Asia increased eightfold, and imports from Southeast Asia increased more than fivefold. There was a doubling (from 11,845 to 23,967 in 1918) of the Japanese population in Southeast Asia in the five years following the war.[14] As Hajime points out, various Japanese organizations for promoting economic ties and facilities for the local Japanese communities were rapidly established and developed in many parts of Southeast Asia during the war and during the 1920s. After the war, new Japanese consulates were opened in Haiphong, Davao, Surabaya, Saigon, Hanoi, and Medan, in addition to those in Manila, Singapore, Bangkok and Batavia, which had been established before the war.

The Japanese became economically involved in Southeast Asia during the war and in the following decade to satisfy requirements for raw materials for the development of heavy and chemical industries, which were considered vital to Japanese industrialization and catch-up with the United States and other Western countries. It was imperative that Japan obtain raw materials from geographically proximate Southeast Asia as well as China to achieve the development of heavy and chemical industries for competition with the West. The import of raw materials produced a perennial excess of imports and aggravated Japan's balance of payments. A solution to this problem called for a vigorous export drive and diversification of export markets in order to acquire foreign currencies. In this context, Southeast Asia emerged as an important market for Japanese cotton textiles.

In the process of emerging from the economic collapse of 1929 and the depression that followed, the formation of economic blocs by the advanced countries of the world increased and brought international economic and political tensions to the surface. As part of this process, Japan began to advance extensively into Southeast Asian markets to acquire a sufficient fund of foreign currencies to construct a Japan-Manchuria-China economic bloc. This was considered vital, given the frailty of international trade generally and the declining volume of business carried on with the United States and China, the more so to Japan after the Manchurian incident of 1931. While Western trade with Southeast Asia declined, Japanese goods, mainly cotton products, aided by a devalued yen, streamed into Southeast Asian markets, where the production of primary products had been seriously damaged by the economic crisis and purchasing power had been lowered. Table 3.2

Table 3.2
Main Export Markets for Japanese Cotton Textiles, 1921–1937

	1921	1929	1937
Market	¥ (Thousands)	¥ (Thousands)	¥ (Thousands)
China	100,987	150,115	11,295
Kwantung Province	15,536	15,342	29,425
Manchuria			55,748
British India	30,465	109,124	63,040
Straits Settlements	3,841	5,787	12,230
Dutch East Indies	25,571	42,269	85,603
Philippines	3,779	5,615	12,056
Siam	609	3,799	16,148
South Africa	—	3,043	10,214
Egypt	—	24,398	10,509
Australia	2,857	2,917	13,527
Argentine	280	4,154	29,294
Total (with others)	203,673	412,706	573,064

Source: Based on Sugiyama and Guerrero, *International Commercial Rivalry in Southeast Asia in the Interwar Period*, 48.

shows the significant decrease in exports to China after the Manchurian incident and the rise of Southeast Asian markets for Japanese cottons. This rapid increase in exports changed the Japanese trade structure with Southeast Asia from one of deficit into one of surplus. This phenomenon made Southeast Asia the scene of international economic frictions between Japan, the Western colonial powers, particularly Britain, and the local economies.

ECONOMIC IMPLICATIONS FOR THE HONG KONG TRADING COMPANIES

A number of factors in the external environment of the period put acute pressures on the British trading companies, including the post–World War I recession, deflated commodity prices, the Great Depression, and the increasing importance of new competitors, specifically the Japanese *sogo shosha*.

Within the overall context of stagnating international trade, British export performance, especially cotton textiles, was especially weak. Although the firms had long since performed tasks other than selling British exports, the declining competitiveness of British goods, the growth of competition, and import substitution in the interwar years adversely affected what had remained a most profitable part of their business before 1914.

In the 1920s Ralli was the leading importer of British textiles into India, followed by Grahams, James Finlay, the Bombay Company, and Forbes, Forbes, Campbell. These firms suffered badly when the postwar recession hit—leaving them with huge stocks.

In India and Hong Kong, trading companies that had traditionally worked as middlemen for British firms sought a more independent role. In Japan, Dodwell, on the other hand, had grown rich. In 1919 the capital of the company was doubled out of accumulated reserves. The trading profit achieved record levels unsurpassed until 1947,[15] largely from Dodwell's shipping interests, which included chartering, bunkering, and the sale of streamers. The Russo-Japanese War of 1904–1905 was a period of great activity for Dodwell in Japan. Numerous time charters were negotiated for the Japanese, and at one time no less than 24 chartered ships were running around the coasts of Japan. By 1914, Japan had entered an era of unparalleled prosperity. Ships were requisitioned from their regular trade, and as scarcities developed, freight rates and prices rose rapidly as the war boom got under way. Freight rates on general cargo from the Far East to London, which had long been £2 per ton, shot up to £50, and even at that figure space was almost unobtainable without payment of a premium. Japan earned increasing profits, not only in freight returns but in constantly rising export prices. Dodwell's shipping business boomed with the chartering and sale of Japanese steamers to the Allied powers and with imports and exports.

After the war, Japan's increasing success and continued struggle for a share of the world's trade made middlemen import and export traders and ship charterers far less desirable than direct dealing with importers and consumers. Dodwell was restricted to steel and lumber. Other sundry imports—chemicals, mill supplies, paints, dyes, and tobaccos—were handled but problematic as the Japanese import business was in the process of change. Increasing competition from Japanese *sogo shosha* with an associated insurance company made Dodwell's insurance operations unprofitable.

In 1927, it was decided that Dodwell limit its future import operations to acting solely as agent to manufacturers abroad selling to Japanese buyers on their behalf for direct shipment. Only a few exceptions were made, for example, for office equipment, where Dodwell held the exclusive agency in Japan.

By 1938 the whole commercial picture in Japan had become very dark. Import restrictions become more and more strict, exchange control was tightened, and in the export trade markets were oversupplied or were adopting measures regulating imports from Japan. Dodwell stuck it out in Japan until 1941, when the last expatriate was imprisoned, interned, and then sent to South Africa under an exchange scheme between the Allies and Japan for national repatriation of noncombatants.

Like Dodwell, Harrisons & Crosfield determined to tough out the grim economic conditions of the interwar period, deepening its involvement in Malaysia, investing in logging, sawmilling, and ship-repairing in Sabah until the Japanese occupation of North Borneo in 1942, and diversified into chemicals in Canada and, later, pharmaceuticals. The firm took an aggressive stand when shrinking margins threatened its plywood business, encouraging area plywood companies to join the Plywood Chest Association to control prices and formulate guidelines for orderly marketing, an arrangement that worked well for 30 years.[16] By 1939 Harrisons & Crosfield had capital available for investment topping trading companies Booker McConnell, Finlays, and Swires.

After making superior profits during the war selling to the military, Jardine Matheson experienced large losses in 1920 through trading in produce and silk, returning to profitability only in 1935. The firm continued to diversify in China, making a large investment in the 1920s in the export of dried eggs and in the 1930s in brewing. The firm also established an engineering affiliate in the 1920s and in the following decade developed an extensive business selling armaments in China. However, Jardine Matheson reduced its activities in markets outside Hong Kong and China at this time.

The major change was that Matheson & Company no longer functioned as a worldwide investment house as it had since 1885. Matheson's performed in London a variety of banking and merchanting services for the parent company, Jardine Matheson, and became closely involved with the dried egg business but no longer scanned the world for business opportunities.

During the 1930s, Swire sought an accommodation between its shipping interests and the Chinese, and Jardine Matheson was considering selling its failing brewing venture in China to the Japanese. In India, British managing agencies like Bird and Gillander were conservative, hostile to import substitution industries, and slow to consider the possibilities of collaborating with Indian business groups.

While the trading companies scrambled to make sense of the interwar economic environment, a new business model with an ancient heritage was emerging to exploit the opportunities for both suppliers and buyers in Southeast Asia.

THE *SOGO SHOSHA*, A NEW COMPETITIVE BUSINESS MODEL

In the interwar period, as the British trading companies were deepening their involvement in their main host country, Japan was emerging from isolation and sending its general trading companies or *sogo shosha* into new markets to sell textiles and finished industrial goods. In return, Japan required low-cost iron and steel. The *sogo shosha*, literally translated from the Japanese, is a company trading in a broad variety of products and services. By 1990, some nine of these companies represented 68% of Japan's imports and 36% of the country's exports for a total of ¥127 trillion.

The evolution of the *sogo shosha* began in the period of the Meiji Restoration of 1868 and had much in common with the contemporaneous development of the private trade in China. What little commerce Japan had conducted with the outside world had been handled by the Dutch through the port city of Nagasaki, and after the Meiji Restoration, Japan's leaders sought to create internal trade vehicles.

Mitsui and Mitsubishi became the prototype trading companies, quickly diversifying into coal, iron, shipping, and other areas. Others included Itochu in textiles and Iwai in manufactured products.

In his analysis of the Japanese commercial community, Shimizu Hiroshi offers a view of world trade, the leaders, and new entrants from 1882 to 1930. Taking 1882–1892 as the base year (equal to 100), from 1910 to 1939 an index of Japan's imports increased to 592.8 and 1729, while exports rose to 643.7 and 2505. In relation to this expansion of Japan's foreign trade, by the end of World War I there had emerged three major trading partners: the United States, the British Empire, and China. They remained very important until the end of the 1930s. In 1929, they together accounted for 84.8% of Japan's total exports and 77.5% of total imports. When the major European powers went to war, they were not in a position to supply the developing countries with large quantities of manufactured goods. This put Japan in an excellent circumstance to maneuver into position. Japan's share of finished industrial goods in total exports rose from 30.5% in 1908–1912 to 43.5% in 1918–1922. Mitsui Mitsubishi, Suzuki Shoten, Gosho, and Nippon Menka made huge profits during the war. Gosho's annual profits rose from ¥61,000 in 1913 to ¥206,000 in 1916 and ¥7,282,000 in 1918, and the firm wanted to expand its business activities in the Dutch East Indies, a source of sugar and other local produce. From the early 1920s large Japanese merchant houses in Japan began increasingly to export finished cottons direct to their foreign markets through representative offices.

During the mid-1950s and early 1970s, Japan embarked on an aggressive, export-led industrialization program, building up its capabilities in synthetic fibers, heavy machinery, and petroleum refining. Gross National Product (GNP) growth averaged 8% in the 1950s and 11% in the 1960s.

The *sogo shosha* imported the raw materials necessary for expansion, brought in the capital goods and technology, and provided one-stop trading services. Simultaneous involvement in importing and exporting enabled them to establish true hedges in foreign exchange risk. At the same time, access to short-term and long-term financing was vital to firm growth through oil and liquid natural gas production facilities, mining, farming, forestry, and fisheries. Acquisitions were usually made in partnership with public or private sector organizations in foreign countries.

The era of high growth for the *sogo shosha* came to a halt with the first oil shock, when the price of oil trebled, but cheap financing made it possible for the *sogo shosha* to bounce back. Access to cheap financing can be explained by the *sogo shosha*'s relationship with a main bank within the overarching *keiretsu* industrial structure. This structure is defined by Michael Gerlach as "institutionalized relationships among firms based on localized networks of dense transactions, a stable framework of exchange, and patterns of periodic collective action."[17] The governance style of the *keiretsu* is explained by Gerlach and by Yoshino and Lifson[18] as midway between Chandler's "visible hand" (formal administration) and Adam Smith's "invisible hand" (autonomously self-regulating, impersonal markets). In Paul Sheard's view, the organization of Japanese industry has been an important factor underpinning the resilience of the economy in the face of external shocks to competitiveness and its propensity to carry out longer-term structural adjustments in response to shifts in competitiveness.[19]

Kenichi Miyashita and David Russell identify the roles of the *sogo shosha*:

If something is bought anywhere in the world, from iron ore to textiles to oil, autos, jumbo jets, or nuclear power plants, the chances are a Japanese trading company is involved at some stage. They not only handle direct imports and exports to and from Japan, but they also handle "third-country" trade, where they act as a middleman even though the transaction has nothing to do with Japan. They purchase raw materials and sell finished products throughout the world, serve as the eyes and ears of major clients, providing them with global market information and analysis . . . they help smooth out the rocky road their clients would face in dealing with foreign languages, foreign currencies and foreign governments. They not only buy and sell but also invest overseas, particularly in fields that promise a steady supply of critical raw materials (such as mining and oil and gas exploration) and in large-scale industrial projects where few other companies have the resources to compete with them.[20]

The *sogo shosha* play an extremely important role in Japanese business by providing credit for small to medium sized companies. Without the *sogo shosha* as financial intermediary, these firms would have to deal directly with the giant city banks, which do not have a reputation for bending over backwards to accommodate small businesses, having to vet the firm's business performance and future prospects, check collateral, and so on. The banks are happier to extend credit to the giant *sogo shosha*.

The Business Value of the *Sogo Shosha*

Paul Sheard focuses on the role of the general trading companies as trade-financing intermediaries in interfirm transactions, particularly in the domestic economy. It is well known that Japanese manufacturing firms make extensive use of trade credit in interfirm transactions. Sheard examines and emphasizes the attributes of the *sogo shosha* as a "quasi insurance agency" in facilitating interfirm transactions involving trade credit. Specifically, he argues that the trading companies are involved as a device for the insurance of default risks in a regime dependent on trade credit.[21]

In studying the *sogo shosha* and its boundary with the market, Sheard and others build implicitly on the transaction cost economizing view of internalization developed by Oliver Williamson.[22] For example, Aoki has noted the tendency of Japanese economic organizations to be characterized by long-term relationships designed to reduce uncertainty and collective risk costs.[23]

The *sogo shosha* are central actors in Japan's industrial groupings and maintain close relations with the respective main bank in the grouping and with other member firms in the *keiretsu* through the extensive use of interfirm trade credits as well as shareholdings. Sheard's conceptual framework proposes an intermediate goods economy where at least some firms buy some of their inputs on credit from supplier firms. He assumes, for the sake of argument, that there is a positive probability that purchasers will default on their liability of trade credit to their suppliers in certain states of the world. Then supplier firms may wish to shed this default risk or diversify the risk in some way. Is it reasonable to assume firms might be risk-averse? What institutional arrangements might be used to shed this risk?

Returning to Williamson's schemes for the governance of contractual relations, the firm might sell its potential default risks to an insurance company, but how can the firm reduce the probability of these risks at all? How might moral hazard and adverse selection be overcome? Make the insurance company a party to the transaction? Sheard finds a precedent in implicit labor contract theory in which the firm simultaneously functions as a purchaser of labor inputs and an insurer of fluctuations in labor income. The firm achieves economies of scope in jointly acting as employer and insurer to workers. In the context of the *sogo shosha*, the trading company exploits certain economies of scope in the joint provision to its customer firms of "regular" marketing services and of insurance against default risks.

The *sogo shosha* enters the transaction as an intermediary between the supplier and the purchaser, accepting payment from the buyer in the form of a bill of payment and issuing its own bill to the supplier. The supplier's extension of credit is to the trading company not to the purchaser. Similarly, the liability of the purchaser is to the trading company rather than to the supplier. The trading company's role is analogous to that of an insurance agency. Although the trading company doesn't receive insurance premiums directly, it receives commission income, usually a small percentage of the value of the transaction.

The Business Value of the Hong Kong Trading Company: A Comparison

From the early history of the agency house, it will be recalled that commissions were charged on every kind of service provided by agents to their principals, including sales of product (3–5%), returned goods (2.5%), insurance (.5%), ships charter (2.5%), inbound freight (1%), outbound freight (5%), settling insurance losses (1%), negotiating bills of exchange (1%), debt recovery efforts (2.5%; if successful, 5%), estate management (2.5%), serving as executor (5%), transshipment (1%). Like the *sogo shosha*, the agency house was primarily a trading firm, although it also acted as banker, bill-broker, shipowner, freighter, insurance agent, and purveyor, maintaining commercial and financial connections with its branch houses or agents all over the world. As Hong Kong developed as an entrepôt center, the value of these services increased, as depicted in Table 3.3.

Underlying these services was a network of relationships built and sustained by frequent communications and the development of logistical and organizational routines to facilitate trade. Yoshino and Lifson identify these as the distinctive competences of the *sogo shosha* and use the expression "coordination of product systems" to describe "the identifiable flows of goods, services and resources among

Table 3.3
Entrepôt Services of the Hong Kong Trading Company

Financier	Direct Investment	
	Indirect Investment	
	Loan Syndication	
Trading Partner	Commodities Trade	
	Services Trade	
Middleman	Commodities Trade	Entrepôt
		Transshipment
		Brokerage in Direct Trade
	Services Trade	Tourism
		Loan Syndication
		Services Trade
Facilitator	Contact Point	
	Conduit for Information	
	Training ground for marketing, production	

Source: Based on Yun-Wing Sung, *The China-Hong Kong Connection: The Key to China's Open Door Policy*, 7.

technologically separable units that transform raw materials into finished products. The product system coordinated by a *sogo shosha* is an intermediate business model between the poles" of corporate administration and market governance, having the organizational routines of the one and the flexibility and low cost of the other.[24] The agency house and the *sogo shosha* represent a common, one-stop shop response to similar business problems.

Although the primary function of the *sogo shosha* is trading—that is, matching buyers and sellers of diverse products—in performing this core activity, it is entrenched in a number of key industries, not on a onetime, ad hoc basis, but on a recurring basis. In various industries the *sogo shosha* is typically involved at different stages of the value chain, from the purchase of raw materials to the marketing of the final product—vertically integrated commodity systems, particularly in basic commodities such as textiles, iron and steel, nonferrous metals, chemicals, and foodstuffs. The *sogo shosha*'s uniqueness lies in its capacity to provide essential links between stages in a product system for a client firm, only one stage of which is trading.

Akira Goto argues that, by organizing collectively, *sogo shosha* are able to avoid the scale diseconomies and the control losses likely in full-scale vertical integration and at the same time to provide benefits not available in unprotected market exchange. As market alternatives, such groups function as an "information club," with close cooperation "secured by a set of tacit, informal rules that emerge through a long history of exchange of information and recognition of interdependence substantiated by financial linkages and interlocking directorates."[25]

Like the *sogo shosha*, the Hong Kong trading companies would build financial linkages with subsidiaries and associated companies, including equity holdings, capital investments, and potential trade synergies. While acquisition and network building began in the 1950s, the period of greatest external network building came in mid-1970s, changing the scale and scope of the Hong Kong trading industry.

NOTES

1. Stephen J. Kobrin, "The Architecture of Globalization: State Sovereignty in a Networked Global Economy," in John Dunning, ed., *Governments, Globalization and International Business* (Oxford: Oxford University Press, 1997), 146–147.

2. E. J. Hobshawm, "The Development of the World Economy," *Cambridge Journal of Economics* 3 (1979): 312–315, 305–318.

3. J. M. Guehenno, *The End of the Nation State* (Ann Arbor: University of Minneapolis Press, 1995).

4. Alan M. Taylor, "Globalization, Trade and Development: Some Lessons from History," Working Paper 9326, National Bureau of Economic Research, November 2002, 5.

5. A. G. Kenwood and A. L. Lougheed, *The Growth of the International Economy 1820–1990* (London: Routledge, 1992), 82.

6. P. Lamartine Yates, *Forty Years of Foreign Trade* (London, 1955), Tables 6 and 7, 32–33, in Kenwood and Lougheed, *The Growth of the International Economy 1820–1990*, 213.

7. A. J. Arnold, "Profitability and Capital Accumulation in Britain," *Economic History Review* 52 (1999): 45. Also Geoffrey Jones, *Merchants to Multinationals* (Oxford: Oxford University Press, 2000), 84.

8. Stephen J. Kobrin, "Beyond Symmetry: State Sovereignty in a Networked Global Economy," Carnegie Bosch Institute for Applied Studies in International Management, Working Paper 95–98.

9. John Dunning, *Multinational Enterprises and the Global Economy* (Reading, PA: Addison-Wesley, 1993), 476.

10. Arnold, "Profitability and Capital Accumulation," 45.

11. Antoni Estevadeordal, Brian Frantz, Alan M. Taylor, "The Rise and Fall of World Trade, 1870–1939," NBER Working Paper No. W9318 (November 2002): 4–5.

12. S. N. Broadberry, "The Emergence of Mass Unemployment: Explaining Macroeconomic Trends in Britain during the Trans World War I Period," *Economic History Review* 43 (1990): 272.

13. Kenwood and Lougheed, *The Growth of the International Economy*, 212–217.

14. Shimizu Hajime, "Japanese Economic Penetration in Southeast Asia," in *International Commercial Rivalry in Southeast Asia in the Interwar Period* (New Haven, CT: Yale University Press, 1994), 13.

15. Edmund Warde, ed., *The House of Dodwell: A Century of Achievement, 1858–1958* (London: Dodwell & Company, 1958), 126.

16. Peter Pugh, *Great Enterprise: A History of Harrisons & Crosfield* (UK: Harrisons & Crosfield, 1990), 115.

17. Michael Gerlach, *Alliance Capitalism: The Social Organization of Japanese Business* (Berkeley: University of California Press, 1992.

18. M. Y. Yoshino and Thomas B. Lifson, *The Invisible Link: Japan's Sogo Shosha and the Organization of Trade* (Cambridge: MIT Press, 1986), 6–7.

19. Paul Sheard, "The Japanese General Trading Company as an Aspect of Interfirm Risk Sharing," *Journal of the Japanese and International Economies* 3 (1989), 308–322.

20. Kenichi Miyashita and David Russell, *Keiretsu, Inside the Hidden Japanese Conglomerates* (New York: McGraw-Hill, 1994).

21. Paul Sheard, "The Japanese General Trading Company." 319.

22. Oliver F. Williamson, *The Economic Institutions of Capitalism: Firms, Markets, Relational Contracting* (New York: Free Press, 1985), 32.

23. Masahiko Aoki, "Towards a Comparative Institutional Analysis: Motivations and Some Tentative Theorizing," *The Japanese Economic Review* 47 (March 1996): 1–19.

24. Yoshino and Lifson, *The Invisible Link.* 43.

25. Akira Goto, "Business Groups in a Market Economy," *European Economic Review* 19 (1982), 63.

4

Jardine Matheson's Blind Ambition: Opportunity and Risk, 1961–2002

Chapter 4 deals with the history of Jardine Matheson and its strategic management, after the near destruction of the firm and its assets and the imprisonment and death of many of the firm's managers in World War II. There was little left after the war beyond the ambition to rebuild in an uncertain environment they believed they knew far better than the Europeans and Americans, who saw advantage in marketing their products in China.

The chapter is an analytical history of Jardine Matheson from 1961 to 2002, touching briefly on the post-war years, including a period of intense acquisition and divestiture activity, 1961–1996. It uses firm history to answer questions about the firm's resource and services choices, the experience of failure, the raising of funds for project investment, and the continued development of market institutions to make trading and investment conditions more reliable.[1]

Well into the 20th century, foreign trade continued to give Jardine Matheson a role in the national agenda of China and its trading partners in the Pacific. Jardine's bread-and-butter business was importing into the Far East hundreds of lines of British, Canadian, and American consumer and capital goods, everything and anything from packages of Ovaltine to Westinghouse transformers. Jardine Matheson acted as principal, consultant, or agent in trading with the Chinese. As an agent for British and Australian companies, it sold to the Chinese livestock, wool, cotton, hides, aircraft, rolling mills, machine tools, and complete chemical plants. As a principal, Jardine bought and resold commodities such as soybeans, broad beans, vegetable oils, hog bristles, and furs, as well as tea, rice, gold, and diamonds.[2]

Day-to-day business in the China trade was volatile and dangerous. In the summer of 1937 Japanese forces attacked China in an attempt to expand Japanese commercial and strategic interests to the Asian mainland. A number of Jardine

Matheson's managers were captured and imprisoned. The company's textile factories were looted, and the Chinese staff was dispersed.

In December 1941, Japanese forces invaded British colonies in Asia, including Hong Kong. Jardine Matheson officials in the colony were again imprisoned. Jardine taipan John Keswick, who had managed to escape to Ceylon, returned to Hong Kong after the war to rebuild the small airline, textile mills, wharves, brewery, and cold storage facilities, which were all that remained of the firm's physical assets. In 1949, Communist forces seized control of the mainland after four years of civil war. Jardine Matheson attempted to build a relationship with the Communist regime. By 1950, new government policies increased taxes, restricted currency exchanges, and banned layoffs. Jardine's Ewo Brewery in Shanghai was forced to reduce its prices by 17% and to remain open at a $4 million annual loss. Companies based in Hong Kong were bound to observe a British trade embargo against China because of the Korean War. Compelled to close its operations in China, Jardine Matheson entered into negotiations with the Communist government and, in 1954, wrote off $20 million in losses. While little of the physical assets remained, the skills of Jardine Matheson's managers were intact, although removed to Matheson & Company, London.

With trade *inside* China closed, Jardine Matheson continued to trade *with* China from its London base, although such trade was limited. To survive and grow in the midst of adversity in China and uncertainty in Hong Kong, the firm investigated new Asian markets, both for itself as principal and for the British, Canadian, and Americans firms for which the firm acted as agent. To do so, it needed an infusion of cash.

Jardine Matheson & Company was 129 years old when it went public in 1961, abandoning the partnership system under which the firm had been administered since 1832. The listing of the company's stock on the Hong Kong Stock Exchange marked the beginning of a search for expansion and diversification fueled by investor capital, which was cheaper than bank loans during the period.

The firm was not alone in its pursuit of other Asian markets at this time. World trade had begun to exceed the growth of world production during the mid-1950s, and by the early 1960s firms sought to grow by direct foreign investment[3]:

- in the developing countries of Japan, Korea, Taiwan, Singapore, and Malaysia across a wide range of industries;
- by exploiting knowledge and expertise gained in one country's markets in other countries at low cost, and
- by offsetting the unavoidable extra costs of doing business in foreign nations.

BUILDING ON HISTORIC CAPABILITIES: STEPPING-STONES PERIOD, 1961–1971

The 1961 stock prospectus described Jardine Matheson as a firm "which participates widely in the commerce and industry of the Far East, in the merchanting of imports and exports, the distribution and servicing of engineering products, the shipping industry, air transport business, insurance, investment management, agency business and general merchant adventure." The new public company was family-owned—the family of James Keswick had bought out the remaining shares of the Jardine family and had arranged the public offering with three London banks. The net operating profit in 1961 was US$161.24 thousand, reflecting the sale of investments sufficient to fund the reorganization of the capital of the company.

The firm was organized along geographic lines and consisted of a head office and a few wholly owned subsidiaries. All of the departments and the subsidiaries reported into the Hong Kong head office. The departments included the Imports and Exports Departments, Jardine Engineering Corporation, Airways and Insurance Departments, Shipping Department, Jardine Dyeing & Finishing Company, Matheson & Company, Ltd. (with investment, shipping and chartering sections) in London, and the China Trading Department (closely allied to Matheson & Company, Ltd.). In addition, Jardine Matheson possessed several wholly owned subsidiaries, including Jardine Matheson & Co., Japan, Ltd.; Jardine Matheson & Company, Ltd.—Taiwan, and Jardine Waugh, Ltd.—Malaysia (expansion of an investment initiated in 1954).

Jardine Matheson embarked on cautious expansion into new geographic markets with existing capabilities—trading, finance, shipping, and insurance services—and extensive investment in unrelated industries in Hong Kong and Australia, as depicted in Table 4.1. The word "cautious" is used because Jardine Matheson and other investors made their plans with an eye toward the turnover in 1997 of lands adjacent to Hong Kong that had been leased to the British. Since Hong Kong was dependent on these lands for water and industrial space, many Hong Kong residents expected that the Colony would be taken over by the Communists. The Cultural Revolution did not assuage their fear. Jardine's caution

Table 4.1
Stepping Stones Period, 1961–1971

Resources/Services		Markets
Forest Products	2	Japan, Malaysia
Construction and Engineering	7	HK, Malaysia, Australia
Manufacturing	9	HK, Australia, Thailand
Shipping, Transportation	22	HK, Australia, Japan, Philippines, UK
Wholesale Trade	18	HK, Australia, Japan, Philippines, US–San Francisco
Finance, Insurance and Real Estate	19	HK, Australia Japan, US–Hawaii, London/UK
Business Services	6	HK, Australia, Fiji

played itself out in two ways: (1) acquirers like Jardine Matheson & Company sought to recoup their investments in three to five years,[4] and (2) acquirers sought to spread their risk by expanding across the Pacific Rim.

Along with caution, there was optimism that Hong Kong would be a financial leader and world light-industrial center. The economy was booming. Corporate income tax was 15%, among the lowest in the world, with no tax levied on dividends, capital gains, or income generated outside the colony. The currency was among the strongest in Asia and was maintained by a colonial policy of virtually uninterrupted budget surpluses. Further, the influx of skilled Chinese workers into Hong Kong from the Mainland, the rising standards of living of the people in the territories (i.e., the New Territories that lie along the border of Kowloon and China), and the accompanying commercial and industrial expansion afforded reason to believe that the Hong Kong home market offered growth opportunities in every area of the economy. Broader trade with Asia depended on the trading requirements of the more prosperous European and North American countries.

Jardine Matheson moved into Australia in 1964, establishing a holding company with interests in importing and exporting, aviation, real estate, textiles, sugar manufacturing, shipping and timber. The firm had very long-term contacts in Australia and interests—some of them dating back to the 19th century—in Japan, Malaysia, Singapore, Brunei, Thailand, Laos, Taiwan, and the Cook and Fiji Islands. The firm used the holding company construct as an anchor for the eventual creation of economic hubs like Hong Kong, located in deepwater ports, such as those in Australia, Japan, South Africa, and Singapore and the Pacific Coast of the United States for shipping, commodities trading, finance, and insurance.

In Hong Kong, the firm acquired a new wholly owned subsidiary, the Empire Finance Co., Ltd., a brokerage firm that traded in Hong Kong and Japanese stocks. Jardine Matheson and the Hongkong Land Company entered into agreement to develop hotel and apartment projects at East Point. Also in Hong Kong, Jardine Matheson & Company took on new insurance subsidiaries like the Lombard Insurance Company (descendant of the 10th Canton Insurance Company), and new acquisitions, like Chinese International Underwriters, Ltd. in the hull insurance-broking field and Hong Kong Security, Ltd. in the field of security services. The firm initiated a new marketing partnership with Alfred Dunhill, Ltd.

At the end of the "stepping-stones" period, consolidated trading profit before taxes was US$12.06 million, an increase of more than 600% since the firm went public in 1961. Fixed assets, mainly ships and property, had increased from US$6.82 million in 1961 to US$23.2 million in 1971. Investments in subsidiary and associated companies increased from US$4.85 million in 1961 to US$48.91 million in 1971. Return on equity increased from 8.51% in 1961 to 18.83% in 1971. Return on total assets increased from 7.82% in 1961 to 16.12% in 1969 and began a slow decline to 15.05% in 1970 and 13.31% in 1971—a decline that became increasingly evident during the 1970s as assets mounted. The sale of stock—some 12 million shares in 1970 and 1971—and the sale of Hong Kong property for redevelopment during the decade created a net capital surplus that went directly to reserves to finance new growth. Added value accelerated the ratio of retained earnings or transfers to reserves over trading profit began the decade at 39% and ended at 47.14%. No turnover data were available until 1972, hence the use of trading profit for added value calculations in Table 4.2.

SPECULATING IN COMMODITIES AND MANUFACTURES: EXPLOIT AND DEVELOP PERIOD, 1972–1977

From 1972 to 1977, the firm pursued two paths toward growth. The first was a continuation of its stepping-stones approach into new markets. The second, concurrent, and radical approach was expansion into 46 markets with product offerings that spanned 152 individual lines of business. One might call the period "Exploit and Develop," based roughly on Birger Wernerfelt's[5] typology in which the growth of the firm involves a balance between the exploitation of existing resources and the development of new ones, as depicted in Table 4.3.

Looking at the firm's investment decisions during this period, we can hypothesize a hybrid growth strategy that executives at Jardine Matheson could summarize as follows:

- We will continue to invest heavily in our home market, Hong Kong;
- We will continue to expand the market reach of our related businesses—trading shipping, finance, insurance, where physical resources and skills are shared;
- We will invest in unrelated businesses where we can't lose and maybe we'll win. Investment prospects with easy exit (high current ratio gives the firm the ability to convert its accounts receivable into cash or borrow to repay current creditors) and high returns on equity (high profit margin, low-cost labor);
- We will exploit our managerial skills (approximately 10% of total employees) in finance, management, marketing, engineering, supply chain/logistics, and industry specialists to simplify and replicate the work effort of unskilled or blue-collar labor common across our businesses (some 90% of employees);
- We will consider that we have succeeded if we achieve 25% return on investment within three years (If yes, exploit, develop, raise ownership percentage, create subsidiary, create holding company for further acquisitions; if not, sell and commit net surplus capital to reserves).

Beginning in 1972, Jardine Matheson experimented with stock sales and long-term debt to finance the acquisition or investment in firms whose products and services were related and complementary to Jardine Matheson's existing products and services—for example, real estate in London's financial district and in Hawaii—and to access additional investment capital for growth. In that year, the firm made the largest acquisition in its history—the London real estate company, Reunion Properties Company, Ltd., reported to be the biggest landlord in London's financial district, for US$23.58 million—for the first time issuing new stock that found ready buyers among institutional investors. Before the year was out, the Re-

Table 4.2
Key Ratios, 1961–1971

	1961	1962	1963	1964	1965	1966	1967	1968	1969	1970	1971
	%	%	%	%	%	%	%	%	%	%	%
ROE	8.51	7.60	10.23	10.49	11.03	11.5	12.27	15.01	18.73	17.76	18.83
ROTA	7.82	7.00	9.47	7.89	7.84	8.97	9.65	12.41	16.12	15.05	13.31
Added Value	39.07	35.24	43.08	45.92	45.18	45.81	41.28	45.84	47.14	—	—

Notes: ROE = Return on equity
         ROTA = Return on total assets
         Added Value = Amount added to reserves or returned earnings over total turnover
         (or total profits in the case of Jardine's financials before 1972).

Table 4.3
Exploit and Develop Period, 1972–1977

Resources/Services	Number of Companies	Markets
Agriculture and Forestry	3	Malaysia, Micronesia, Philippines, Singapore
Mining	6	HK, S. Africa
Construction and Engineering	10	HK, Australia, Fiji, Malaysia, Singapore, Taiwan
Manufacturing	75	HK, Indonesia, Malaysia, Philippines, Singapore, South Africa
Shipping, Transportation	92	HK, Australia, Japan, Kenya Liberia, Malaysia, Mozambique, S. Africa, Taiwan, US–San Francisco
Wholesale Trade	54	HK, Australia, Japan, Fiji, Philippines, Singapore, South Africa, Taiwan, UK, US–San Francisco
Retail Trade	5	HK
Finance, Insurance and Real Estate	142	HK, Australia, Bermuda, Indonesia, Japan, Malaysia, Netherlands Antilles, Philippines, Singapore, South Africa, Swaziland, Taiwan, Transkei, UK, US–San Francisco
Business Services	50	HK, Fiji, Kenya, Lesotho, Philippines, Rhodesia, South Korea, Swaziland, Transkei, UK

union deal was followed by a US$9.75 million takeover bid for Theo. H. Davies & Co., Ltd., an old Hawaii trading company with sugarcane and real estate holdings. This was Jardine Matheson's first major acquisition in the United States and, again, was made possible by issuing new stock. For the first time since the Communists seized its vast Shanghai holdings after 1949, Jardine Matheson held greater assets outside Hong Kong than it held in the Crown Colony.

The availability of cheap labor and raw materials, coupled with increasing, although limited, GDP, justified the firm's diversification into unrelated product/services in the emerging markets of Asia (Thailand, Korea,) and Africa (South Africa, Zambia, Zimbabwe, Lesotho) and its investment of low-cost capital into high-risk, high-potential positions in forest products, sugar, and oil exploration. Jardine Matheson & Company's U.S. development program was also well under way with four initial investments in real estate, building materials, tourist services and computer components. By the end of 1972, net operating profit was US$3.28 million, 60% over the previous year. The compound growth rate in adjusted earnings per stock unit was now 27% per annum. Stockholders equity was US$20.31 million in 1972 and increased to US$56.42 million in 1973. The announcement of a cease-fire agreement in Vietnam improved the political climate throughout the Far East and raised investor confidence in Asia as a place to do business.

The firm continued to grow its historic shipping, financial services, and insurance operations by initiating joint venture arrangements with other overseas and Hong Kong partners who had leading positions and expertise in their own subsector—be it deposit and foreign exchange-broking, hire purchase finance, stock-broking, or bullion dealing; financial, insurance, or transportation services subsector—including life, marine, fire insurance, or reinsurance; or transportation—including containerization, freight forwarding, and other shipping agency services.

The organization—as well as the capital structure—of the firm was beginning to change from a purely geographic to a functional alignment. The Hong Kong Head Office, first referred to as "the parent company" in 1972, was changing from an operating company to an active holding company, with a strong focus on better balance sheet management of the parent and of the principal operating subsidiaries and associates of the firm. While the Hong Kong office continued its long-standing departmental activities, four departments had been spun off as public companies with subsidiaries and associates of their own: Jardine Industries, Ltd. (trading, manufacturing, and real estate); the Indo-China Steam Navigation Company, Ltd. (shipping); the Lombard Insurance Company, Ltd. (insurance); and Jardine Securities, Ltd., an associated company (investment).

By mid-1973 the net assets of Jardine Matheson & Company, Pty. Ltd. were US$33.07 million, and those of Matheson & Company, Ltd. approximately US$68.09 million, representing the parent company's equity and loan funds. The firm continued to increase its overseas assets. Chairman Henry Keswick explained, "Our immediate objective is to consolidate our position as a major international trading, services and financial group with headquarters in Hong Kong and operating throughout the Pacific region and in the United Kingdom."

In 1974, Jardine Matheson & Company's capital expenditures totaled US$73.55 million. Investments had been made in ships, existing property ventures, and acquisition of minority interests in subsidiary companies in the oil servicing industries. These investments had been funded largely from internal resources and term finance. The major portion of Jardine Matheson & Company's total fixed assets was in property and dry cargo ships. In the next three years, some US$25.52 million was invested in modernizing the sugar plantations and sugar mills of Theo. Davies & Company, the firm's acquisition in Hawaii.

Capital expenditures continued in 1975, including the acquisition of all the issued capital of Gammon (Hong Kong), Ltd., a leading Hong Kong construction and civil engineering group with substantial commercial property holdings; the successful cash and share offer for 75% of Zung Fu Company, Ltd., a firm with widespread automotive, engineering, trading and aviation interests in Hong Kong and Australia; and the acquisition for US$35.49 million of 53% of Rennies Consolidated Holdings, Ltd., a firm operating in eight South African countries in shipping, transportation, trading and light industry, hotels, and tourism.

To provide additional financial strength and flexibility, the firm issued US$102.04 million in 7.5% convertible subordinated unsecured loan stock due 1990, with the intention of refinancing on improved terms its short-term and medium-term debt and providing more working capital for continued growth and investment. Jardine Matheson consolidated its shipowning and marine insurance in Hong Kong in 1976, acquiring for cash all the outstanding shares of two previously publicly quoted subsidiaries, the Indo-China Steam Navigation Company (Hong Kong, Ltd.) at a cost of US$6.12 million and Lombard Insurance Company, Ltd. at a cost of US$3.47.

The firm made another striking geographical move in 1976 with its first major investment in the Middle East, a significant minority shareholding in Transportation and Trading Company (TTI), a company affiliated with the Olayan Saudi Holding Company, which operated through subsidiaries and associates, principally in Saudi Arabia and Kuwait. TTI was involved in the distribution and marketing of construction and engineering equipment, vehicles and machinery, food products, transportation and contracting. At the close of 1976 an agreement was reached with Diamond M. Drilling Company of Houston, Texas, to manage the drill ship in which Jardine Matheson & Company had a substantial minority shareholding through International Petroleum, Ltd., now operating in the Far East. In the same year in Hong Kong, Jardine Matheson & Company went into partnership with Barclays Bank International, Ltd. as Jardine Barclays, Ltd. to acquire Union Dominion Trust, Ltd. This company provided consumer finance services through two local joint ventures—United Merchants Finance, Ltd in Hong Kong and Jardine Manila Finance Inc., the Philippines.

By 1977, turnover (reported as of 1973, previously called consolidated trading profit) was US$948.28 million, reflecting the contribution of subsidiary and associated companies. Fixed assets continued to rise from US$54.96 million in 1972 to US$547.42 million in 1977. Investments in subsidiary and associated companies increased from US$74.11 million in 1972 to US$298.71 million in 1977. Return on equity was 16.06% in 1972 and 15.33% in 1977. Return on total assets was 13.40% in 1972 and 10.89% in 1977. Added value continued to decline from 6% in 1973 to 5% in 1977, reflective of high growth and high expenses in the face of mounting assets. See Table 4.4. The ratio of debt to equity, which was 40% in 1972, increased to 53.8% in 1977. Sales margins declined from 14.5% at the beginning of the period to 10.8% in 1977. Working capital to sales declined from 10.8% at the beginning of the period to 7% in 1977.

Between 1972 and 1977 a total of 437 acquisitions were made for a total investment of US$1634.25 millions in finance, transportation, trade and service, manufacturing, and natural resources. Through investments and acquisitions, Jardine Matheson was now represented in 46 markets.

RATIONALIZING COMMODITIES AND MANUFACTURES: HARVEST AND DIVEST PERIOD, 1978–1983

From 1978 to 1983, the firm began to rationalize products and markets, building a more focused portfolio that could be replicated in each market. This period was characterized by two waves of divestitures, the first from 1978 to 1979 and the second wave from 1981 to 1983. The interpretation of this period, which we'll call Harvest and Divest, is based on the diversification and divestiture research of Hoskisson, Johnson, and Moesel and D. D. Bergh and G. F, Holbein,[6] which relates divestiture to deliberate, voluntary resource reallocation and strategy choices. Hoskisson et al. describe a phenomenon they call "strategic divestiture," the reshuffling of asset portfolios through divestiture and voluntary restructuring linked to strategy formulation. What sets the Hoskisson research apart is its finding that strategic decisions—more than performance and weak governance—are the primary cause of high levels of divestment intensity.

A voluntary restructuring program aided by input from McKinsey and Company accompanied the first wave of Jardine Matheson's divestitures during 1978–1979. The second wave of divestitures was initiated to get the company out of high debt, caused by its stock swap with the Hongkong Land Company. Table 4.5

Table 4.4
Key Management Ratios, 1972–1977

	1972	1973	1974	1975	1976	1977
ROE	16.06%	9.40%	11.70%	13.30%	15.19%	15.33%
ROTA	13.40%	7.91%	18.54%	9.97%	10.39%	10.89%
Added Value	—	0.06	0.058	0.05	0.03	0.05

Table 4.5
Harvest and Divest Period, 1977–1983

Resources/Services	Number of Companies	Markets
Agriculture and Forestry	0	
Mining	6	S. Africa, US
Construction and Engineering	3	HK, Netherlands Antilles, Singapore
Manufacturing	13	HK, Brazil, Philippines, Malaysia, US
Shipping, Transportation	44	HK, Germany, Holland, Liberia, Netherlands Antilles, Panama,Philippines, Singapore, Taiwan, Thailand, UK, US–San Francisco and Hawaii
Wholesale Trade	13	HK, Japan, Zimbabwe
Retail Trade	9	HK, Australia, Malaysia, Singapore, UK, US–San Francisco and Hawaii, Zimbabwe
Finance, Insurance and Real Estate	111	HK, Bermuda, Germany, Japan, Netherlands Antilles, Panama, Philippines, Singapore, US–San Francisco and Hawaii, UK
Business Services	24	HK, Japan, UK, Zambia

presents the scope of Jardine Matheson's divestments during the period 1978–1983.

With fixed assets and returns on invested capital more or less static, and the firm's debt-to-equity ratio at 54.8%, it is not surprising that Jardine Matheson & Company turned to management consultant McKinsey & Company in 1978 to restructure the firm. The result was to place more of the day-to-day business with the operating companies and the activities of the chairman and his team of senior managers on planning and policy issues and overall firm strategy, which included exploration of growth opportunities in China.

Through its investments in commodities, the firm's earnings had become subject to widespread political, economic, and monetary uncertainty. After a meteoric rise to over 60 US cents per pound, the world price of sugar fell to 15 US cents in six months, taking the profits of Jardine Matheson & Company's Hawaii and Philippines operations with it. A sharp deterioration in the South African economy dealt a similar blow to Rennies. The Organization of Petroleum Exporting Countries (OPEC) oil shock and near collapse of Indonesia's state oil company sent troubling ripple effects through the economies of Hong Kong and South East Asia.

In Hong Kong, Jardine Industries, Ltd.'s shareholdings in three companies in three consumer electronics manufacturing companies were sold, taking Jardine Industries out of the manufacture and sale of consumer electronics. In 1979, the firm disposed of US$42 million in investments, including Promet Engineering Pte, Ltd. and Toft Bros. Industries, Ltd. and their subsidiaries, shipbuilders. With a depression in local property markets, Jardine Matheson & Company sold Reunion Properties as well as its shareholding in Singapore Land Ltd. and its interests in the Gotanda office building in Tokyo, and the Excelsior Hotel and Shopping Center complex in Hong Kong.

The emergence of China from the anarchic Cultural Revolution to the more stable era of the Four Modernizations appeared about to open China's untapped consumer market. Indeed, Jardine Matheson expanded its China Trading Division to support and benefit from the government's modernization program, which included the expansion of foreign trade, among its Four Modernizations. Jardine's Beijing office became the focal point of the effort. A second office was added in Guangzhou (Canton) to deal with traditional export and import activities as well as joint-venture industrial investments and commodities trading. Jardine Matheson and its joint-venture partner A. M. Schindler, with the China Construction Machinery Corporation, established the China Schindler Elevator Co. Ltd. in March 1980 to manufacture and distribute lifts and escalators for sale within China as well as for export.

Overseas Chinese seeking secure investments and business developers created additional demand for Hong Kong property. As a result, the last years of the 1970s had seen an unprecedented property boom in Hong Kong. Rents rose from some US$1.21 per square foot in 1975 to nearly US$6.03 in 1980, and the price of a luxury flat rose from US$304.2,000 in 1975 to US$1.6 million in 1980. The Hongkong Land Company held a unique portfolio of top quality office and residential property and was very active in property development. Its other main interests included the Mandarin Oriental group of deluxe hotels and the Dairy Farm food distribution group with major supermarket chains in Hong Kong, Australia, and Singapore.

When Hongkong Land signed a cooperative agreement with its rival, Cheung Kong Holdings Ltd., which had been raiding property companies in Hong Kong, Jardine Matheson—then owning 26% of Hongkong Land—sprang into action to avoid what it anticipated to be a takeover bid. In the late summer and early autumn of 1980, Jardine increased its holdings in Hongkong Land to 32%, financing the purchase by property sales, and the sale of a large block of shares and warrants in the Hongkong & Kowloon Wharf & Godown Company Ltd. On the morning of 3 November, amid intense speculation and press comment and following the expenditure of US$442.6 million in the stock market that day, Jardine Matheson & Company announced that the firm now owned 40% of Hongkong Land. Concurrently, Hongkong Land was also increasing its holdings in Jardine Matheson & Company and, following a series of corporate moves and acquisitions through the stock market, Hongkong Land announced that it owned approximately 40% of Jardine Matheson & Company, making Hongkong Land the firm's single largest shareholder. Compounding what amounted to a mutual hostage-taking situation, Jardine invited two of Hongkong Land's senior directors to join the board of Jardine

Matheson & Company, namely, Trevor Bedford, managing director of Hongkong Land, and George Ho, deputy chairman and managing director of Hongkong Commercial Broadcasting Company, Ltd. and a director of Hongkong Land. Their appointments paralleled the appointments of two Jardine Matheson & Company directors to the board of Hongkong Land, David McLeod and R. C. Kwok.

The year saw a significant increase in investments of US$1012 million and of additions (and fewer disposals) to fixed assets of US$63.58 million, funded by cash generated from operations of US$236.4 million, increases in term debt of US$602.81 million and the issue of shares totaling US$151.50 million. Total term debt rose to US$788.93 million by 31 December, 1980, with two-thirds of that largely in medium-term debt.

With a substantial drop in property trading profits, 1982 proved a very bad year for Hongkong Land. Local property markets declined. Several of Hongkong Land's joint ventures in Hong Kong with other partners met with serious difficulties because of the depressed state of the property market and the failure of partners to meet their commitments. Hongkong Land conducted a thorough review of all its joint ventures and decided to make substantial extraordinary provisions where either the project in its current form was not viable or its partners unable to meet their obligations. Due to Jardine Matheson & Company's new equity accounting procedures, these provisions now showed up on Jardine Matheson & Company's accounts where they had a negative effect on results. They did not, however, show up on Hongkong Land's accounts.

During 1983 Jardine Matheson disposed of surplus assets to raise cash, extended regional joint ventures to breathe new life into two businesses—Lombard Insurance and the Indo China Steamship Company—that needed access to specialist skills and further capital to expand, and trimmed overheads. In February 1983, Jardine reached agreement with the Continental Corporation to develop jointly their insurance underwriting interests in the Asia Pacific region. This amounted to the Lombard Insurance Company, formerly a wholly owned subsidiary, being owned 60% by Continental and 40% by Jardine Matheson & Company. The Indo-China Steamship Company, a wholly owned subsidiary of Jardine Matheson, was sold. Jardine Matheson's sale of its 53% stake in Rennies Consolidated Holding for US$175.20 millions generated a surplus over book value of US$104.68 million.

By the end of December 1983, Jardine had reduced its debt to equity ratio from .81 to .75. But the moves made during 1983 were insufficient to solve Jardine Matheson & Company's problems—low working capital to sales, high assets to sales—low profitability in the face of high debt and interest expenses. The firm announced its intention to put more effort into developing several of its functional businesses to the point where they could stand alone. Insurance brokerage was already in this position. Following its acquisition of Bache Insurance Brokers Inc, now renamed Jardine Insurance Brokers Inc., Jardine had become a major international insurance-broking business in most of the countries in which it operated. Now, the firm intended to develop its freight forwarding and shipping agency interests along similar lines.

In January 1984, Jardine Fleming & Company Ltd. arranged on behalf of Hongkong Land a needed U$512.16 million, eight-year syndicated bank loan, secured mainly against properties in Hong Kong's Central District. This loan replaced some of Hongkong Land's short-term borrowings and meant that all of its current borrowing requirements for its Hong Kong Telephone, Hongkong Electric and Exchange Square real estate purchases could be met by medium- to long-term financing.

Jardine Matheson & Company would take further steps in 1984 to manage its balance sheet, making more provisions against property and shipping. While Jardine Matheson & Company's ship management and shipping agency businesses would continue to be developed, the firm would progressively withdraw from shipowning activities, including those related to offshore oil servicing.

The asset sales of the late 1970s were, in fact, followed by asset acquisitions in 1980–1981, notably in real estate, as Jardine Matheson built up extensive holdings in Hongkong Land at a time when the cost of funds was high. The firm's debt-to-equity ratio was .87:1.00 in 1981. By 1984, total debt was more than two times equity. Return on assets in 1984 declined 50% from peak 1981 levels. This reflects the firm's high debt and low income levels and points to an unrealistic dividend payout policy in the face of rising debt and reduced earnings. Return on equity dropped from a high of 11% in 1982 to 1.89% in 1984. This reflects the firm's high debt and low income levels. (See Table 4.6.) The firm's ratio of assets to revenues was low throughout the period, approximately 1.18 in 1984, dropping from a high of 1.29 in 1981. A low asset-to-revenue ratio meant that Jardine Matheson could make an easy exit from investments. Net cash flows during the period were far lower than expected, but not in deficit, despite net sales growing 20% a year and the relationship of cost of goods sold to sales at 93.5%.

EXPERIENCE OF FAILURE: FOCUS ON DISTINCTIVE CAPABILITIES PERIOD, 1984–2002

The acquisition by Jardine Matheson & Company of 40% of Hongkong Land Company and vice versa had long-range management consequences for both companies. Jardine and Hong Kong Land had made their acquisitions near the peak of Hong Kong's land boom. The subsequent collapse in the property market and

Table 4.6
Key Management Ratios, 1978–1983

	1978	1979	1980	1981	1982	1983
ROE	14.51%	15.25%	10.02%	10.63%	11.26%	2.64%
ROTA	11.33%	11.84%	8.88%	9.65%	9.65%	5.65%
Added Value	5.4%	5.5%	11%	6.8%	0	0

soaring interest rates became the single largest burden on Jardine. When earnings plunged and debt soared, local entrepreneurs like Li Ka'shing and Y. K. Pao began to view Jardine Matheson (and Hongkong Land) as takeover targets. Jardine had to sell valuable—and profitable—assets to survive. A major reorganization plan was deployed with changes amounting to the dismantling of Hongkong Land and the creation of a complex web of mutually owned corporations, fortifying the firm's defenses against future takeovers and strengthening the firm's governance in innovative ways.

The Hongkong Land affair was the firm's first truly major and unanticipated taste of failure. In addition to winding up, or disposing of, those projects and businesses for which Jardine saw no promising future, both companies used favorable market conditions to raise capital or to sell assets, such as Atlas House in London and Hongkong Land's shareholdings in Hong Kong Telephone and Hongkong Electric, where the investments, although of high quality, were not integral to operations. To spread business risk, Jardine also introduced partners to some of Jardine Matheson & Company's businesses where management considered that their specialized expertise and capital would be on value.

From 1984 to 1996, business interests were reduced and new governance schemes introduced to protect information and closely monitor expenses and investments. Growth continued, but far less visibly, through related diversification strategies pursued by subsidiary and associated companies as depicted in Table 4.7.

In 1985, Hongkong Land's residential real estate portfolio was sold to Australian investors and in 1986, Hongkong Land's Dairy Farm food subsidiary and Mardarin Oriental hotel chain were spun off as separate companies. Hongkong Land's remaining interest in Jardine Matheson was contributed to a new investment company, Hongkong Investors, Ltd. The new company was merged with Jardine Securities, Ltd. to form Jardine Strategic Holdings, Ltd. Jardine Strategic, with net assets of more than US$705.12 million, was the single largest shareholder in Jardine Matheson, Hongkong Land, Dairy Farm and the Mandarin Oriental hotel chain. Like Jardine Matheson Holdings, Jardine Strategic was incorporated in Bermuda. At its founding in 1986, Jardine Strategic had a 25% stake in Jardine Matheson; 15% stake in Hongkong Land; 27% stake in Dairy Farm; and 35% stake in Mandarin Oriental. Unlike Hong Kong-based investment concerns, Jardine Matheson had the right to repurchase its own shares—and did so repeatedly through 1996. Simon Keswick removed David Newbigging as taipan. Keswick cleaned house of 40 other executives at Jardine Matheson responsible for lines of business that had been discontinued with the asset sales of the late 1970s.

The capital base of a number of Jardine Matheson's affiliated companies was enlarged, including the placement of 30 million new shares with Jardine Strategic for US$76.92 million. Jardine Strategic raised $US200 million (HK$1400 million) in the Euromarket, and Dairy Farm placed new shares valued at US$58.20 million with Jardine Strategic. The purpose of these issues was to take advantage of favorable market conditions to build group equity to finance acquisitions and expansion without excessive borrowing. Jardine Matheson entered a joint venture with

Table 4.7
Focus on Distinctive Capabilities Period, 1983–1997

Resources/ Services	Number of Companies	Markets
Agriculture and Forestry	1	Japan
Mining	1	US–Houston
Construction and Engineering (largely acquisitions made by Jardine Pacific)	3	HK, Singapore
Manufacturing	6	HK
Shipping, Transportation (largely acquisitions made by Jardine Pacific)	12	HK, Singapore
Wholesale Trade (largely acquisitions made by Jardine Pacific)	20	HK
Retail Trade (largely acquisitions made by subsidiaries: Dairy Farm, Jardine International Motors)	20	HK, Australia, Canada, China, Japan, India, Malaysia, NE Asia, Singapore, and UK
Finance, Insurance and Real Estate (largely acquisitions made by subsidiaries Jardine Fleming Financial Services, Jardine Lloyd Thompson Insurance, Hongkong Land)	87	HK, Australia, Bermuda, Japan, UK

Moet Hennnessy S.A. and United Distillers Group of Guiness Plc for the distribution of an expanded range of brands on long-term contracts in Japan, Hong Kong, and Northeast Asia. The firm also expanded its franchise interests through the acquisition of additional fast-food and convenience store franchises in Hong Kong, the United Kingdom, Canada, and Australia. In the United Kingdom, Dairy Farm acquired 25% of Kwik Save Group, Plc, a leading discount supermarket operator.

Compared with 1986's consolidated net earnings of US$61.41 million, Jardine Matheson recorded earnings of US$100.64 million in 1987—a 64% increase. Net extraordinary profit of US$35.73 million in 1987—compared with US$6.6 million in 1986—arose mainly from three items: the company's share of Hongkong Land's property, land bank sales, and profits arising from business restructuring within Jardine Matheson, less a provision against the company's investment in Jardine Strategic.

Beginning in 1988, Jardine Matheson continued to strengthen its shareholding in major affiliates—a policy and program, according to Simon Keswick, "that enabled the firm to increase its share of current profits and the future growth of businesses which we know well and for which we see promising prospects." In 1989 Jardine Strategic increased its share of Dairy Farm from 27% to 41%, permitting Dairy Farm to acquire from Jardine Matheson & Company the firm's 7-Eleven franchises in Hong Kong, Singapore, and Malaysia for a consideration of US$51.69 million to be satisfied mainly by the issue of 67.1 million new Dairy Farm shares.

In terms of managerial structure, the most significant event of 1989 was the formation of Jardine Pacific, which grouped together all of Jardine Matheson's Asia Pacific businesses into a regionwide trading and services operation. By 1990, Jardine Pacific had created joint ventures in life assurance, air conditioning, and security and increased its investment in restaurant franchises in Australia and Taiwan.

Jardine Matheson's motor vehicle operations in Hong Kong, China, Australia, and the United Kingdom were amalgamated to form Jardine International Motor Holdings Limited. Jardine Insurance Brokers continued to enlarge its network of acquisitions in the United States, Australia, and Singapore, while Jardine Fleming consolidated its position as one of the leading investment and merchant banking houses in Asia Pacific.

Dairy Farm completed two new strategic acquisitions in 1990, buying major supermarket chains in Spain and New Zealand. In March 1993, Eurodollar convertible preference shares were issued to raise some US$200 million for Dairy Farm and US$350 million for Jardine Strategic. Dairy Farm intended to deploy the proceeds of its issue to fund its expansion program, including a joint venture with Nestle to manufacture dairy products in Hong Kong and China and the acquisition of the Cold Storage retail chain in Singapore. Jardine Strategic's issue would provide funds for its portion of Dairy Farm and its refinancing of the company's investment in Cycle & Carriage to 16%.

On 1 July, 1994, the Bermuda Takeover Code, which provided statutory takeovers protection for the company's shareholders equivalent to London's City Code on Takeovers and Mergers, came into force. The law formalized the protection Jardine Matheson & Company had required in undertaking its move to Bermuda in 1984. In 1994, Jardine Matheson & Company's secondary listing on the Hong Kong stock exchange was withdrawn, and Asian time zone trading in the company's securities began to take place mainly on the Singapore Stock Exchange; the company's primary listing on the London Stock exchange and its other secondary listings were not affected.

In 1996, Jardine Matheson & Company had 60,000 employees in Hong Kong—200,000 overall in its subsidiary undertakings and associates. With interests in 30 countries, Jardine Matheson & Company derived 80% of its profit from the Asia-Pacific Region. The firm's business lines included Jardine Pacific, the group's Asia-Pacific trading and services business. Its activities fell into five industry groupings: Marketing & Distribution, Engineering & Construction, Aviation & Shipping Services, Property Services, and Financial Services. The firm provides 26% of the group's profits and is 100% owned by Jardine Matheson & Company. Jardine Pacific accounts for 16% of the parent's equity. Jardine International Motors is a Hong Kong listed company engaged in the sale and service of quality motor vehicles, with an emphasis on Mercedes-Benz. It has operations in Asia, Europe, and the United States. The firm provides 14% of the group's profits and is 75% owned by Jardine Matheson & Company. Jardine International Motors accounts for 8% of the parent's equity. Jardine Fleming, a joint venture with Robert Fleming of London, was a leading financial services group in Asia Pacific. It undertakes investment management, securities broking, corporate finance, capital markets, and banking. This joint venture provides 15% of the group's profits and is 50% owned by Jardine Matheson. Jardine Fleming accounts for 7% of the parent's equity. Jardine Lloyd Thompson is a listed international specialist insurance broker. The recently merged company combines specialist skills in the London insurance market with an international network, especially in the Asia-Pacific Region. The firm provides 1% of the group's profits. Jardine Lloyd Thompson accounts for 1% of the parent's equity. Dairy Farm is a listed international food retailer with supermarket and other interests across Asia, in Australasia, and in Europe. It has joint-venture interests in restaurants through Maxim's in Hong Kong and in manufacturing through Nestle Dairy Farm. The firm provides 10% of the group's profits and is 52% owned by Jardine Matheson & Company. Dairy Farm accounts for 9% of the parent's equity. Hongkong Land is a major listed property group, with some 5 million square feet of prime commercial property in the heart of Hong Kong. The group is focusing on high-quality property and infrastructure investments in Asia. The firm provides 21% of the group's profits and is 32% owned by Jardine Strategic. Hongkong Land accounts for 46% of the parent's equity. Mandarin Oriental manages a group of luxury hotels principally in the Asia Pacific region. The listed company holds equity in most of its hotels, which include Mandarin Oriental, Hong Kong, and the Oriental, Bangkok. The firm provides 5% of the group's profits and is 51% owned by Jardine Strategic. Mandarin Oriental accounts for 9% of the parent's equity. Cycle & Carriage is a leading Singapore-listed company with two core business areas: motor vehicles, with operations in Singapore, Malaysia, Australia, New Zealand, Thailand, and Vietnam; and property investment and development in Singapore and Malaysia. The firm provides 5% of the group's profits and is 23% owned by Jardine Strategic. Cycle & Carriage accounts for 4% of the parent's equity.

In 1996, 64% of Jardine Matheson's profit came from Hong Kong and China; 14% from the greater Asia Pacific area, 6% from Europe, and 16% from North America for a total of $US356 million. Jardine Matheson & Company drew 60% of its equity from Hong Kong and China, 22% from the rest of Asia Pacific, 8% from Europe and 10% from North America and liquid funds, for a total of US$4,096 million. South East Asia remained a focus, as highlighted by the acquisition of a 23% interest in Cycle and Carriage in Singapore and more recent investments in EON Berhad in Malaysia (9% shareholding acquired in June 1995) and Tata Industries in India (20% shareholding acquired in March 1996).

By 1996 all eight of Jardine's core companies—Jardine Pacific, Jardine International Motors, Jardine Fleming, Jardine Lloyd Thompson, Dairy Farm, Mandarin Oriental Hotel, Cycle and Carr, and HongKong Land—were pursuing expansion abroad and generating significant returns on shareholder equity, as depicted in Table 4.8. Hongkong Land with nearly half the prime real estate in Hong Kong's Central District was pursuing investments in Philippines, Singapore, Vietnam as well

Table 4.8
Return on Equity (%) of Jardine, Matheson Businesses 1987–1996

Year	Jardine Matheson	Jardine Strategic	Hongkong Land	Dairy Farm	Mandarin Oriental	Jardine International Motors	Jardine Lloyd Thompson	Cycle & Carriage
1996	9.12	7.64	8.69	2.71	6.05	19.91	0.12	17.15
1995	12.87	7.42	2.83	13.6	5.49	39.56	34.03	17.5
1994	16.67	10.15	4.77	25.68	5.85	37.21	32.31	14.04
1993	21.07	14.07	10.16	25.93	6.27	51.51	41.93	11.37
1992	21.1	14.92	7.01	55.43	6.23	128.19	44.22	12.29
1991	27.68	17.96	9.87	30.57	5.87	34.21	47.07	15.96
1990	15.54	8.97	8.29	22.75	9.58	23.57	48.71	15.79
1989	21.45	10.52	3.57	18.09	7.65	58.02	51.96	12.43
1988		9.75	5.11	18.01		48.64		7.12
1987		27.41	15.95	40.36		44.18		5.84

Source: Worldscope. Comparable data not available for Jardine Fleming.

as China. Jardine Pacific was investing in toll roads in Indonesia, water treatment plants in China, and drugstores in Singapore (see Table 4.8).

MODELING JARDINE MATHESON'S STRATEGIC DECISIONS

Had Jardine Matheson continued to pursue its horizontal and vertical acquisition program, what would have been the firm's value in 1985, and what risk would banks have been willing to take for further unrelated diversification? Model 4.1 values the firm as though the Exploit and Develop scenario (1972–1977) had continued through 1985. The valuation methodology is based on the following assumptions:

- Horizon Period: The number of years for which current strategies will continue to add value to the company. The number is usually 6 to 10 years. Our model uses 6 years.

- Forecasts: For each of the years in the horizon period, operating and investment cash flows are forecast based on known operating and investment cash flows. In Model 4.1, a linear regression of actual cash flows from 1970 to 1979 was used to produce a growth rate that assumed the same broad "Exploit and Develop" acquisition strategy for the next six years.

- Cash Flow to the Firm: Profit available for appropriation or earnings before interest and tax [(EBIT) (1-tax rate) + depreciation] minus capital expenditures, minus

Model 4.1
Continuation of Exploit and Develop Acquisition Strategy

Actual Historic Cash Flows 1970–1979 (US$Millions)

	1970	1971	1972	1973	1974	1975	1976	1977	1978	1979
Profit Available	46	58	92	137	215	265	259	367	432	495
+/- Fixed Assets		64	114	717	49	1,030	346	-201	-554	-86
+/-Net Working Capital		39	-29	236	110	393	-80	-44	314	45
Net Cash Flow		-45	7	-816	56	-1,158	-7	612	672	536

Projected Cash Flows 1980–1985 (US$Millions)

		1980	1981	1982	1983	1984	1985
Projected Cash Flow		577	695	814	932	1,051	1,169
Discounted at 10% WACC		525	574	612	636	652	660
Total Present Value	'80–'85	3,659					
+Present Value of Terminal Value		6,600					
Entity Value- Total Liabilities	Funds Employed	10,259– 5136					
Accumulated Added Value		5,123					

Actual Cash Flows 1980–1985 (US$Millions)

	1980	1981	1982	1983	1984	1985
Profit Available	525	723	708	139	80	157
+/- Fixed Assets	154	437	684	-801	205	-1,035
+/-Net Working Capital	-269	729	-254	47	-640	-462
Net Cash Flow	640	-443	278	893	515	1,654

change in working capital. Where it appears, the change in assets is due to cash conversion, not to write-offs.

- Discount Rate: Each year is discounted back to the present using a discount factor based on the weighted average cost of capital (WACC). The WACC is estimated at 10%.

- Terminal Value: The final year's cash flow is capitalized using the long-term cost of capital (net operating profit after taxes X 10). This gives the terminal value at the end of the horizon period.

- Total Enterprise Value: The terminal value is discounted back to the present again, using the WACC; cash flows are added, including the terminal value, to produce the total enterprise value.

- Added Value: Liabilities are subtracted from the total enterprise value to derive accumulated added value. In the context of cash flow analysis, added value is what the banks would be willing to lend for unrelated diversification.

Actual cash flows for 1980–1985 fell below those projected for 1981–1984, a consequence of high assets to sales, itself a consequence of Jardine Matheson's very aggressive acquisition program.

To meet its cash flow projections and avoid raiding reserves, the firm might have reduced its growth to a level it could safely absorb by increasing retained profits (e.g.,, through additional asset sales) or by reducing internal costs, specifically the cost of sales, which is captured in its assets to sales ratio—or by instituting a combination strategy to wipe out the cash deficit and restore a balance between profits, assets, and growth. This balance is what Ciarin Walsh calls "growth equilibrium," defined as the rate of growth that a company can sustain from its operating cash flow. Following Ciarin Walsh, decreasing assets, increasing owners' funds, or both would have improved Jardine Matheson's cash flows financials. (See Table 4.9.)

As discussed, Jardine Matheson made significant divestitures between 1978 and 1979, including its investments in shipping and overseas properties that were unprofitable, as well as its interests in several subsidiaries. The firm expected that these asset sales would be sufficient to increase working capital and cash flows (200% increase by 1985). The growth rate was anticipated to be approximately 14% from 1980 to 1985, close to the actual Heng Seng Index (HSI) earnings growth rate of 16%. However, the Hong Kong Land stock swap put additional demands on Jardine Matheson's cash flow and debt coverage.

To understand the impact, if any, of Jardine Matheson's reorganization in 1985, the firm was modeled as is. Using 1985 as the starting year, Model 4.2 allows us to see the impact, if any, on cash flow of Jardine Matheson's asset sales and stricter cash management.

The debt/equity ratio was reduced dramatically from an average 66% in the early 1980s to 10% in the last four years of the decade and return on equity (ROE) from a low of 1.89 in 1984 to 14% in 1989. Beginning with the reorganization of 1985, Jardine Matheson had begun to increase owner's funds. The five-year average in 1989 was 21.89% (versus—0.13% over the five years beginning 1982–1987).

Table 4.9
Growth Rate Sustainable by Internal Operations—Sensitivity Analysis (US$Millions)

	1980	1981	1982	1983	1984	1985
Current Assets	796	1,525	1,271	1,318	678	216
Sales	7,467	9,266	11,240	10,644	8,881	10,497
Owners Funds	5,235	6,600	6,288	5,261	4,224	4,774
Retained	815	633	-177	-113	834	-310
Current Growth is	**15.5**	**9.5**	**-2.8**	**-2.1**	**19.7**	**-6.4**
Asset cost of ea. $1 sale	0.106	0.164	0.113	0.123	0.076	0.02
Retained earnings generated by $1 sale	0.109	0.068	-0.015	-0.01	0.093	-0.029
Sales this year required to fund $1 additional sales next year	.97	2.41	-7.53	-12.3	0.817	-.689
Rate of growth that can be funded from retained earnings	103%	41.4%	N/A	N/A	122%	N/A

Note: Acquisitions and divestitures affect year-to-year figures.

Model 4.2
Harvest and Divest, without Reorganization

Projected Cash Flows 1986–1990 (US$Millions)

	1986	1987	1988	1989	1990
Projected Cash Flow	946	1,024	1,102	1,180	1,259
Discounted at 10% WACC	860	846	827	806	781
Total Present Value 1986–1990	4,120				
+Present Value of Terminal Value	7,817				
Entity Value	11,937				
-Total Liabilities (Funds Employed)	8,426				
Added Value	3,511				

Actual Cash Flows 1986–1989 (US$Millions)

	1986	1987	1988	1989
Profit Available	479	785	1,113	1,577
+/- Fixed Assets	-222	351	262	329
+/- Net Working Capital	758	-5	-580	-239
Net Cash Flow	-57	439	1,431	1,487

Going forward, Jardine Taipan Keswick looked to unique governance structures to manage risk. In 1986, a new structure was introduced linking the subsidiaries to Jardine Strategic and Jardine Matheson & Company by ownership percentage. Here, a new holding company, Jardine Strategic, manages businesses, which formerly belonged to Hongkong Land (as well as some of the newer ventures, not mentioned here). Jardine Matheson Holdings manages the older portfolio, consisting of Jardine Pacific, Jardine Insurance Brokers, Jardine Fleming, Jardine Strategic, and other interests. From a qualitative viewpoint, Jardine Strategic imposes a layer of management between higher-risk businesses and Jardine Matheson Holdings. Management theorists and equity analysts might view Jardine Strategic as a cost center, draining resources from the Jardine Group—as indefensible as corporate services are to value-minded management. Using 1992 as an average year (in terms of ownership percentage), Figure 4.1 shows that Jardine Strategic is worth more to Jardine Matheson Holdings than the individual companies it manages, contributing 100% of the profits expected but at less risk. The role of Jardine Strategic—indeed, the role of any of the firm's holding companies in governing Jardine Matheson's widespread interests—is an example of organizational innovation. In a unique way a holding company can become a vehicle for creating more value for Jardine Matheson and for its subsidiaries than would be created by market mediation or internalization. Critical is the ability of the subsidiary to raise shareholder capital in excess of Jardine Strategic's ownership percentage.

Figure 4.1
Ownership Structure of Jardine Matheson & Company, 1992

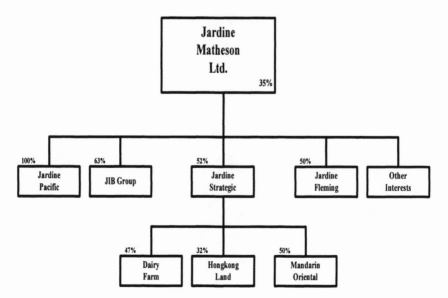

Model 4.3 uses after-tax operating profit for each of Jardine Matheson's subsidiaries from 1986 to 1996 to calculate the variability of annual results. Jardine Strategic's profits are calculated over the same period. With less variability, Jardine Strategic contributes 100% of profit while taking only 86% of the risk.

To understand the contribution of mutual ownership to firm value, imagine a company named Jardine Matheson Direct (a veiled reference to Jardine Matheson Holdings and all the companies it manages, minus Jardine Strategic) with investments in three companies, Jardine Pacific, Jardine Fleming, and Jardine Insurance Brokers.

Model 4.4 uses 1991 betas (derived from DataStream) and 1992 earnings as reported in the Jardine Matheson & Company Annual Report and Heng Seng Index. The Capital Asset Pricing Model (CAPM) is calculated thus: CAPM = Risk-free rate + ß (Market Rate - Risk free rate). The risk-free rate is estimated at .06, and the

Model 4.3
Is Jardine Strategic Worth More Than Its Pieces?

(US$ Millions Based on After-Tax Operating Profit)

Year	Jardine Pacific	Jardine Insurance	Jardine Fleming	Dairy Farm	Hongkong Land	Mandarin Oriental	Jardine Strategic
1986	10	9.6	26	37.5	111	18.5	72.19
1987	43.75	10	48	58	123.5	31	107.61
1988	72.5	12	46	100	154	44.5	153.61
1989	87.5	15.66	67	125.2	194	50.5	190.73
1990	98	19.5	73	150.2	267	45	228.41
1991	100	35.5	83	147	277.5	38	232.85
1992	107	31.5	80	303	301	40	314.1
1993	109	32	200	189	517.5	41	353.25
1994	126	38	208	224	371	48	334.64
1995	145	34.5	123	187	262.5	54	276.91
1996	93.5	26.5	82.1	105	649.4	60.6	339.34
N	11	11	11	11	11	11	11
M	90.2	24.06	94.1	147.8	293.4	42.92	236.69
SD	37.41	10.96	59.7	76.1	166.2	11.4	97.03
SD/M	0.41	0.45	0.64	0.52	0.57	0.27	0.41
.41/.4736 =	86% of average variation	100% of profits taking only 86% of risks					

Model 4.4
Impact of Holding Company on Overall Earnings Stability

US Millions	Jardine Pacific	JIB	Jardine Fleming	Jardine, Matheson Direct
ß	3.04	3.37	1.55	2.08
Earnings	107	31.5	80	166.8
Fraction Owned by Jardine, Matheson Direct	1	0.63	0.5	
$M to Jardine Matheson Direct	107	19.8	40	166.8
CAPM	0.49	0.53	0.28	0.35
Cost	220	37	144	
Total	401			
Total Value	474.94			

market return is estimated at .20. If Jardine Matheson Direct had to buy these investments on the open market, the cost would be $474.94 million, a savings of $73.94 million to Jardine Matheson Direct—and an increase to Jardine Matheson Direct of 18.4% added value.

Another scenario, Model 4.5, proposes a company called Jardine Strategic Direct, with investments in Dairy Farm, Hongkong Land, and Mandarin Oriental, using 1991 betas from DataStream and 1992 earnings.

In each scenario, the fractional ownership of high-risk businesses affords Jardine Matheson Direct and Jardine Strategic Direct added value at less risk. Was the governance structure designed for this purpose? Certainly, the foregoing makes the case that Jardine Matheson & Company's complicated ownership structure was designed for this purpose. Whether or not the evidence proves design, this is certainly an example showing that added value could occur due to governance structure, that is, due to firm architecture.

Based on actual cash flows from 1990 through 1996, Model 4.6 values the firm to the year 2002, based on current strategies. Following the asset sales of the late 1970s and early 1980s, the firm has focused on a limited portfolio of business services and high-margin, consumer businesses.

The reported 1996 market value of Jardine Matheson was $36 billion. Cash flow analysis suggests that Jardine Matheson & Company is in a strong bargaining position for loans for unrelated diversification. The firm has made a solid comeback after the asset sales of the late 1970s and early 1980s. The firm's value has doubled with anticipated growth of 10%. Despite the firm's commitment to Hong Kong and investment in China, much of the actual revenue growth over the period

Model 4.5
The Effect of Jardine Strategic on Earnings Stability, Overall Beta

US$Millions	Dairy Farm	Hongkong Land	Mandarin Oriental	Jardine Strategic Direct
ß	1.33	1.07	0.32	1.01
Earnings	303	301	40	255.7
Jardine Strategic Direct Ownership Fraction	0.46	0.32	0.5	
$M to Jardine Strategic Direct	139.38	96.32	20	255.7
CAPM	0.25	0.21	0.1	0.2
Cost	566	459	191	
Total	1,216			
Total Value	1,269			
Added Value	4.5%			

Model 4.6
Actual and Projected Cash Flows 1990–2002 (US$Millions)

Actual	1990	1991	1992	1993	1994	1995	1996
Cash Flow	6.4	134.4	344.1	-182.3	1,070.2	1,131.8	1,193.7
Projected	1997	1998	1999	2000	2001	2002	Total Value
Present Value Next 5 Years	1,426	1,650	1,875	2,000	2,323	2,548	25,480
Discount at 10% WACC	1,296	1,364	1,408	1,366	1,442	1,438	14,380
Total Present Value 1997–2002	8,201						
+Present Value of Terminal Value	14,380						
Total Value 1996	22,581						
- Liabilities	7,788						
Added Value	14,793						

1990–1996 came from investments outside Hong Kong, which had averaged 9.69% from 1982 to 1987; 56.29% from 1985 to 1990, and 69.64% from 1991 to 1996. Foreign sales as a percentage of total sales over the same period increased to 68.08% from 1991 to 1996. Foreign income as a percent of total income increased from 45.47% from 1982 to 1987 to 279.69% from 1991 to 1996.

NOTES

1. In this chapter, the source of all product/market expansion and financial data is the collection of Jardine Matheson & Company Consolidated Annual Reports from 1961 to 1996. Because Jardine Matheson & Company and its major subsidiaries are domiciled offshore, there is no requirement that Annual Reports be housed in a central repository. The collection was assembled by the author from the U.S. Library of Congress, Harvard University Library, and Washington University, St. Louis. The performance ratios, financial analyses, and cash flow models are the result of the author's own analysis, based on Consolidated Annual Report data.

2. Allen T. Demaree, "The Old China Hands Who Know How to Live with the New Asia," *Fortune* (November 1971): 133.

3. Edward Chen, "Economic Restructuring and Industrial Development in the Asia Pacific: Competition or Complementarity?," *Business & the Contemporary World* (Spring, 1993): 68.

4. Demaree, "The Old China Hands Know How to Live with the New China," 134.

5. Birger Wernerfelt, "A Resource-Based Theory of the Firm," *Strategic Management Journal* (1984).

6. Bergh, Donald D. and Gordon F. Holbein, "Assessment and Redirection of Longitudinal Analysis: Demonstration with a Study of the Diversification and Divestiture Relationship," *Strategic Management Journal,* 18 (7), 561; Hoskisson, Robert E., Richard A. Johnson, Douglas D. Moesel, "Corporate Divestiture Intensity in Restructuring Firms: Effects of Governance, Strategy and Performance," *Academy of Management Journal* 37 (5) (1994): 1208.

5

INDUSTRIAL LOGIC: ACQUISITION AND DIVESTITURE STRATEGY

The extraordinary range of relationships created through investment and product/market choices made by Jardine Matheson during the period covered in Chapter 4 might be explained by a loss of focus with painful consequences, leading to a reexamination and refocusing of the company along the lines of its historic capabilities. While the final outcome was indeed a refocusing, the internal and external factors responsible for the firm's choices defend their logic, consistency, insight into industrial development, and real productive opportunity for extending historical capabilities and relationships into new business areas. Hence, Chapter 5 contributes to the architecture of this study by offering an in-depth analysis of the firm's investments, its acquisitions, and divestitures from 1972 to 1996 to understand the industry (external) and skills (internal) factors responsible for Jardine Matheson's resource and services choices.

From 1961 to 1996, Jardine Matheson made approximately 850 acquisitions or investments at 20% of book value or more in very diverse businesses across the Pacific. Jardine Matheson exploited sectoral opportunities in the ASEAN where these existed, while it supported the continued development of Hong Kong as an industrial district.

Without industry and market understanding, such frenetic activity, followed by rationalization in the mid-1980s, would appear to be a matter of vaulting corporate ambition with no clear and pragmatic strategic intent, until high debt and eroding profit necessitated a return to core competences.

A resource-based interpretation argues that a firm grows by building on its resources and capabilities, transforming its physical and skill resources to create new products and markets. Firms might use equity, debt, and trading relationships to extend their resource and capabilities outreach, building a network that extends well outside the firm—an external organization, as it were, governed by long-term relationships with well-known expectations and financial rewards, utilizing virtually frictionless contracts.

To find a diversification pattern—or pathways—and ultimately understand the relationships between associated companies, their customers and even their competitors, this study used as its starting point a standard industrial classification (SIC)-based methodology. The SIC has been widely adopted as the standard coding system used to define and analyze industry structure. With SIC code analysis, materials, processes, logistics, and end-uses emerge as connections between businesses and related skills.

The precedent for SIC code analysis to establish the relatedness of businesses was set by the empirical research of Amit and Livnat,[1] Krishna Palepu,[2] Chatterjee and Wernerfelt,[3] and Grant, Jammine and Thomas.[4] Moshe Farjoun[5] broadened the discussion to include the relationship of skills required by each industry. He used SIC codes to establish business relatedness—and U.S. Bureau of Labor Statistics data to identify the skills required for each SIC code—and compared them for manufacturing businesses.

Like Farjoun's analysis, this study then progressed to a consideration of the skills required by each industry. Finally, the study looked to national and sectoral characteristics and foreign direct investment flows to establish a diversity pattern. The diversification and diversity patterns were then compared with those of other companies during the same time periods.

The chapter begins with an analysis of acquisitions and divestments by industry group and major category over each of the strategic subperiods, identified in Chapter 4. The chapter then identifies and compares the skills required by the firm's manufacturing, resource, and services acquisitions with those required by Jardine Matheson's core businesses. The geographic spread of Jardine Matheson's acquisitions and divestitures is then analyzed, including the entry and exit strategies of the firm. Jardine Matheson's pattern of acquisition activity is compared with that of other multinationals for the same periods. The chapter concludes with an examination of the advantages to Jardine Matheson of its "external organization," that is, its network of equity and trade relationships, versus market transactions.[6]

JARDINE MATHESON'S ACQUISITIONS AND DIVESTITURES BY INDUSTRY

This section analyzes Jardine Matheson's acquisitions and divestments, fitting them into industry group and major category to understand how industries were structured; to asses how close to or distant they were from Jardine Matheson's core businesses; to measure the extent of continued investment in core businesses versus new and unrelated businesses; to discover the logic of Jardine Matheson's divestitures over the same period; and to discern how Jardine Matheson's senior leadership may have assessed the productive opportunity afforded by the 850 investments made during 1972–1996.

To define and analyze industry structure and compare Jardine's investments, the SIC was used. The first two digits of the SIC code system, called major group, divide economic activity into the following 10 major divisions. Note that not all two-digit classifications fall within a major group. (See Table 5.1.)

The third digit subdivides activity into a more specific industry group, and the fourth digit defines a particular industry. This progressive refinement is illustrated by the example of wholesale trade, in Table 5.2.

The four-digit SIC code is assigned on the basis of what the business does. If a corporation has subsidiaries, it is assigned a four-digit SIC code based on its own activities and the activities of its direct and indirect subsidiaries. Subsidiaries are assigned four-digit SIC codes solely on the basis of their own activities unless they, in turn, have subsidiaries.

When a company's activities cover multiple SIC codes, they are listed in descending order of importance, measured by the percent of total dollar volume pro-

Table 5.1
Stand Industrial Classifications (SIC) at Two-Digit Level—Major Groups

Division	Title	Two-Digit Major Group
A	Agriculture, Forestry and Fishing	01–09
B	Mining	10–14
C	Construction	15–17
D	Manufacturing	20–39
E	Transportation, Communication, Electric, Gas and Sanitary Services	40–49
F	Wholesale Trade	50–51
G	Retail Trade	52–59
H	Finance, Insurance and Real Estate	60–67
I	Services	70–89
J	Public Administration	91–97

Table 5.2
Stand Industrial Classifications (SIC)—Wholesale Trade Example at Two-, Three-, and Four-Digit Levels

Division F	Wholesale Trade	
Major Group	Wholesale Trade-Durable Goods	50
Industry Group	Machine Equipment and Supplies	508
Industry	Industrial Machinery and Equipment	5084

duced or the order of importance cited by management when the exact percentage is not provided.

All of Jardine Matheson's acquisitions and investments from 1961 to 1996 were charted along with country of operations, year acquired, year divested, percent owned, line of business, and primary SIC code. Only those investments valued at 20% or more of book were reported in the firm's consolidated Annual Report; lesser holdings were not reported. The research supporting this analysis looked at the total number of acquisitions and divestitures by year, 1972–1996; total acquisitions by four-digit SIC code, number of acquired firms and description of activity; total acquisitions by major group by year; total divestitures by major group by year; total number of acquisitions; and divestitures within division and within major groups during substrategic periods: Exploit and Develop (1972–1977); Harvest and Divest (1978–1983); Focus on Distinctive Capabilities (1984–1996).

A preliminary period identified was one of sequential growth to 1971, during which time the firm used its trading, shipping, finance, and insurance core businesses to move into new markets and establish a representative office, usually a holding company, often by investing in, or acquiring, a local trading business. For purposes of classification, I called this period "Stepping Stones."

The next period from 1972 to 1977 was characterized by very aggressive growth pursued simultaneously along two paths. The first path was a continuation of its Stepping Stones approach into new geographic markets. The second path involved building chains of related businesses or clusters within specific industries and across geographies. A total of 427 acquisitions or investments were made (and 93 divestitures). Some 65.5% of acquisitions during the period were in finance, insurance, and real estate; transportation and trading/wholesaling; and primary goods, machine tools, and other manufacturing interests, as well as retail sales (some 35.5% of acquisitions, including 17% manufacturing, 12.6% in retail, 2% primary goods). I called this period "Exploit and Develop," because the firm was building or extending existing capabilities to new markets while acquiring new capabilities. (See Table 5.3.) Of the divestitures made during this period, 70% were of non-performing assets in core businesses.

From 1978 through 1983, the firm began to rationalize products and markets, building a more focused portfolio that could be replicated in each market. A total of 223 acquisitions were made, compared with 317 divestitures. Of acquisitions, 75% were in core businesses (50% in finance, insurance, and real estate; 20% in transportation; and 5% in wholesaling). Of divestitures, 74% were in core businesses, 12% in manufacturing, and 10% in services. I classified this third period "Harvest and Divest." (See Table 5.4.) The period was characterized by exit from businesses the firm believed to be no longer strategic and the spin-off of successful businesses to new owners, including Swire, Hutchison, and Old Mutual/Safren.

From 1984 to 1997, Jardine Matheson's business interests were reduced. Growth continued, but far less visibly, through the diversification strategies of subsidiary and associated companies. The firm continued on this track through 1996 (the end of the period covered by this book). During this time, 46% of acquisitions and 52%

Table 5.3

Acquisitions and Divestitures—Exploit and Develop Period, 1972–1977

	Acquisitions	Divestitures
Agriculture and forestry (01–09)	3	0
Mining (10–14)	6	1
Construction (15–17)	10	0
Manufacturing (20–39)	75	14
Shipping, Transportation (40–49)	92	19
Wholesale Trade (50–51)	54	16
Retail Trade (52–59)	5	0
Finance, Insurance and Real Estate (60–67)	142	30
Business Services (70–89)	50	13
Other (91–97)	0	0
Total	437	93

Table 5.4

Acquisitions and Divestitures—Harvest and Divest Period, 1978–1983

	Acquisitions	Divestitures
Agriculture and forestry(01–09)	0	1
Mining(10–14)	6	4
Construction(15–17)	3	7
Manufacturing(20–39)	13	41
Shipping, Transportation (40–49)	44	69
Wholesale Trade(50–51)	13	47
Retail Trade(52–59)	9	1
Finance, Insurance and Real Estate(60–67)	111	112
Business Services(70–89)	24	35
Other (91–97)		
Total	223	317

of divestitures were in financial, insurance and real estate; 24% of acquisitions were in retail and services. I classified this period Focus on Distinctive Capabilities, because the firm's intention was to limit investment to a few core businesses, while the experimentation and innovation was taking place at the level of the firm's associated companies. (See Table 5.5.)

SKILLS REQUIRED BY ACQUIRED BUSINESSES; COMPARISON WITH SKILLS REQUIRED BY HISTORIC CORE BUSINESSES

Moshe Farjoun's 1998 study presents an analysis of skills required across manufacturing businesses. Farjoun used SIC codes to identify individual lines of business within a firm and U.S. Bureau of Labor Statistics Occupational Employment Survey (OES) data to identify the skills required within those lines of business. The similarity in required skills was used as an indirect indicator of diversification related to firm-specific resources. After a discussion of Farjoun's methodology, the same methodology will be applied to an analysis of the skills required by Jardine Matheson's acquired businesses.

Looking at manufacturing firms only (SIC codes 20–39), Farjoun drew a sample of firms from the TRINET data set[7] and Fortune 500 manufacturing firms. Using a skill-based approach, he characterized each industry by its underlying profile of specialties, defined as the different types and extent of human skills required in the industry, as identified by occupational distributions. Farjoun then grouped industries with similar skill profiles. To measure the human skills requirements, Farjoun

Table 5.5
Acquisitions and Divestitures—Focus on Distinctive Capabilities Period, 1984–1997

	Acquisitions	Divestitures
Agriculture and forestry (01–09)	1	0
Mining (10–14)	1	1
Construction (15–17)	3	2
Manufacturing (20–39)	6	9
Shipping, Transportation (40–49)	12	12
Wholesale Trade (50–51)	20	10
Retail Trade (52–59)	20	13
Finance, Insurance and Real Estate (60–67)	87	67
Business Services (70–89)	26	16
Other (91–97)	1	1
Total	188	128

used OES data, which define industries at the three-digit SIC code level of detail. The OES contains data about the percentage distribution of 480 occupations in all industries. The occupational employment ratios are an indicator of both the different types of human expertise needed in industry and the extent to which they are required.

In developing skills profiles, Farjoun used all major groups of occupations employed in manufacturing, from management to marketing and sales, administration, service, production, and agriculture—38 types of skills in all—to create an industry-by-industry "similarity-in-skill matrix" that would subsequently be used to cluster businesses within manufacturing. Farjoun's matrix groups each occupational variable by its Major Group affiliation. It further details the distribution of the standardized occupational variable in each of eight skill-related industry groups identified in the cluster analysis. Farjoun's cross-tabulation of skills and industries captures both physical and skill-based systems. The skill-based system uses skill profiles to group industries that require similar production skills, scientific and engineering know-how, and administration and, to a lesser extent, service and marketing skills. The physical-based system captures similarity in raw materials, physical production processes, and end use. Farjoun correctly predicted that these two systems—physical and skills-based—will agree that industries are related when they employ similar production technology, require similar skills, and use similar physical processes and that the classifications will disagree when the grouping is based on an aspect that is specific to only one system.

Skills Required for Jardine Matheson's Manufacturing Acquisitions

It is valuable to an understanding of Jardine Matheson's diversification during the Exploit and Develop phase (1972–1977) to plot the firm's manufacturing acquisitions using Farjoun's approach. For comparison with Farjoun's data, only those acquisitions were plotted that corresponded to the subset of manufacturing industry SIC codes Farjoun studied, as well as the OES data relating to those codes.[8]

The skills required by Jardine Matheson's manufacturing acquisitions are identified in Table 5.6 In the table, the first column identifies the number of manufacturing firms acquired by Jardine Matheson from 1972 to 1977. The middle column identifies the industry (industries) and related three-digit SIC codes, and the far righthand column summarizes the skills required for each industry cluster over and above those for manufacturing as a whole.

Some 50 of Jardine Matheson's manufacturing acquisitions during the study period fall into Farjoun's cluster 2, with helpers and laborers and transport and materials movers preponderant, and 24 of Jardine's manufacturing acquisitions fall within cluster 4, with top management and precision workers preponderant. The skills required for cluster 2 are common across frozen food, textiles, concrete and asbestos, primary metal industries and iron and steel foundries. The skills for cluster 4 are common across conveying equipment, elevator and moving machinery,

Table 5.6

Jardine Matheson's Manufacturing Acquisitions and Required Skills, 1972–1977

#	Industry (3-digit SIC)	Skills Required (Farjoun Category)
3	Logging, Sugar Growing, Rubber (072-085)	Agriculture, forest, fishing; transport & materials moving; top management; technicians (1)
50	Dairy products; preserved fruits; grain mill products; bakery products; sugar; beverages; misc. food; tobacco; floor covering; misc. textile; sawmills; wood building; pulp and paper mills; converted paper; paperboard; misc. petroleum; rubber products; misc. plastic products; flat glass; glass & glassware; concrete & gypsum; other clay; blast furnaces; iron & steel foundries; other primary metals; metal cans; ships & boats (SIC Codes: 202, 203, 204, 205, 206, 208, 209, 210, 227, 229, 242, 245, 261, 264, 265, 295, 302, 307, 321, 322, 327, 329, 331, 332, 335, 336, 339, 341, 347, 373)	Helpers & laborers; transport & materials moving; other machine setting; metal & plastic work; supervisory blue-collar; mechanics & installers (2)
4	Meat products; weaving; knitting mills; apparel; misc. apparel; millwork; wood containers; household furniture; partitions; office furniture; commercial printing; blankbooks; all other printing; footwear; luggage (SIC Codes: 201, 221, 225, 231, 239, 243, 244, 251, 252, 254, 275, 278, 279, 311, 313	Top management; other precision products; textiles & related workers; helpers & laborers (3)
24	Cutlery; plumbing & heating; fabric. Structural metal; screw machine prod. ordnance; misc. fabric metals; engines & turbines; farm & garden mach.; construction mach; spec. indus. mach; gen. Indus. mach; refrigeration; misc. indus mach; electric distr. equipment; electric ind. app; household appliances; electric lighting eq.; electric household eq; misc. electric eq; motor vehicles; all other transportation; jewelry; toys; other manufacturing (SIC Codes: 342, 343, 344, 345, 348, 349, 351, 352, 353, 354, 355, 356)	Top management; precision metal work; machine tool cutting; precision assemblers; other assemblers (4)
5	Office & computer equipment; communications equipment; electrical components; engineering instrumentation; measuring devices; medical instrumentation; etc. (SIC Codes: 357, 366, 367, 381, 382, 389)	Financial managers;public relations (5)
1	Aircraft & parts; guided missiles (SIC Codes: 372, 376)	Aeronautic engineers, chemical engineers, other engineers; physical scientists, other natural scientists, technicians; management, purchasing managers, management support (4)
1	Industrial inorganic chem.; plastics materials; drugs; soap; paints; indus. org. chem.; agri chem., etc. (SIC Codes: 281, 282, 283, 284, 285, 286, 287, 289, 291, 301, 386)	Chemical engineers, life scientists, physical scientists, technicians, plant & systems (7)
1	Newspapers; periodicals; books; misc. publishing (SIC Codes: 271, 272, 273, 274)	Social Science & professionals, marketing& sales, top management, administrative support, supervisory blue-collar, printing workers (8)

Source: Based on Moshe Farjoun analysis and the author's analysis of Jardine Matheson's Annual Report Data.

machine tools, special industry machinery, and printing equipment. Together, they represent 67% of Jardine Matheson's manufacturing acquisitions between 1972 and 1977. Cluster 4 makes the tools and moving equipment used by businesses in cluster 2.

There is a close relationship as well between Farjoun's clusters 4, 5 and 6 and Jardine Matheson's core transport business, in which engineers predominate. See Table 5.7 for relative percentage of engineers employed in transport versus other businesses. Jardine Matheson's manufacturing and core businesses required a heavy concentration of engineering talent. For comparison purposes, the cross-industry average for engineering employment according to OES data is .26%.

Skills Required by Core Jardine Matheson Businesses Compared with Those Required for Manufacturing and Service Business Acquisitions

What is the relationship between the skills required for Jardine Matheson's original and core businesses and those required for manufacturing acquisitions from 1972 to 1977 and service acquisitions during the same and later periods? Table 5.8 uses OES data to track skills required by Jardine Matheson's original businesses and service acquisitions in the 1970s and 1980s. Concentrations of skills appear in bold. A few industries outside Jardine Matheson's acquisitions portfolio—namely, pharmaceuticals, electric services, and telecommunications—were introduced for possible comparison.

Table 5.7
Engineers as Percent of Total Employment by Industry

Industry	Percent Engineers of Total Employment
Shipping	3.94
Motor vehicles and equipment	3.7
Aircraft and parts	3.65
Electronic components and accessories	3.62
Personnel supply services	2.13
Electric services	2.13
Measuring and controlling	1.95
Computer and office equipment	1.89
Wholesale trade	1.89
Medical Instruments and supplies	1.52
Photographic equipment	1.25
Computer and data processing services	1.23
Crude petroleum, natural gas	0.85

Table 5.8
Skills Required Across Jardine Matheson's Original and Acquired Businesses

Types of Skills in International Trade Industry/Skills	%
Security and Commodities Brokers	
All other management support workers	12.33
Securities and financial services sales workers	8.82
Secretaries, except medical and legal	8.43
General managers and top executives	7.71
Brokerage clerks	6.39
General office clerks	5.56
Financial Managers	5.06
Clerical supervisors and managers	4.46
Bookkeeping, acct. and auditing clerks	4.15
Commercial Banks	
Bank tellers	27.27
New accounts clerks, banking	5.66
Loan and credit clerks	5.13
All other transportation and material moving, equipment operators	3.85
General managers and top executives	2.97
Non-Bank, Insurance & Real Estate	
Insurance adjusters, examiners, investigators	12.18
Insurance policy processing clerks	6.73
Underwriters	6.64
Insurance sales workers	6.39
Clerical supervisors and managers	4.99
General office clerks	4.73
Secretaries, except medical and legal	4.45
Claims examiners, property and casualty	4.28
Insurance claims clerks	4.17
General managers and top executives	2.81
Freight Transport Services	
General office clerks	9.15
General managers and top executives	7.02
Billing, cost and rate clerks	5.71
Clerical supervisors and managers	4.93
Communications, transport, and utilities, operations manager	4.86
Bookkeeping, acct. and auditing clerks	4.65
Water Transportation	
Freight, stock, and materials moving	13.88
Able seamen, ordinary seamen	11.03
Captains and pilots	6.94
All other material, moving equipment operators	6.2
All other food preparation and service workers	4.24
Mates, ship, boat and barge	4.06
Ship Engineers	3.94
Blue collar worker supervisors, movers, hand	3.31
Maintenance repairers, general utility	2.32
General office clerks	2.29
All other transportation and material moving, equipment operators	2.20
Communications, transport, and utilities, operations manager	2.08
Traffic, shipping and receiving clerks	1.50
General managers and top executives	1.42

Table 5.8 continued

Types of Skills in International Trade	
Industry/Skills	%
Wholesale Trade	
All other sales and related workers	19.22
General managers and top executives	5.84
Truck drivers, light and heavy	5.34
General office clerks	3.58
Traffic, shipping and receiving clerks	3.52
Freight, stock, and materials moving	3.22
Order fillers, wholesale and retail sales	2.95
Bookkeeping, acct. and auditing clerks	2.85
Retail Trade	
All other sales and related workers	13.51
Driver/sales workers	6.32
Adjustment Clerks	6.32
Coin and vending machine servicers, repairers	3.61
Salespersons, retail	3.53
General managers and top executives	3.38
General office clerks	3.38
Traffic, shipping and receiving clerks	3.26
Order fillers, wholesale and retail sales	3.12
Dairy Products Wholesale and Retail	
Packaging and filling machine operators and tenders	8.75
Truck drivers, light and heavy	7.29
Driver/sales workers	4.57
Blue collar worker supervisors, movers, hand	4.31
Freight, stock, and materials moving	3.74
Hand packers and packagers	3.62
Industrial machinery mechanics	2.92
Traffic, shipping and receiving clerks	2.45
All other sales and related workers	2.06
General managers and top executives	1.72
Hotels	
Janitors and cleaners, incl. Maids, housekeeping	23.62
Waiters and waitresses	9.45
Hotel desk clerks	8.24
Food preparation workers	4.01
Cooks, restaurant	3.93
Maintenance repairers, general utility	3.28
General managers and top executives	1.79
Motor Vehicles Dealers	
Salespersons, retail	21.33
Automotive mechanics	17.84
All other sales and related workers	6.30
General managers and top executives	4.20
General office clerks	4.19
Bookkeeping, acct. and auditing clerks	4.04

Overall, Jardine Matheson's move into service businesses required skills that the company had accumulated in its core businesses. Each acquisition in a new industry added a few asset specific skills to the top or middle management requirements (Table 5.9) providing insight into the capital and skill intensity of Jardine Matheson's bread and butter businesses. Note that import/export, shipping, finance and insurance are significantly more capital- and skill-intensive than manufacturing exports.

This suggests that the former required a higher investment in assets and human resources which Jardine Matheson found justifiable because trading, transportation, and financing continued to generate higher profits than the firm's other business lines. These were the core businesses of the firm and a source of long-term competitive advantage. Table 5.8 shows that several skills were common across these core businesses, specifically, management, marketing, and finance. The expertise would likely be shared across businesses, as fast-track executives from functional disciplines were given additional market or business experience.

Note that manufacturing exports and wholesale and retail trade require comparatively low capital investment and far less costly skills. These were businesses that could provide Jardine Matheson with a high return on sales—but with very easy exit, if the venture proved unsuccessful after three years. By the end of the 1970s, Jardine Matheson had begun to rationalize its manufacturing, shipbuild-

Table 5.9
Capital and Skill Intensity of Selected Hong Kong Industries

Industry	Depreciation/Labor Expressed in HK$/Employee	Skill Ratio (Professionals in Major SIC Group/Total)
Manufacturing Exports	2,683	2.49
Import/Export Trade*	5,328	7.03
Wholesale Trade	2,945	2.9
Retail Trade	2,851	2.03
Shipping*	21,160	5.16
Air Transport	9,465	12.23
Communication	16,146	12.4
Storage	12,992	2.85
Finance*	5,706	5.52
Insurance*	4,618	8.12
Business Services	11,989	29.95

* The firm's original and core businesses.

Source: Yun-Wing Sung, The China–Hong Kong Connection: The Key to China's Open Door Policy, 33

ing/shipowning and natural resources interests and refocus the enterprise on services, which could be standardized and replicated at low investment and operating costs and staffed by local nationals. This format is characteristic of Jardine's extension of Jardine, Fleming; shipping services; Securicor and Securair security services; Jardine Insurance Group; the Mandarin Oriental Chain of hotels; Franklins and Kwik Save Supermarkets; industrial laundry and contract cleaning services; Taco Bell; and other franchises.

GEOGRAPHIC SPREAD OF JARDINE MATHESON'S ACQUISITIONS AND DIVESTITURES

Jardine Matheson's desire to broaden its outreach in Asia and reduce its dependency on Hong Kong and China is clear from a geographic, market-by-market review of the firm's acquisitions and divestitures. While committed to building its presence in Hong Kong, the firm was not alone in its pursuit of other Asian markets at this time. World trade had begun to exceed the growth of world production during the mid-1950s, and by the early 1960s firms sought to grow by direct foreign investment in the developing countries of Japan, Korea, Taiwan, Singapore, and Malaysia across a wide range of industries. The strategy was to exploit knowledge and expertise gained in one Pacific market elsewhere in the region.[9] At the same time, it is obvious from the breadth of acquisitions that Jardine Matheson wanted to sustain its competitive advantage in Hong Kong, where GDP was rising 10% per year, interest rates were low, and the island was emerging as an important regional finance center.

This section establishes the factors responsible for GDP growth and the flow of foreign direct investment into the ASEAN and Hong Kong from the 1960s through 1990s and reviews Jardine Matheson's investments in the area and contribution to GDP growth from 1961 to 1996.

GDP Growth and Foreign Direct Investment in Hong Kong and the ASEAN

Brunei, Indonesia, Malaysia, the Philippines, Singapore, and Thailand—the original member states of the ASEAN—experienced dramatic growth in real GDP. Between 1965 and 1985, average annual GDP rose 4.8% in Indonesia, 4.4% in Malaysia, 2.3% in Philippines, 7.6% in Singapore, and 4.0% in Thailand, largely from corporate foreign direct investment, a significant portion of which came from Hong Kong firms.[10] Between 1967 and 1993, Japan and Hong Kong were the two largest investors in Indonesia, measured in terms of foreign direct investment and in terms of *cumulative* foreign direct investment, Hong Kong was among the top three largest investors in Indonesia, the Philippines, and Thailand. Between 1967 and 1997, Hong Kong invested some US$14.6 billion in Indonesia; in Malaysia, Hong Kong's paid-up capital in approved foreign direct investment projects in the manufacturing sector was US$256 million (or 4.2% of the total). In the Philippines, Hong Kong firms invested up to US$233 million (or 6.3% of the total) in cumulative foreign equity investment between 1965 and 1991. In Singapore, Hong Kong's cumulative foreign equity investment between 1981 and 1994 was US$3.3 billion, or 2.5% of the total.

Hong Kong firms looked to ASEAN countries for specific sectoral advantages: Indonesia and the Philippines offered greater competitiveness in resource-rich primary and labor-intensive manufacturing industries. Malaysia and Thailand were more competitive in manufacturing industries that required higher technological and capital inputs. In cumulative terms, from 1967 to 1993, some 70% of Hong Kong's foreign direct investment in Indonesia was concentrated mainly in six industries—textiles (US$838 million); office building (US$792 million); paper (US$658 million); hotels and restaurants (US$606 million), the chemical industry (US$604); and the basic metal industry (US$596 million). The top four manufacturing industries are related to resources abundant in Indonesia. For the textile industry, the availability of labor is an important factor, whereas the availability of natural resources is crucial to the chemical and basic metal industries.

In Malaysia, between the years 1975 and 1994, the majority of Hong Kong's foreign direct investment went into five industries: textiles, chemicals, electronics, food manufacturing, and wood products. These five industries accounted for 94% of total Hong Kong foreign direct investment in 1975 and 87% in 1994. The textile, electronics, and wood industries were the top employers in Malaysia—some 35,000 were employed by Hong Kong firms, the largest employer in that industry.

In the Philippines, agroindustries, mining/ mineral, and chemical industries attracted most of the Hong Kong foreign direct investment from 1972 to 1987. Since 1982, the service sector has absorbed 51% of Hong Kong's total foreign direct investment. As early as 1963, Hong Kong's foreign direct investment in Singapore's manufacturing sector represented 9% of total manufacturing foreign direct investment. Since 1985, the leading sector for Hong Kong's foreign direct investment has been financial and business services.

In 1970, Hong Kong's foreign direct investment in Thailand was concentrated in three sectors—trade, industry and construction, representing 87% of Hong Kong's total foreign direct investment. In 1980, the commercial and services sectors reemerged as the leading sectors for foreign direct investment. The five major industries or sectors were financial institutions; trade; services; housing; and hotels. In the manufacturing sector, electrical appliances and chemicals were the leading industries for Hong Kong's foreign direct investment in 1980. From 1980 to 1995, the service sector dominated, at some 63% of total foreign direct investment, with financial institutions and real estate the two largest recipients of foreign direct investment.

Jardine Matheson's Investment and Acquisition Strategy in Hong Kong and the ASEAN

Hong Kong had been Jardine Matheson's home market for 129 years, and the firm enjoyed a formidable reputation for financial strength and political influence.

From 1961 to 1974, Jardine expanded its interests in Hong Kong, acquiring firms engaged in finance, insurance, and real estate, as well as manufacturing, construction, transportation, wholesale and retail, and personal and business services.

Jardine Matheson began the decade with investments in finance (a new investment management and financial services joint venture with Robert Fleming & Co., London and the Empire Finance Company), insurance-broking (Turnbull Gibson and Lombard), shipowning (Indo-China Steam Navigation Company), engineering (Jardine Engineering) diamond trading (Gregory), marketing (Harry Wicking, Inc., Dunhill, Inc.), and security services (Hong Kong Security, Chubb).

By 1974 the firm began to expand its range of transportation services to accommodate Hong Kong's entrepôt trade, buying container operations (Dominion Line), and container services (Hui Kong), container reconditioning and expanding into air charter operations (Eupo-Air), air cargo forwarding (Freight Express), cargo handling and storage (Gateway), and air cargo terminal (Hong Kong Air Cargo terminal). Jardine Matheson had seven Hong Kong–registered shipowning companies in 1974.

By the same year, the firm had acquired six financial services, merchant banking, or securities firms and 11 property and insurance companies, reflecting confidence in the development of Hong Kong as a major economic center and entry point for international firms looking to do business with Asia, but with limited risk. Jardine Matheson had five insurance underwriting and brokerage firms in Hong Kong in 1974—Turnbull Gibson, Lombard Insurance Company, Chinese International Underwriters, Jardine Matheson Insurance Brokers, and Hong Kong Fire Insurance Company. In addition to its real estate investments, Jardine Matheson invested in a number of construction companies beginning in 1974 (Schindler and Gammon).

Taking advantage of low-cost labor and the reexport market, the firm invested in local manufacturing businesses, including jewelry manufacture, office partitioning, toys and radios for export, precious and semiprecious stones, canvas and webbing equipment, watch parts manufacture, rainwear, and electronic plating, as well as business services, hospital and contract cleaning, car park and garage (Zung Fu Motors), hotels (Excelsior), and TV rentals (Rentacolor).

Table 5.10 reveals that some 75% of Jardine Matheson's acquisitions were made in Asia, including 40% in Hong Kong or China and 25% in Southeast Asia. Hong Kong predominates with 226 service area acquisitions. But Singapore, Malaysia, Philippines, Japan, Thailand and Indonesia—and even more prominently South Africa—were also major markets for Jardine Matheson's investment, particularly in manufacturing and services. Jardine Matheson's manufacturing investments in the ASEAN supplied product to the firm's Hong Kong's wholesale and retail trade investments.

By 1974, Jardine Matheson had made significant investments in Singapore in shipowning, container freight stations, road transportation, agricultural industry manufacturing, textiles, scientific equipment, and medical and hospital supplies. The firm invested in oil exploration in 1974 and bought three Singaporean compa-

Table 5.10
Geographic Spread of Manufacturing, Service and Natural Resources Acquisitions and
Investments, 1961–1984

Region	Manufacturing	Services	Resources
Africa	7	119	4
Hong Kong/China	24	226	
Singapore	18	46	5
Malaysia	9	35	3
Philippines	16	17	
Europe		120	
US	8	46	7
North East Asia		14	1
Other	5	107	19
Total	87	722	39

nies engaged in oil industry supplies, manufacturing, and servicing. In 1975, Jardine Matheson acquired two firms to manage its oil interests and service oil rigs. Also in 1975, the firm brought in Jardine Fleming, Schindler Elevators, Rentacolor and a Hongkong Land-type property company, Singapore Land. Jardine acquired Promet Berhad, a company that undertook civil engineering and construction, steel fabrication, and marine transportation.

Jardine Matheson entered the Philippines with the acquisition of two life insurance companies and holdings in three sugar-milling companies, an air-conditioning and TV manufacturing company, a joint venture with Sherwin Williams to manufacture industrial machinery, and the acquisition of a machinery distribution company. In 1975 Jardine Matheson established Jardine, Davies, a holding company with Theo. Davies, long associated with sugar plantations in the East Indies, to manage a portfolio of food and kindred products, timber trading, clothing and machine tools manufacture. Shipbuilding and repair were added in the same year. Financial services were added in 1978.

Jardine entered South Africa in 1974 with the acquisition of Holiday Inn franchise licenses and local companies engaged in clothing, luggage, and outdoor equipment manufacture. In 1975, Jardine Matheson acquired 53% of Rennies, a 165-year-old trading conglomerate, based in Johannesburg with interests in shipping, shipowning, and tourism. The association quickly became extremely profitable, with the subsidiary contributing 12% to parent company profits by the end of the decade and operating in eight African nations. From 34 acquisitions by the end of 1977, the firm reduced its holdings to 23 in 1979 and had sold off all of its African holdings by 1980.

Like other Asian, European Community, and U.S. investors during the early 1970s, Jardine Matheson made a significant investment in Australia. It was Jardine's plan to create another Hong Kong, that is, another home base in Australia. In what became the firm's signature style, Jardine Matheson established holding companies in anticipation of exporting its finance, insurance, and retail "brands." By 1977, Jardine had acquired 18 firms engaged in finance, insurance, and real estate—ship owning, shipping services, airways, security services, sugar harvesting equipment manufacture (to accommodate the firm's sugar-milling businesses elsewhere in the Pacific), commodity-broking, sanitation services, and refuse removal and other personal and business services, as well as manufacturing businesses. From 22 businesses acquired during the Exploit and Develop period, Jardine Matheson's holdings in Australia were reduced or consolidated to 7 in the Harvest and Divest period and to 5 in the Focus on Distinctive Capabilities period, ending up with 1 in financial services; 1 in property, 1 in holding, and 2 in supermarkets. Jardine Matheson went from 22 wholly owned subsidiaries in 1978 down to 6 in 1980 and 2 in 1996.

Jardine Matheson Contribution to GDP Growth in Hong Kong and the ASEAN

In 1972, 82% of the firm's profits derived from Hong Kong, as well as 78% of its equity. In the same year, Northeast Asia (largely Japan) contributed 7% to profits and represented 2% of firm equity. Southeast Asia (largely Singapore, Indonesia, Malaysia, and the Philippines) contributed 3% to profits and represented 3% of firm equity. But by 1978, Hong Kong was contributing 45% to profits and represented only 37% of equity. Japan was contributing 12% to profits and represented 5% of equity; Singapore, Indonesia, Malaysia, and the Philippines were contributing 6% to profits and 12% of equity.

Indeed, Jardine Matheson had an extraordinary impact on the national economies in which it invested so heavily. With Hong Kong representing 37% of turnover in 1977, Jardine Matheson represented 3.9% of Hong Kong's GDP. With Singapore, Indonesia, Malaysia, and the Philippines representing 4% of turnover in 1977, Jardine Matheson represented 2% of their combined GDP. South Africa represented 5% of the firm's turnover in 1977 and 2% of the nation's GDP.

During the period examined in this study (1961–1996) peer firms like Swire and Hutchison Whampoa never took the multimarket approach of Jardine Matheson, making it part of their strategy to focus on Hong Kong and China. Only in the mid-1970s, when Swire was issuing shares, did Swire's contribution to Hong Kong GDP began to rise to 1.9% at the end of the decade. By 1984, Swire had eclipsed Jardine Matheson's contribution to the colony. By 1986, Hutchison Whampoa was contributing 2.1% to Hong Kong GDP.

COMPARISON OF JARDINE MATHESON'S ACQUISITION/DIVESTITURE STRATEGY WITH THAT OF OTHER MULTINATIONALS IN THE SAME TIME FRAME

This section looks at trends and patterns of acquisition activity across industries and geographies for the same period. A study by R. S. Khemani[11] of recent world-wide trends in merger and acquisition activity classifies merging parties into 29 industrial categories for the consolidated years of 1978–1979, 1983–1984 and 1988–1989. Within manufacturing, the categories correspond generally to the two-digit SIC (major group) codes, whereas outside manufacturing they represent one or more industrial divisions (i.e., several major groups). Hence, the number-ing system used by Khemani is unique to this investigator, but the industrial cate-gories correspond to the verbal descriptions of the two-digit SIC codes, which have been used throughout this chapter. Khemani's industrial categories are:

1. Agriculture	16. Primary Metals
2. Forestry	17. Metal Fabricating
3. Fishing and Trapping	18. Machinery
4. Mines, Quarrying, Oil Wells	19. Transportation Equipment
5. Food and Beverages	20. Electrical Products
6. Tobacco Products	21. Nonmetallic Mineral Products
7. Rubber	22. Petroleum and Coal Products
8. Leather	23. Chemicals and Chemical Products
9. Textiles	24. Misc. Manufacturing
10. Knitting Mills	25. Construction
11. Clothing	26. Transportation, Construction, Utilities
12. Wood	27. Trade
13. Furniture and Fixtures	28. Finance, Insurance, and Real Estate
14. Paper	29. Community, Business, or Personal Services
15. Printing, Publishing	

It is notable that the majority of mergers and acquisitions studied by Khemani over the time period tend to be broadly horizontal—approximately 57% of total activity in the years 1978–1979 and 1983–1984, and at a significantly higher level of 66% in 1988–1989. But there is considerable variation in horizontal merger activ-ity within different industry categories during the three time periods.

Also of interest is the variation in total merger activity in the different industry categories; that is, the level tends to be high when the *acquiring firm* falls into one of the following categories: Transportation, Communications and Utilities; Whole-sale and Retail Trade; Finance, Insurance and Real Estate; and Community, Busi-ness and Personal Services. The number of mergers and acquisitions is also high in mining—Mines, Quarrying and Oil Wells, particularly in the years 1978–1979 and 1988–1989. Toward the end of the 1980s, mergers and acquisitions activity was also pronounced in the Food and Beverage Sector, most of which tended to be horizontal.

Acquisitions in the wholesale and retail trade categories increased from 14% in 1978–1979 to 70% in 1983–1984 and were at 57% in 1988–1989. This may reflect forward integration of economic activity by firms located in different industries. Also striking is the number of acquisitions made by firms in Finance, Insurance, and Real Estate spanning the broad spectrum of the nonfinancial sector. The magnitude of these mergers and acquisitions increased from 17% to 82% and then dropped to 62% over the three time periods. This trend reflects the changing regulatory environment, which governs the operation of financial companies and the removal of certain barriers between different segments of financial markets.

Using Khemani's methodology and the same industrial categories and charting formats, Jardine Matheson's acquisitions were tracked over five periods. Two earlier periods were included, because Jardine Matheson's acquisition strategy was well under way in 1972–1974 and at its apex in 1975–1977. As noted earlier, the firm made a total of 437 acquisitions—32.5% in finance, insurance and real estate; 21% in transportation, 17% in manufacturing and 13.5% in wholesale and retail trade, 11.4% in services, 2% in mining and agriculture. (See Tables 5.11 and 5.12.) Jardine's very broad horizontal M&A activity, including 18% in manufacturing and resources, is similar to that of the trading and financial companies Khemani studied. Overall, a full 32% of Jardine Matheson's acquisitions were horizontally distributed.

In Tables 5.13–5.15, Jardine Matheson's activities are highlighted in gray and can be compared directly with Khemani's findings for the same time sequences. In reviewing these tables, it should be noted that the totals along the diagonal in these figures represent the number of acquiring and acquired firms that fall into the same broad industrial category. The transactions may be viewed as "broadly horizontal" in nature (i.e., where the firms have operations in the same or similar products). The industry categories are sufficiently broad; however, these numbers include related product diversification as well. The totals at the base of the columns indicate the industry categories in which the target (acquired) firms operate. Similarly, the totals at the end of the rows indicate the total number of firms in each industry category in which the acquiring firms are based. The number of mergers and acquisitions not located on the diagonal suggest the extent of nonhorizontal activity; these include transactions that are conglomerate and vertical (forward-backward) in nature.

By 1978–1979 Jardine Matheson's M&A activity in manufacturing and resources was reduced. As previously noted, the firm had reduced many of its noncore holdings. The 1983–1984 and 1988–1989 tables reflect reduced and highly focused M&A activity in the areas of finance and transportation, retail and services. (See Tables 5.14 and 5.15.) Hence, the overall shape of Jardine Matheson's acquisition pattern was familiar to that of trading and financial firms studied by Khemani, broadly horizontal at the outset (for Jardine Matheson this was 1972–1977, not 1978–1979) with increasing contraction through 1988–1989.

Table 5.11
Jardine Matheson & Company Compared to Global Firms, Trends in Merger and Acquisitions, 1972–1974

Acquired Firm Industry Category

	1	2	3	4	5	6	7	8	9	10	11	12	13	14	15	16	17	18	19	20	21	22	23	24	25	26	27	28	29	(Total)
1																														0
2																														0
3																														0
4																														0
5																														0
6																														0
7																														0
8																														0
9																														0
10																														0
11																														0
12																														0
13																														0
14																														0
15																														0
16																														0
17																														0
18																														0
19																														0
20																														0
21																														0
22																														0
23																														0
24																														0
25																														0
26																														0
27																														0
28	1	2			4		2	1	2		4	1	1		1	1		5	1	1	1			4	3	36	35	58	20	183
29																														0
	1	2	0	0	4	0	2	1	2	0	4	1	1	0	1	1	0	5	1	1	1	0	0	4	3	36	35	58	20	183

Source: Jardine Matheson Annual Report Data

1. Agriculture; 2. Forestry; 3. Fishing and Trapping; 4. Mines, Quarrying, Oil Wells; 5. Food and Beverage; 6. Tobacco Products; 7. Rubber; 8. Leather 9. Textiles; 10. Knitting Mills; 11. Clothing; 12. Wood; 13. Furniture and Fixtures; 14. Paper; 15. Printing, Publishing; 16. Primary Metal; 17. Metal Fabricating 18. Machinery; 19. Transportation Equipment; 20. Electrical Products; 21. Non-metallic Mineral Products; 22. Petroleum and Coal Products; 23. Chemicals and Chemical Products; 24. Miscellaneous Manufacturing; 25. Construction; 26. Transportation, Communication, Utilities; 27. Trade; 28. Finance, Insurance, Real Estate; 29. Community, Business or Personal Services

Table 5.12
Jardine Matheson & Company Compared to Global Firms, Trends in Mergers and Acquisitions, 1975–1977

Acquired Firm Industry Category

	1	2	3	4	5	6	7	8	9	10	11	12	13	14	15	16	17	18	19	20	21	22	23	24	25	26	27	28	29	(Total)
1																														0
2																														0
3																														0
4																														0
5																														0
6																														0
7																														0
8																														0
9																														0
10																														0
11																														0
12																														0
13																														0
14																														0
15																														0
16																														0
17																														0
18																														0
19																														0
20																														0
21																														0
22																														0
23																														0
24																														0
25																														0
26																														0
27																														0
28				8	5				1		2	4				2	2	1	4	2	1			3	4	48	24	48	30	189
29																														0
	0	0	0	8	5	0	0	0	1	0	2	4	0	0	0	2	2	1	4	2	1	0	0	3	4	48	24	48	30	189

Source: Jardine Matheson Annual Report Data

1. Agriculture; 2. Forestry; 3. Fishing and Trapping; 4. Mines, Quarrying, Oil Wells; 5. Food and Beverage; 6. Tobacco Products; 7. Rubber; 8. Leather 9. Textiles; 10. Knitting Mills; 11. Clothing; 12. Wood; 13. Furniture and Fixtures; 14. Paper; 15. Printing, Publishing; 16. Primary Metal; 17. Metal Fabricating 18. Machinery; 19. Transportation Equipment; 20. Electrical Products; 21. Non-metallic Mineral Products; 22. Petroleum and Coal Products; 23. Chemicals and Chemical Products; 24. Miscellaneous Manufacturing; 25. Construction; 26. Transportation, Communication, Utilities; 27. Trade; 28. Finance, Insurance, Real Estate; 29. Community, Business or Personal Services

Table 5.13

Jardine Matheson & Company Compared to Global Firms, Trends in Merger and Acquisitions, 1978–1979

Acquired Firm Industry Category

	1	2	3	4	5	6	7	8	9	10	11	12	13	14	15	16	17	18	19	20	21	22	23	24	25	26	27	28	29	(Total)
1	4				1																					2		5		12
2												1																		1
3			1																											1
4				67		1										1					1	2			1			14		86
5	2				40	1																						5		48
6																														0
7							5											2												7
8								2																						2
9									9														1			1		1		12
10																														0
11											3									1		1	1				1	5		9
12												23	10	5	3					1		1	2				1	8		36
13													10											2				2		15
14												2		5	16	2								1		2	1	5		11
15					1										16											1	1	1		25
16																2	1													5
17													4	3		1	27	3	2	1			2	1	2	1	5	8	1	57
18					1												1	17	5	2		1		1		1	1	6	2	36
19																	3	1	14					2				6	1	26
20				1													1	3	1	19		1			2			6		32
21				3																	7	4				1		9		22
22				1				1																						6
23				2	2				1		1	1		1			2			1		2	29	12		1	1	10	1	50
24				2				1				1					2			1			1				1	11		30
25																									12	55				14
26			1	1	3					1	1			1	1		1	1	1							55	1	8	1	73
27				4	5	1		2	1		1			1	4	1	8	18	5	10	1	4	14	13	1	1	80	41	2	216
28				2											1		1	1	2		1		2	2		1	1	54	1	65
29				1	4										2		1	3	2	1		2		2	1	8	6	20	9	45
	6	1	2	84	57	2	5	5	10	0	5	27	14	10	27	5	45	48	32	37	10	16	50	37	16	74	100	266	79	1070

Source: R. Khemani's analysis, Merger Register, Bureau of Competition Policy, 1978, 1979; Jardine Matheson Annual Report Data   Diagonal Total: 582

1. Agriculture; 2. Forestry; 3. Fishing and Trapping; 4. Mines, Quarrying, Oil Wells; 5. Food and Beverage; 6. Tobacco Products; 7. Rubber; 8. Leather 9. Textiles; 10. Knitting Mills; 11. Clothing; 12. Wood; 13. Furniture and Fixtures; 14. Paper; 15. Printing, Publishing; 16. Primary Metal; 17. Metal Fabricating 18. Machinery; 19. Transportation Equipment; 20. Electrical Products; 21. Non-metallic Mineral Products; 22. Petroleum and Coal Products; 23. Chemicals and Chemical Products; 24. Miscellaneous Manufacturing; 25. Construction; 26. Transportation, Communication, Utilities; 27. Trade; 28. Finance, Insurance, Real Estate; 29. Community, Business or Personal Services

Table 5.14

Jardine Matheson & Company Compared to Global Firms, Trends in Merger and Acquisitions, 1983–1984

Acquired Firm Industry Category

	1	2	3	4	5	6	7	8	9	10	11	12	13	14	15	16	17	18	19	20	21	22	23	24	25	26	27	28	29	(Total)
1	3																													3
2		3																												3
3																														0
4			4	28	1													3		2	1		2				1	1	3	46
5					27													1					1				5		3	37
6						2																					1			3
7							1	1																						2
8																														0
9									11	1											1								1	14
10										1																				1
11											6																1		1	8
12												8																		8
13									1			1	3											2			3		1	11
14					2							1	1	21				2						2			1			30
15															28			2		1							3		3	37
16																														0
17					1								1			1	41	2		1	1		1				7			56
18																1	1	32	1	2			2				10		1	50
19																1	1	1	20	1	1		1				8		1	35
20																				43	7		1				25		7	83
21																				1	15	1	3				2		1	23
22																						1					7		1	9
23			1													3			2				46	1			12		8	73
24				1			1	1								3	1		1				1	14			16		3	42
25																1	1								12				1	15
26														1										1		53	4	1	2	62
27				2	1						1						1	2	2		1		1	2		1	74		4	92
28		1	7	15	1		2		1		3	4	1	7	2	2	20	8	8	12	9	1	18	13	4	9	57	59	84	336
29																						1					6	5	155	167
(Total)	3	4	12	46	32	2	4	4	14	2	10	14	5	29	31	11	68	56	32	63	34	3	77	38	19	69	258	84	278	1299

Source: R. Khemani's analysis, Merger Register, Bureau of Competition Policy, 1983, 1984; Jardine Matheson Annual Report Data.

Diagonal Total: 710 (excludes unclassified)

1. Agriculture; 2. Forestry; 3. Fishing and Trapping; 4. Mines, Quarrying, Oil Wells; 5. Food and Beverage; 6. Tobacco Products; 7. Rubber; 8. Leather; 9. Textiles; 10. Knitting Mills; 11. Clothing; 12. Wood; 13. Furniture and Fixtures; 14. Paper; 15. Printing, Publishing; 16. Primary Metal; 17. Metal Fabricating; 18. Machinery; 19. Transportation Equipment; 20. Electrical Products; 21. Non-metallic Mineral Products; 22. Petroleum and Coal Products; 23. Chemicals and Chemical Products; 24. Miscellaneous Manufacturing; 25. Construction; 26. Transportation, Communication, Utilities; 27. Trade; 28. Finance, Insurance, Real Estate; 29. Community, Business or Personal Services

Table 5.15
Jardine Matheson & Company Compared to Global Firms, Trends in Mergers and Acquisitions, 1988–1989

Acquired Firm Industry Category

	1	2	3	4	5	6	7	8	9	10	11	12	13	14	15	16	17	18	19	20	21	22	23	24	25	26	27	28	29	(Total)
1	5																													5
2																														0
3		2																												2
4				152	1						1	1			2		1	2		1	1		2	2		2	3	3	1	175
5	1				95										2						1		1	1		1	7		4	109
6					1																									1
7							2		1																		6			9
8								1																				1		2
9									1	1			1														1			4
10																														0
11											8				1													1		9
12												14	8				2										1		1	17
13												1	8														1			9
14												2		14			1		4				1	2		1	1			21
15				1											72	1	32	1		2				2		1	1		2	84
16															1	4	4	3	4	1			1				8	1	1	38
17															1	1	1	19	19							2	2		1	23
18							1										2	1	2	1				1		5	19	3		25
19				1								1			1					33			1		2	11	19	14		31
20				4																1	26		1				2			87
21				1													1					1	2				12	2	1	34
22							2							1	1			1	1				30	19	7		19	1	4	19
23																							1				7	1	3	57
24				1								1					1	1		1			1			103	3	1	9	31
25				1	4										2		1	3		1			1				116		8	13
26		2	1	10	10		2	1	1	1	1	1	2	5	10	1	14	9	13	9	3		9	14	3	17	48	149	63	124
27																	1									2	9	14	2	133
28											1											1					6		6	398
29	7	2	3	175	109	0	6	2	3	1	11	20	11	19	89	7	61	39	43	48	30	1	51	42	12	139	278	178	256	1643

Source: R. Khemani's analysis, Merger Register, Bureau of Competition Policy, 1988, 1989; Jardine Matheson Annual Report Data

1. Agriculture; 2. Forestry; 3. Fishing and Trapping; 4. Mines, Quarrying, Oil Wells; 5. Food and Beverage; 6. Tobacco Products; 7. Rubber; 8. Leather 9. Textiles; 10. Knitting Mills; 11. Clothing; 12. Wood; 13. Furniture and Fixtures; 14. Paper; 15. Printing, Publishing; 16. Primary Metal; 17. Metal Fabricating 18. Machinery; 19. Transportation Equipment; 20. Electrical Products; 21. Non-metallic Mineral Products; 22. Petroleum and Coal Products; 23. Chemicals and Chemical Products; 24. Miscellaneous Manufacturing; 25. Construction; 26. Transportation, Communication, Utilities; 27. Trade; 28. Finance, Insurance, Real Estate; 29. Community, Business or Personal Services

Alan Rugman and Leonard Waverman[12] examined merger and acquisition activity over two time periods, 1975–1985, and 1985–1990, trying to identify sectoral and geographic convergence or divergence among U.S., European, and Japanese acquiring firms. From 1974 to 1985, 74% of Japanese firms' acquisitions were in the services sector, compared to 48% of American and 54% of European acquisitions. Some 39% of European Community acquisitions were in manufacturing, compared to 46% of American and 16% of Japanese acquisitions. Between 1985 and 1990, service sector acquisitions by Japanese firms represented 66% of all acquisitions; American and European Community service sector acquisitions were 51% and 56%, respectively. Manufacturing acquisitions were 36% for European Community firms, 41% for American firms, and 32% for Japanese firms. Resource acquisitions tallied 6% for European Community firms, 8% for American firms, and 2% for Japanese firms.

Compare Jardine Matheson's acquisitions over the same time period: 74% of Jardine Matheson's acquisitions were in the services sector (including transportation and financial services, as well as personal and business services); 16% in manufacturing; and 5% in resources. Like Japan, Jardine Matheson was still heavily invested in trade, with 14.4% of its acquisitions coming from the wholesale or retail trade subsector. From 1985–1990, 92% of Jardine Matheson's acquisitions were in the services sector.

COULD JARDINE MATHESON LEVERAGE ITS CAPABILITIES MORE EFFECTIVELY THROUGH AN EXTERNAL ORGANIZATION THAN THROUGH MARKET MECHANISMS?

To examine the kinds of strategic choices Jardine Matheson made during the period, we examined the firm's investment in associated and subsidiary firms across 152 business lines, the relationship between businesses and required skills, and Jardine's choice of geographic markets. This section examines the advantages to Jardine Matheson of its "external organization," an "industrial district" spread across the Pacific, linked by shipping, insurance, finance, and distribution services.

This section first examines the clustering within geographic markets of skill sets held by associated and subsidiary firms and available to the business as a whole. The section also examines the financial benefits of interorganizational contracting for the parent firm and its associates, justifying the mutual advantage of what may be described as an "external organization," in the Marshallian sense of a pattern of relationships within and outside the business.

Industrial Clusters

One can look at the three-digit SIC codes represented among Jardine Matheson's investments—that is, major industry—and plot these by stage in the value chain (primary goods or resources; manufacturing; services) and by geography. This shows the interdependence of Jardine Matheson's acquired companies within product systems for materials and metals (the steel product system), forest products, transportation, textiles, oil and gas and sugar, producing what might be called "Industrial Clusters."

The analysis of these "Industrial Clusters" revealed that many firms acquired by Jardine Matheson between 1972 and 1977 were steel-dependent. Included were oil refining, shore drilling and offshore services, construction and elevator installation, sugar-milling, sugar-harvesting equipment manufacture, shipbuilding and repair, steel foundry, piping and components, machine parts, agricultural equipment manufacturing, air-conditioning manufacturing, electricity and supply, motor distribution, steel fabrication, hydraulic components, crane and winch trading, industrial equipment, oil equipment and services. (See Table 5.16.)

Further, this analysis shows how the separate product systems actually related to each other and to Jardine Matheson's own historical capabilities. For example, the steel product system supplied flexible steel for cladding and decking to the transportation (shipbuilding) product system; machinery to both oil and gas as well as sugar product systems. The steel product system also supplied piping and aluminum components to the oil and gas product system, and the transportation product system supplied shotblasting and marine engineering services to that product system. A dramatic example of product system interdependencies was the impact of the energy price crisis of 1973 on shipbuilding and—domino-like—on the steel industry. The energy crisis hit the automobile industry and the housing industry in the industrialized West (United States, UK, Europe) and in Japan; demand for steel slumped. But in the newly industrializing nations of Australia, Malaysia, Philippines, Singapore, and South Africa demand for steel produced and used in the same region accelerated with GDP growth—and Jardine Matheson was there with the capabilities to take advantage of a spectacular opportunity.

While Jardine Matheson was largely involved in its core activity of matching buyers and sellers of diverse products, the firm was also entrenched in a number of key industries. This was not on a onetime, ad hoc basis but on a recurring basis and at very different stages of the value chain. Relying on its broad architecture, its relational contracts, Jardine Matheson would purchase raw materials, assemble them, coordinate their flow from firm to firm, through the production and distribution chain, using its own vessels and supporting the effort with its own marketing services. The firm would not only buy and sell the product at various stages but arrange the logistics and handle the foreign exchange aspects, documentation, customs clearance and other details.

Financing was another important aspect of Jardine Matheson's service to client and associated firms. The firm acted as a retailer of loans, borrowing wholesale at preferential rates and re-lending the money to finance the trade. Because of its intimate customer contact and its insurance-broking services, Jardine Matheson had the highest-quality credit information on current and prospective clients. The firm's capacity to gather and distribute information was an important commodity.

How was clustering an advantage to Jardine Matheson, the parent company? The range of related services that Jardine provided to firms in its network generated commissions to Jardine and its shipping/transportation services, financing, insurance, distribution, and marketing businesses. At each stage, from production to final sale, Jardine Matheson both provided value—knowledge and know-how—and extracted value as a buyer or a seller, on its own account or as a broker or shipper, operating on commission and absorbing the risk for companies in the chain. Using 1977 as an example, Table 5.17 illustrates how Jardine Matheson's value chain for steel offered at least 61 separate points at which the firm could extract value, make a commission, as it were, going back to the firm's history in the commission business.

Looking back at the classification scheme used earlier in this section to discuss Jardine Matheson's growth periods, it is evident that the opportunities that the firm and its managers saw for capturing value changed dramatically between 1974 (Exploit and Develop) and 1978 (Harvest and Divest period). The data derive from the firm's Annual Reports: in 1974, the firm made 19 cents of every dollar buying and selling the manufactures of associated firms; 22 cents on transporting goods; 2 cents on financial services. By 1978, the firm was making 30 cents on every dollar from making and selling manufactures, 29 cents from transportation, and 22 cents on financial services to its associated firms. By 1981 this configuration had changed. The firm had divested its manufacturing interests and divested its shipowning interests and was building a business concentrating on service delivery. For every dollar of profit generated in 1981, 77 cents was derived from services, versus 53 cents in 1974 and 61 cents in 1979.

The External Organization as Quasi Insurer

As noted in an earlier section, some 75% of acquisitions were made in the Asia Pacific Region, 40% in Hong Kong and China, and 25% in Southeast Asia. Northeast Asia represented only 10% of acquisitions because import quotas and trade restrictions limited entry.

The availability of low-cost labor in the Asia Pacific was attractive to Jardine Matheson, particularly when the firm was entering manufacturing and resource businesses, unrelated to its core finance, insurance, shipping, and trading businesses. Entry into unrelated businesses depended on ease of exit (reflected in a low current ratio) and the potential for high returns. In geographies where labor and energy costs were low, the firm could expect to appropriate more of its total revenue. With low exit costs, the firm could easily divest a nonperforming investment and add proceeds to reserves to fund future growth. As documented earlier in this chapter, half as many divestitures as acquisitions were made from 1972 to 1996.

Knowledge about investment opportunities and available returns was obtainable on-site through the firm's trading and shipping experiences. In cases like Rennies of South Africa, Guthries of Singapore, and Theo. Davies of Hawaii, the acquired firms were large trading firms that shared scope of activity and long expe-

Table 5.16

Jardine Matheson & Company—Industry Clusters

Industry	Primary Goods	Machinery	Services	Markets
Materials and Metals	**Raw Iron and Steel:** Promet Steel Foundry; Singapore Steel	Jardine Schindler Lift Installation Equipment	Jardine Engineering	Singapore Hong Kong
	Fabricated Ironand Steel: Promet Steel Products Mfg Diaward Steel Works Khinko Sdn. Bhd. **Non-Ferrous Metals:** Pipes and aluminum components **Metal Manufactures:** Flexible steel	Toft Bothers Industries Sugar Harvesting Equipment Studenberg Co. Sugar Harvesting Machine Parts Hilo Iron Works Machine Tools	Pacific Machinery Distribution Services P.J. Jaya Mandarin Agung Engineering Sales & Distribution Sherwin Williams Marketing & Distribution	Australia Singapore Brazil Hawaii Indonesia Philippines Hong Kong Malaysia Fiji
Forest Products	**Timber:** MacMillan Jardine		MacMillian Jardine Marketing	Malaysia Hong Kong
	Forest Products: Pagadanan			Philippines
	Fabricated Wood: Cemac Office Partitions Acme Plywood & Veneer **Paper:** MacMillan Bloedel			Hong Kong Philippines Canada Japan
	Wood Manufactured Goods: MacRall Holdings, Wooden containers, pallets			South Africa
Petroleum	**Oil and Gas Exploration:** Diamond M, TTI Jardine Drillships Investment Co.	**Oil Service Equipment:** Jardine Fearnley Antah Holdings Jack Enen & Co. Oil Industry Suppliers	Arrow International Logistics Promet Contactors Offshore Services Oil Rig Broking Offshore Vessel Operation Management of Oil Interests Compania Progress Co.	United States Tehran Singapore Hong Kong Bermuda Malaysia Netherlands Antilles Panama

Industry	Primary Goods	Machinery	Services	Markets
	Oil Refining: Diamond M			United States
Transportation	Shipbuilding: Promet Dynamarine	Marine Equipment: Mandarin Coatings Steel Ship Coating Promet Marine	Ship Owning & Chartering: Elegance Citation Compania Progress Matheson Chartering Indo-China Steam Navigation Co. Jardine Shipping Agencies	Singapore Philippines Liberia Panama Hong Kong Thailand
		Construction & Engineering: Promet Shotblasting Engineering Redland Jardine Industrial Services		
Textiles	Fabrics: Isherwood & Dreyfuss			Australia
	Apparel Manufacturing: Jardine Wicking Spencer Hay International Garment Company Jordon & Co. Shoes		Harry Wicking Marketing & Distribution Rennies Marketing & Distribution	Hong Kong South Africa Philippines
	Luggage: Rennies Luggage Holdings			South Africa
Sugar	Plantations: Honokaa Sugar Co. Laupahoehoe Jardine Davies	Hawaiian Fluid Power Co. Hawaiian Irrigation		Hawaii Philippines
	Sugar Milling: Bogo Medellin Honokaa Sugar Co. Laupahoehoe Sugar Co. San Carlos Milling Hawaiian-Philippine Co.	Sugar Harvesting Machinery: Toft Brothers		Australia Philippines Hawaii Philippines
	Sugar Good Mfg.: Associated Bakeries			Fiji

Table 5.17
How Jardine Matheson Extracted Value at Each Stage of the Steel Value Chain

Stages	Buy Oportunities	Sell Oportunities
Iron Ore	Local and international Own account Broker Ship Finance, insure	Local and international Own account Broker Ship Finance, insure
Blast Furnace	Product mix Contract	Product mix Unused Capacity Contract
Steel Ingots	Local or International Own account Broker Contract Ship Finance, insure	Local or International Own account Broker Contract Ship Finance, insure
Manufactures	Local or International Own account Broker Contract Ship Finance, insure	Local or International Own account Broker Contract Ship Finance, insure
Engineering and Construction	Local or International Own account Broker Contract Finance, insure	Local or International Own account Broker Contract Finance, insure

rience with Jardine. Jardine Matheson also had access to information brokers like Lloyd's List and Drewry's Shipping Consultants. The value to Jardine Matheson of dependable, long-term relationships with businesses in Asia Pacific was higher returns and lower-cost interfirm transactions. Lower-cost interfirm transactions were also of direct benefit to Jardine's associated firms.

To evaluate the ability of the Jardine Matheson network to retain more profitable revenue than any individual firm, we looked at the ratio of taxes paid to profits, reserves to stockholders funds, and operating profits to operating costs; see Table 5.18.

During 1972–1977, Jardine's taxes paid as a percentage of earnings were dramatically lower than for individual firms engaged in manufacturing or resource industries, an average of 29.32% (excluding the outlier 1974) versus 33.35%. The highest taxes affected the resource group, which averaged 46.61% during this period. Jardine Matheson also achieved a higher operating profit-to-costs ratio—an average of 16.78% per annum versus 15.14% per annum. For a comparison with individ-

Table 5.18
Higher Profits, Lower Costs Available through Jardine Matheson's External
Organization during Exploit and Develop Period, 1972–1977

		1972	1973	1974	1975	1976	1977
Taxes/		19	34	239	90	94	112
Profit Attributable		92	137	215	265	259	367
	Ratio	20.6%	24.8%	111%	34%	36.2%	30.5%
Trans. to Reserves/		73	128	149	129	227	280
Stockholders Funds		573	1,458	1,637	1,993	1,988	2,048
	Ratio	13%	8.7%	9%	6.4%	11.4%	13.6%
Operating Profit		117	184	479	400	461	482
Cost of Operations			1080	1844	2535	3508	3937
	Ratio		17%	26%	15.7%	13%	12.2%

Source: Based on Jardine Matheson Annual Reports.

ual, publicly traded firms within industries included in Jardine Matheson's portfolio, see Table 5.19.

Experienced financiers and insurers, Jardine Matheson achieved higher profits, retained more income for future growth, and maintained lower operating costs overall as a member of an external organization than the average individual firm dealing with suppliers on a contract basis. The anticipated financial value would have been important to Jardine Matheson, but also minimizing the peaks and valleys of profits and costs in an uncertain environment would have been important both to Jardine and to its associated firms.

Comparison of Jardine Matheson's Internal and External Organization with the Japanese *Sogo Shosha*

In studying Jardine Matheson & Company and its external organization, it is useful to compare this firm with the Japanese general trading company, or *sogo shosha*. Both share a similar history: the *sogo shosha* came into being in Japan at the same time as the agency house in Canton.

Like Jardine Matheson, the primary function of the *sogo shosha* was trading, that is, matching buyers and sellers of diverse products. In performing this core activity, it was entrenched in a number of key industries, at different stages of the value chain, from the purchase of raw materials to the marketing of the final product. It played a role in vertically integrated commodity systems, particularly in basic commodities such as textiles, iron and steel, nonferrous metals, chemicals and food-

Table 5.19

Profits and Costs Available to Individual Firms, Across Business Sectors, 1967–1983

Industrials Composite							
	1967	1972	1973	1974	1975	1976	1977
Taxes/Profit Attributable	29%	30.4%	32%	36.5%	35.2%	35%	26.4%
Operating Profit/Ops Cost	15.55%	15.06%	15.84	15.36	14.38%	14.42%	14.36%
		1978	1979	1980	1981	1982	1983
Taxes/Profit Attributable		33.5%	33.3%	31.7%	29.1%	25.6%	26.5%
Operating Profit/Ops Cost		14.40%	14.37%	13.16%	12.92%	12.78%	13.64%
Resources Composite							
	1967	1972	1973	1974	1975	1976	1977
Taxes/Profit Attributable	23.3%	37%	39.5%	52.7%	53%	48.3%	49.2%
Operating Profit/Ops Cost	21.55%	22.32%	25.22%	22.89%	19.87%	17.37%	16.48%
		1978	1979	1980	1981	1982	1983
Taxes/Profit Attributable		46.1%	47%	44.8%	38.9%	34.6%	34.5%
Operating Profit/Ops Cost		16.04%	18.09%	15.53%	13.87%	13.86%	16.29%
Machinery							
	1967	1972	1973	1974	1975	1976	1977
Taxes/Profit Attributable	39%	39%	39%	34.7%	32.3%	33%	34%
Operating Profit/Ops Cost	15.81%	17.71%	17.38%	16.01%	15.79%	15.35%	16.43%
		1978	1979	1980	1981	1982	1983
Taxes/Profit Attributable		37.9%	34.65	34.1%	35.1%	30.3%	48.2%
Operating Profit/Ops Cost		12.55%	12.48%	11.46%	12.35%	9.81%	7.36%
Iron & Steel							
	1967	1972	1973	1974	1975	1976	1977
Taxes/Profit Attributable	14%	15%	23.6%	32%	17.7%	7.1%	-30%
Operating Profit/Ops Cost	14.75%	11.26	12.04%	14.54%	10.30%	8.64%	5.59%
		1978	1979	1980	1981	1982	1983
Taxes/Profit Attributable		15.2%	2.7%	6.8%	30.4%	-55.5%	-17.4%
Operating Profit/Ops Cost		8.91%	7.97%	6.45%	7.81%	2.28%	4.23%
Paper & Forest Products							
	1967	1972	1973	1974	1975	1976	1977
Taxes/Profit Attributable	23.2%	20.7%	27%	32%	26.7%	25.3%	23%
Operating Profit/Ops Cost	14.49%	12.24%	14.67%	16.43%	15.50%	15.69%	14.87%
		1978	1979	1980	1981	1982	1983
Taxes/Profit Attributable		254.2	28,3%	22.5%	28.3%	10.5%	12.7%
Operating Profit/Ops Cost		14.55%	13.69%	11.94%	10.60%	8.42%	10.72%

Source: Standard & Poors Data, 1967–1983.

stuffs. The *sogo shosha*, like Jardine Matheson, provided essential links between stages in a product system for a client firm, only one stage of which was trading.

The Japanese general trading company entered the transaction as an intermediary between the supplier and the purchaser, accepting payment from the buyer in the firm of a bill of payment and issuing its own bill to the supplier. The supplier's extension of credit was to the trading company, not to the purchaser. Similarly, the liability of the purchaser was to the trading company rather than to the supplier. The trading company's role was analogous to that of an insurance agency. Although the trading company did not receive insurance premiums directly, it was actually in the insurance business and received commission income, usually a small percentage of the value of the transaction.

A recent study by Chee Ng et al.[13] uses SIC code analysis to identify the length of credit terms extended by the *sogo shosha*. It was possible depending on the extent of value chain activities—raw materials, manufacturing, wholesale, services, and transportation between points—that as much as two years of credit was extended by the trading firm, which brokered all of the transactions.

Importantly, both Jardine Matheson and the *sogo shosha* were linked to the associated and subsidiary firms in their network as well as to national GDP through trade, through investment, through trade credits, and through employment. The impact of the six major *sogo shosha* on Japan's GDP was estimated by Sheard at 28% per annum in 1979. Jardine Matheson's contribution to Hong Kong's GDP was 4% in that year, and to Singapore 2% and South Africa.

While the similarities between Jardine Matheson and the *sogo shosha* were extraordinary, the differences are also interesting. Unlike the *sogo shosha*, Jardine Matheson was in business to maximize retained earnings for growth. While the *sogo shosha* did not aim to maximize trading profit by buying low and selling high into the market, Jardine Matheson 's basic modus operandi was to comb the market looking for the opportunities with the best prospect for high yields. While the *sogo shosha* was compensated for acting largely as a purchasing agent for a relatively fixed group of long-term clients, for which it received a predetermined, volume-based commission or a relatively modest trading profit, Jardine Matheson knew that its share value and market capitalization were critical to draw investors to its subsidiary businesses. Table 5.20 reflects differences in the management and measurement styles of Jardine Matheson and the leading *shosha*.

During the mid-1970s, the Japanese general trading companies and Jardine Matheson were most similar in their activities, and both were concentrated in the basic sectors of the newly industrializing ASEAN economies—metals, fuels, food, fibers, machinery, and construction. To Jardine Matheson's advantage, the *sogo shosha* supplied only the Japanese market at this time. That left Jardine Matheson to explore other Pacific markets as well as to deepen its relationship with Hong Kong.

Jardine Matheson offered something more to its customers and investment partners than the *sogo shosha*. While the sogo shosha did relatively little business involving brand-name consumer products that required extensive advertising and service, Jardine Matheson built an Asian presence and awareness for international brands like Dunhill, Moet-Hennessy, Caterpillar, Sherwin Williams, and MacMillan Bloedel. More recently it did the same for KFC, Taco Bell, and Ikea. Its point of differentiation was its superior marketing ability. Jardine Matheson's advertising joint venture, MacMillan Jardine, provided marketing and advertising services to a raft of brand names handled by Jardine.

JARDINE MATHESON'S INDUSTRIAL LOGIC: A RESOURCE-BASED INTERPRETATION

A central theme of this study has been the resource-based view that Jardine Matheson developed a pattern of relationships within and outside the business that would foster the flow of information, the knowledge with which to interpret it, the ability to influence others, and the reputation to attract and retain trading partners. Chapter 5 took an in-depth look at the equity-based relationships Jardine Matheson built with hundreds of firms engaged in a cluster of industries to understand how the businesses related to each and the unique role they played in their industry.

From 1972 to 1996, Jardine Matheson made half as many divestitures as acquisitions, 300 of which were in broadly horizontal businesses and 500 in vertical businesses. There was a significant increase in divestiture activity during the Harvest and Divest period 1978-1984, particularly among Jardine's manufacturing and resource acquisitions, but divestment was integral to firm strategy throughout the study period.

Chapter 5 closely tracked Jardine Matheson's vertical industry acquisitions and divestitures to uncover the relationship, if any, between businesses within the same industry. The firm made 146 investments in the transportation industry, including

Table 5.20
Sales, Profits, Assets and Margins of the Six Largest *Sogo Shosha* in 1979—Comparison with Jardine Matheson's Financials

Company	Sales	Profits	Assets	Net Margin %	Employees (thousands)
Mitsubishi	48,325.2	77.4	18,824	0.2	13.0
Mitsui	44,886.6	54.1	20,964	0.1	13.6
C. Itoh	35,490.7	10.9	13,614	0.0	9.8
Marubeni	33,592.6	38.3	14,322	0.1	10.0
Sumitomo	30,438.9	40.3	8,637	0.1	10.0
Nissho-Iwai	23,106.8	17.5	8,541	0.1	8.3
Jardine Matheson	14,540.0	99.0	344	6.8	50.0

warehouses, container ports, containers, transshipment, air freight, and security services for container ports—some 28 four-digit SIC codes in all—across Hong Kong and China, Singapore, South Africa, Australia, and the Philippines. On average 20% or more of every transaction Jardine Matheson made between 1972 and 1984 derived from transportation services.

Finance, insurance (major category 60–67) accounted for 198 of the acquisitions Jardine Matheson made during the period. These acquisitions involved some 16 four-digit SIC codes. From the beginning of the decade, when 2% of every transaction, to the end of the 1970s, when 29% of every transaction involved financial or insurance services, financing was a very important aspect of Jardine Matheson's service to client and associated firms. The firm acted as a retailer of loans, borrowing wholesale at preferential rates and re-lending the money to finance the trade. Because of its intimate customer contact and its insurance-broking services, Jardine Matheson had the highest quality credit information on current and prospective clients. The firm's capacity to gather and distribute information was an important commodity.

In studying the skills associated with Jardine Matheson core trading, finance, insurance, and transportation businesses and comparing these skills with the requirements of Jardine Matheson's manufacturing, resource, and later retail and other businesses, it is striking that Jardine Matheson's trading and financial services core businesses put a high demand on top management, marketing, and financial management skills that were transferable across the firm's newly acquired businesses. While Jardine Matheson's manufacturing acquisitions relied on low-cost labor available in the ASEAN between 1972 and 1977, the firm's expansion into new retail and grocery industries in the 1980s required investment in industry-specific skills.

Jardine Matheson's reasons for divesting its manufacturing and resource acquisitions in the late 1970s are not too different from its reasons for divestment—the critical dependencies that could provide additional sources of value to the firm could also destroy value all along the value chain. For example, the steel product system supplied flexible steel for cladding and decking to the transportation (shipbuilding) product system and machinery to both oil and gas, as well as sugar product systems. The steel product system also supplied piping and aluminum components to the oil and gas product system, and the transportation product system supplied shot-blasting and marine engineering services to that product system. A dramatic example of product system interdependencies was the impact of the energy price crisis of 1973 on shipbuilding and—domino-like—on the steel industry.

Jardine Matheson retreated from manufacturing and focused on services acquisitions about five years before this became an acquisition strategy of the international firms studied by Khemani, whose activities are detailed in this chapter. Jardine Matheson closely resembles the Japanese acquirers studied by Rugman and Waverman who invested far more heavily in service sector firms than their European Community and American peers.

Jardine Matheson was a creator of clusters of industries within a very large industrial district framed by the Pacific, Indian, and South Atlantic Oceans. Jardine

Matheson sought to create hubs very similar to Hong Kong—with deepwater ports and facilities for finance, insurance, and transportation—in Australia , Singapore, South Africa, and Hawaii.

In Hong Kong and elsewhere in the Pacific, the geographic spread of Jardine Matheson's acquisitions and the firm's strategy of pursuing only minority equity holdings do not support that interpretation. Instead, the clustering of resources in deepwater ports around the Pacific created an "industrial district," in the Marshallian sense, where shipping, financing, insurance, distribution, and marketing were the lingua franca for transportation, oil servicing, sugar, leather, textile, and other industries in which Jardine Matheson invested.

As noted here, the dense network of relationships Jardine Matheson built with associated firms is reminiscent of the Japanese *sogo shosha*, the general trading company whose relationships with firms in the *keiretsu* were likewise built on trade, equity, and credit.

Jardine Matheson was compared with the Japanese general trading company, acting as a quasi insurance agent, providing trading and production credits to customer and supplier firms and deriving competitive advantage, from a hybrid governance arrangement that was neither internalization (vertical integration) nor market governance (commodities purchase in the open market).

Jardine Matheson was far more interested in potential profits coming from the knowledge of its subsidiaries and associates than the government-sponsored *sogo shosha*. Chapter 6 continues the discussion of Jardine Matheson's internal and external organization and its contribution the management of uncertainty.

NOTES

1. Amit, R. and J. Livnat, "Diversification Strategies, Business Cycles and Economic Performance," *Strategic Management Journal*. 9 (2): 99–110.

2. Krishna Palepu, "Diversification Strategy, Profit Performance and the Entropy Measure," *Strategic Management Journal* 6 (3): 239–255.

3. Sayan Chatterjee and Birger Wernerfelt, "The Link between Resources and Type of Diversification: Theory and Evidence," *Strategic Management Journal* 12 (1): 33–48.

4. Grant, R.M., A.P. Jammine, and H. Thomas, "Diversity, Diversification and Profitability among British Manufacturing Companies, 1972–1984, *Academy of Management Journal*, 31 (4): 771–801.

5. Moshe Farjoun, "The Independent and Joint Effects of the Skill and Physical Basis of Relatedness in Diversification," *Strategic Management Journal* 19 (7): 611–630.

6. The author's analysis of acquisitions and divestitures in Chapter 5 is derived from a close reading of the "Principal Subsidiary and Associated Companies" section of the individual Consolidated Annual Reports of Jardine Matheson & Company. All subsidiary or associated companies in which the firm has acquired a 20% or greater interest are listed there.

7. Davis, R. and I. M. Duhaime, "Diversification, Industry Analysis and Vertical Integration: New Perspectives and Measurement," *Strategic Management Journal*. 13 (7): 511–524.

8. Farjoun identified eight clusters of skills, based on an analysis of how frequently the skills were required to perform manufacturing jobs.

9. Edward Chen, "Economic Restructuring and Industrial Development in the Asia Pacific: Competition or Complementarity?" *Business & the Contemporary World* (Spring, 1993): 68.

10. Henry Wai-Chung Yeung, *Transnational Corporation and Business Networks* (London: Routledge), 18–19; 86.

11. R. S. Khemani, "Recent Trends in Merger and Acquisition Activity in Canada and Selected Countries," *Corporate Globalization through Mergers and Acquisitions* (Calgary: University of Calgary Press, 1991), 1–22.

12. Alan M. Rugman and Leonard Waverman, "Foreign Ownership and Corporate Strategy," *Corporate Globalization through Mergers and Acquisitions* (Calgary: University of Calgary Press, 1991), 78–79.

13. Ng Chee et al., "Evidence on the Determinants of Credit Terms Used in Inter-Firm Trade," *The Journal of Finance* (1 June, 1999): 1118.

6

LEVERAGING RELATIONSHIPS AND BUILDING CAPABILITY

The Hong Kong trading firm's ability to grow depended on the capability and experience of its managers—including the ability to foster the flow of information, the knowledge with which to interpret it, the ability to influence others, and the reputation to attract and retain trading partners. Chapter 6 contributes to the architecture of the current study by focusing on the organizational structure of the firm, including both internal and external organizations that allowed for consistent business routines and promoted organizational learning. The chapter deals with organizational learning from the viewpoint of management processes, including the training of high-potential management; the involvement of the firm's senior managers on the boards of influential external bodies; and the surfacing, review, and approval of new investment ideas. The chapter also covers the management processes that protected the company from ill-considered or opportunistic projects sponsored by departments or by associated or subsidiary firms.

The ability of a sprawling international conglomerate like Jardine, to invest in—and manage its affairs through—joint ventures and acquisitions in multiple locations imposes a challenge to firm governance, resource use, and information sharing.

This chapter seeks answers to two questions: What was the organizational structure of the firm, including both internal and external organizations that allowed for consistent business routines and promoted organizational learning? How did Jardine Matheson promote managerial initiative while curbing opportunism?

Chapter 6 focuses on both internal and external institutional mechanisms and is divided into sections as follows: "Interpersonal Networks" tracks some 200 of Jardine Matheson's managers from 1972 to 1996 to determine how managers contribute to the intra- and interfirm network. "Intrafirm Relationships: Parent and Subsidiary Firms—Affiliational Ties" discusses resource dispersion and networks at Jardine Matheson. "Encouraging Initiative While Curbing Opportunism" discusses the role of boards in decision making at Jardine Matheson. "External Relations—Impact on Influence and Reputation" discusses the information gathering, influence, and decision-making roles played by Jardine Matheson executives on the boards of government, bank, and social/political clubs. "The External Organization and Growth" discusses the roles of organization and managerial initiative in firm strategic management.

INTERPERSONAL NETWORKS

The internal and external organization of Jardine Matheson & Company has been an important factor underpinning the firm's resilience in the face of external shocks to competitiveness and its propensity to carry out longer-term structural adjustments in response. Jardine's organization is based on flexible institutional mechanisms well suited for adaptation to change. The emphasis is on resilience, sustainability, not success, or sustainable competitive advantage.

Interpersonal networks connect Jardine Matheson's vast geographically dispersed and internally differentiated businesses. Given the impossibility of building a fully connected network across all the individuals within the organization, the alternative is a network that relies on having at least a few individuals in each subsidiary who have a wide range of ties, what might be called "social capital" within and across the subsidiaries' boundaries.

The actual movements of 200 of Jardine Matheson's managers were charted from 1972 to 1996 on a spreadsheet. Almost all of Jardine Matheson's new hires or "cadets" were drawn from Oxford and Cambridge. They undertook a three-year training program and were mentored by senior managers. But that was only the starting point. To assess the on-the-job development of "social capital" within Jardine Matheson & Company, I looked at:

- average tenure, based on the notion that individuals with longer tenure will have a greater range of both interdepartmental and intersubsidiary contacts;
- amount of time prior to promotion to associate or director;
- how managers on a "fast track" were assigned to multiple geographic and functional posts—and the number of moves made, pursuing the idea that the greater the number of departments an individual worked in, the larger the range of interdepartmental contacts, and the greater the number of subsidiaries an individual has worked in, the larger the range of intersubsidiary contacts;
- the extent to which headquarters and subsidiaries were represented on the firm's multiple boards of directors; the process by which investment decisions were made—top-down, bottom-up, composition of review councils, and so on;
- the role of senior executives on government and investment councils and their role in decision making;
- The extent of local autonomy and local resource availability.

The Jardine Matheson & Company Annual Reports 1972–1996 are a rich source of information on management movements. It was important for the firm's external contacts to know the rank and decision-making authority of their local Jardine Matheson contact. Each annual report included names of the members of the parent board, regional and Hong Kong boards, and heads of local offices, making it possible to see which individuals got promoted, how fast and with what cross-geographic or cross-functional skills. (See Table 6.1.)

The findings are interesting. Some 40 of Jardine Matheson managers went on to become members of the parent board. On average, Jardine's managers enjoyed a length of service of 20 years or more. They made an average of three cross-functional moves, most often from finance, most often to general management, at a regional office. Jardine's managers made on average of three cross-geographic moves in their career. A senior manager at Jardine (associate director and above) reached board level in four years. In any year, two new members were added to the board, and two retired. The number of outsiders on the board at any time was two. The average tenure of board members was 12 years. The percentage of expatriates in

Table 6.1
Jardine Matheson, Management Development and Succession Planning
1971–1996—Key Findings

Total number of managers surveyed	200
Number of managers promoted to Jardine Matheson Holdings Board of Directors	40
Average tenure with the firm	20 years
Number of cross-functional moves at executive level (AD and above)	3—Usually Finance, General Management, Regional Office
Number of cross-geographic moves at executive level (AD and Above)	3
Years from AD to Board	4
Number of executives named to the Board each year	2
Number of retirees from the Board each year	2
Number of outsiders named to the Board each year	2
Average tenure of members of Jardine Matheson Holdings Board of Directors	12
Percent of expatriate Board Members	90%
Knowledge/skills at a premium for Board Membership	Experience in key markets like Japan, Hong Kong, Australia; and management of important profit centers, like Jardine Fleming, Hongkong Land, Dairy Farm

board seats was 90% as late as 1996. Experience in key markets and businesses were critical to board appointments.

For example, Nigel Rich was a general manager for finance in the Hong Kong office in 1975. Rich had one-year stints in South Africa and the Philippines prior to his appointment to associate director, Philippines, in 1979. In 1981, he moved back to the Hong Kong chairman's office and in 1982 was put in charge of property and hotels. Rich was appointed an executive director and member of the parent company board in 1983. When Jardine Matheson created the Asia Pacific Regional Board to validate proposals prior to presentation to the parent company board, Rich was appointed a director of the new board. He became managing director of Jardine Matheson Holdings in 1988, a position he held until 1992, when Alasdair Morrison replaced him.

Alasdair Morrison was appointed general manager, Jardine Industries in 1975, an umbrella group newly established to provide management oversight to small manufacturing and trading companies. In 1979, he became general manager, Philippines, under Nigel Rich. Morrison was appointed general manager, Europe, in 1982 and appointed associate director in 1983. He was appointed a director of the company and member of the parent company board in 1984. He became a member of the Asia Pacific Regional Board in 1987 and was named to the board of Hongkong Land in the same year. In 1993, Morrison became managing director, Jardine Matheson Holdings and continued in that position until 1999.

Anthony L. Nightingale was appointed general manager, Japan in 1979, a post he held for two years before becoming general manager, Hong Kong, in 1981. Nightingale was appointed associate director, Middle East, in 1982. In 1987, he was appointed a director of the Asia Pacific Board and, in 1991, appointed director, Jardine Pacific. He became an executive director of the parent company board in 1991 and continued in that role through 1996.

Long-term employment, single-firm careers were and remain the norm at Jardine Matheson & Company. To manage relations with subsidiaries and associates, Jardine Matheson's directors were selected for representation on the subsidiary's Board of Directors. Since Jardine Matheson's directors were responsible for firm strategy, they played an additional role representing the subsidiary's interests in Hong Kong, in Asia Pacific regional and global Jardine Matheson strategy.

Beginning in 1992, the practice changed somewhat as Dairy Farm, Cycle & Carriage and Jardine International Motors went through a rapid succession of chief executives. The board of each of these public companies remained essentially the same, while the changing chief executive guard reflected Jardine Matheson's desire to change the public image of these companies.

Despite the exceptions, the 1999 appointment of Percy Weatherall to the position of managing director reinforces the original model. He is a long-term Jardine Matheson man, born in Dumphries, extensive experience in Hong Kong Land and Dairy Farm before his appointment.

INTRAFIRM RELATIONSHIPS: PARENT AND SUBSIDIARY FIRMS—AFFILIATIONAL TIES

The relationships among Jardine Matheson's associated and subsidiary firms involved highly localized networks of dense transactions, creating a stable framework of exchange—with periodic collective action, as in the case of the Jardine Pacific and Asia Pacific Board activities noted earlier. Former managing director Jeremy Brown contrasted Jardine's style of governance with that of Hong Kong rival, Hutchison Whampoa. The latter's acquired firms were autonomous, while Jardine Matheson's governance style was midway between Chandler's "visible hand" (formal administration) and Adam Smith's "invisible hand" (autonomously self-regulating): "We imposed some organization and controls on our subsidiaries, while Hutchison's subsidiaries rode off in all directions at once."[1]

Governance was based on the nature of Jardine Matheson's acquisitions and the firm's expectations of its acquisitions, specifically:

- Jardine Matheson chose high-potential acquisition prospects that would benefit from an infusion of cash, but could be expected to yield high returns within a relatively short period;
- Jardine Matheson owned 40% or less of roughly half the firms it acquired. The firm expected acquisitions to raise additional equity capital;
- Half of all acquired firms were or became subsidiaries, if they met the firm's 25% hurdle rate within three years.
- Divested firms continued to be successful—like Rennies and Hong Kong Electric and Gas, among others—and Jardine Matheson enjoyed a continued relationship with these firms.
- Resources were very widely dispersed among associated and subsidiary firms.

In fact, part of the selection process for such firms was their ability to provide resource access in a part of the world where access was needed. Associates and subsidiaries were expected to participate in Jardine Matheson's interfirm market, that is, the identifiable flows of goods, services, and resources among technologically separable units that transform raw materials into finished products. The product systems referenced in an earlier section and coordinated by Jardine Matheson constituted an intermediate business model between the poles of corporate administration and market governance. It had the organizational routines, information sharing, and flexibility of the former and the cost advantages of the latter.

For example,

- Jardine Matheson ran sugar plantations in Australia, the Philippines, and Hawaii. The firm harvested its own sugar as well as sugar from other plantations with equipment from the sugar-harvesting equipment plants it owned. Jardine sent the raw sugar to one of three sugar-milling firms it owned and shipped the sugar to world ports in its own vessels or stored it in its own container terminals. The sugar process involved the interaction of some four to six Jardine subsidiaries.

- Jardine Matheson had a cluster of services available to its business lines in each major market. Jardine Fleming financed the bailout of Hongkong Land. Jardine Engineering Corporation was awarded construction projects by Gammon Construction and the elevators installed were Schindler Lifts.

- In transportation and shipping services, Jardine Matheson and its subsidiaries provided ship management and shipping agencies, terminal operations, logistics services (including air freight, warehousing, and distribution from locations in China, Hong Kong, Taiwan, Singapore, Malaysia, and the Philippines).

To each of its subsidiaries and to the firms for which it acted as principal and agent, Jardine Matheson provided a cluster of capabilities that included trading, banking, maritime insurance, and shipping—the same services historically known in the China trade as "agency services." Underlying these was a network of relationships built and sustained by frequent communications and the development of logistical and organizational routines to facilitate trade. Jardine Matheson not only handled direct imports and exports to and from Hong Kong but also handled third country trade, where the firm acted as a middleman. Jardine purchased raw materials and sold finished products throughout the world, served as the eyes and ears of major clients, provided them with global market information and analysis through its associates and subsidiaries, and helped smooth out the rocky road their clients faced in dealing with foreign languages, foreign currencies, and foreign governments.

To manage relations with subsidiaries and associates, Jardine Matheson's directors were selected for representation on the associate or subsidiary's Board of Directors. Jardine Matheson & Company never held an interest without voting power in an associated firm. Jardine's directors were responsible for setting financial goals and communicating overall firm strategy, and they represented the associate's interests on the Hong Kong, Asia Pacific regional, and Jardine Matheson Holdings boards.

For example, M.A.R. Young-Herries joined Jardine Matheson in 1948 and served in Hong Kong, Japan, and Singapore. Herries was appointed managing director in 1962 and chairman and managing director in 1963. A 1971 biography describes Herries as chairman of these Jardine Matheson Holdings:

Bangour Investments

Empire Finance Co., Ltd.

Ewo Breweries Ltd.

Harry Wicking & Co, Ltd.

Hongkong & China Property Co. Ltd.

Hongkong Clays & Kaolin Co., Ltd.

The Hongkong Fire Insurance Co., Ltd.

Hongkong & Far Eastern Investment Co. Ltd.

The Hongkong & Kowloon Wharf & Godown Co. Ltd.

The Hongkong Land Investment & Agency Co., Ltd.

Hongkong Tramways Ltd.

The Indo-China Steamship Co., Ltd.

International Pacific Securities Co., Ltd.

The Jardine Engineering Corporation, Ltd.

Jardine Matheson & Co. (Australia) Ltd.

Jardine Matheson & Co. (Japan) Ltd.

Jardine Matheson & Co. (Taiwan) Ltd.

Jardine Waugh Ltd.

Lombard Insurance Co. Ltd.

Pedder Industries Ltd.; Pedder Ventures Ltd.

The Shanghai & Hongkong Wharf Co. Ltd.

Plantation Agencies Ltd.

The "Star" Ferry Co., Ltd.

Young-Herries is listed as alternate chairman of Eastern Securities Co. Ltd, Hong Kong and Aircraft engineering Co. Ltd. He is listed as director of Dairy Farm Ice & Cold Storage Co. Ltd.; Dominion Far East Line Pty. Ltd; Harbour Center Development Ltd; the Hongkong Electric Co. Ltd.; the Hongkong Telephone Co. Ltd.; the Hongkong & Shanghai Banking Corporation; MacMillan Jardine Ltd.; Mercantile Bank Ltd.; Shanghai Dockyards Ltd.; the Sheko Development Co. Ltd.; and the South China Morning Post. The historical practice of interlocking directorates continues. Table 6.2 shows the interrelatedness of Jardine's subsidiary businesses in 1992, a small slice of the overall picture but evocative of the principle in practice.

RECRUITING AND TRAINING

During the period 1972–1977, a total of 437 acquisitions were made for a total investment of HK$8253 millions in finance, transportation, trade and service, manufacturing, and natural resources. Through investments and acquisitions, Jardine Matheson was now represented in 46 markets. Indeed, such aggressive expansion required what David Newbigging called "management in depth."

In a 1975 interview, David Newbigging painted a picture of organizational life and culture in the mid-1970s. Jardine Matheson had 13 directors, one of whom was Chinese, and 140 managers, all expatriates, recruited from Oxford and Cambridge, on a three-year contract with the firm. A consequence of the imprisonment of Jardine's managers during World War II and casualties during the war and the Korean conflict, the company's "old guard" had been replaced by a cadre of very young graduates, who reported to managers only slightly older and were responsible for very large profit centers. Newbigging commented, "We drop them in at the deep end. We say, 'okay, you think you are good, now prove it.' "[2]

Table 6.2
Jardine Matheson & Company—Cross-Board Seat Holdings, 1992

Director	Jardine Matheson Holdings	Jardine Strategic	Dairy Farm	Hongkong Land	Matheson & Company	Mandarin Oriental
Henry Keswick	Chairman	Chairman	Director	Director	Chairman	Director
Nigel Rich	Managing Director	Managing Director	Managing Director	Managing Director		Managing Director
C.I. Cowan	Director	Director	Director			
R.C. Kwok	Director	Director	Director	Director		Director
R.E. Moore	Director	Director	Director	Director		
Gregory Terry	Director		Director			Director
George Ho				Director		
Simon Keswick			Chairman	Chairman	Director	Chairman
C.G.R. Leach		Director	Director	Director	Director	Director
Sir Charles Powell			Director	Director		Director

Jardine's departments and subsidiaries were run as profit centers. Tight financial control and reporting systems ensured that no profit center could fall behind even for one month and pass unnoticed. Each was submitted to the discipline of forecasting three years in advance on a monthly basis. Henry Keswick pushed through strict cash control and reporting measures: "If I want to know the overheads of our air conditioning plant in Thailand, I can find it straight away. Every month we produce group results. I can see how a profit center has done, compared with budget, and the financial people highlight what has gone wrong. Every month we update our forecast for the year. And every quarter."[3]

The firm's management structure was informal. There were no organization charts, only a single-sheet list of directors' responsibilities on which the directors were listed not by name but by initial with instructions to "liaise with."

Executive directors assembled by 9 A.M. every workday—and Jardine's 30 associate directors met weekly—for a meeting known as "prayers," to tell each other what they had done the previous day—or the previous week. Once a month, everyone who headed a profit center in Hong Kong—10 directors, 50 department heads—came together for their version of the "prayers" meeting.

The branch offices kept in touch with headquarters through regular weekly telephone calls in which the head of the profit center in, say Singapore, would speak to the director in Hong Kong, to whom he reported.

ENCOURAGING INITIATIVE WHILE CURBING OPPORTUNISM

David Newbigging noted in an interview that Jardine Matheson's interests could have been rationalized, that if the firm had existed in London, it might have been divisionalized. In Newbigging's view entrepreneurship depended both on responsibility and on incentive. He said, "There are benefits in having many companies, particularly if you have joint ventures. And if you want to bring in an expert and give him a slice of the action, the only way to do it is to have a separate company."[4]

Prior to 1980, Jardine Matheson & Company was organized on a functional basis in Hong Kong and on a geographic basis overseas. After 1983, functional management and grouping of related activities took priority over geographic organization. Distinct business units within Jardine Matheson's core businesses were run as profit centers. The Board of Directors gave the managing directors of operating units near autonomy in running their businesses. Subsidiaries and associates made their own operating decisions. The parent company board approved every major investment decision. New investment opportunities were generated in two ways:

- Markets were identified where expertise in an existing core business would give the firm a competitive advantage and
- Key geographical areas were selected for expansion and viable businesses subsequently identified for investment.

Acquisitions and investments had to have board approval and followed a standard process for assessing the current financial health/operating effectiveness of the target firm. First, Jardine Matheson would send in a team to look at prospects. Members might include an operational director, finance director, and legal and tax men. With smaller acquisition prospects, the examination of the books might be left to an accountant and a management representative.

Responsibility for presenting the investment proposal to the board lay with the board member responsible for a function (business line) or geography. Jeremy Brown, former managing director of Jardine Matheson during the mid-1970s confirms, "There tended to be over that period an alternation between a regional and a functional basis for management control purposes but, however they were defined, each area was always the responsibility of a main board director."[5] Functional and geographic organizations reported to an executive director. Executive directors were members of the board. Figure 6.1 shows functional and geographic organizations reporting to an executive director.

In 1986 an additional board was created, the Asia Pacific board, consisting of the managing director of Jardine Matheson Holdings and the heads of Jardine's regional offices. Its purpose was to review the investment proposals, examining their potential impact on the region as a whole and assuring that the required supporting information and documentation had been evinced before a presentation was made to the Jardine Matheson Holdings Board. This additional review opportu-

Figure 6.1
Organigram 1984—Microcosm of Jardine Matheson & Company

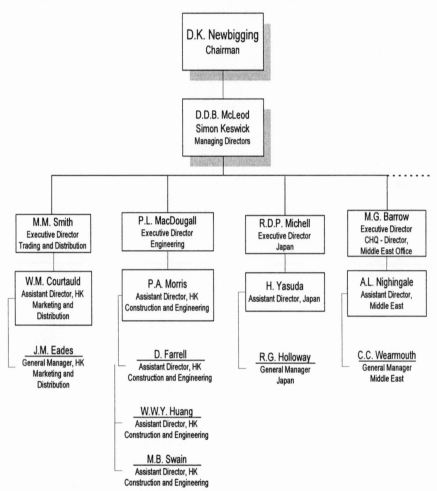

nity—or approval layer—was one of several corrections made in the aftermath of the Hongkong Land stock swap. It was intended to ensure that information critical to decision making was shared and evaluated across the company.

Consider the hypothetical situation of an investment proposal for a new container port in Hong Kong. The Hong Kong head office, specifically the Ship Management Group, generates the initial investment proposal. The proposed container port will impact much of the import/export trade of Jardine Pacific; hence, Jardine Pacific vets the proposal. The port will handle reexports from a number of Asia Pacific countries in which Jardine Matheson has interests.

The proposal goes next to the Asia Pacific board, where the container port's consequences for the broader Pacific region are considered. The new Hong Kong container port is seen to have a potentially heavy impact on Jardine Matheson's trade with Southeast Asia, which is expected to grow by 10 to 14% through the year 2006. The investment will give Jardine Matheson a significant edge in Southeast Asia over container competitor Hutchison Whampoa. The cost of the new container project—and its potential profit for Jardine Matheson—gets discussed next by the Jardine Matheson Holdings Board of Directors and by Matheson & Company, which is always involved in investment and borrowing decisions.

The participants in the container port discussion would have represented a cross-section of the firm's interests and some very senior managers. Jardine Pacific, which included the firm's transportation, trading, and distribution interests, had the largest membership—reflecting the dependence on these Pacific Rim services by Jardine's geographic and functional businesses around the world.

The ability of groups of executives with increasing oversight to examine the potential consequences of an investment decision on the firm, its subsidiaries, and the Asia Pacific region as a whole was a source of strategic strength to Jardine Matheson and characteristic of the firm's use of its "feet on the ground"—its country offices and subsidiaries—as an information club. Table 6.3 lays out who would have been involved at each stage of the discussion.

EXTERNAL RELATIONS—IMPACT ON INFLUENCE AND REPUTATION

Jardine Matheson's senior executives also played important external roles on behalf of the company and its influence in Hong Kong, as well as in London's financial district.

Until 1997, the "unofficial" members of the Governor's Council were representatives of Hong Kong business and banking. "Unofficial" was an actual title. Two of the 13 unofficial members of the Legislative Council were appointed as a result of an election by the Unofficial Justices of the Peace and by the Hong Kong General Chamber of Commerce. From 1958 to 1962, H.D.M. Barton of Jardine Matheson held a seat. From 1962 to 1968, S. S. Gordon, a chartered accountant, former chairman of the Hong Kong General Chamber of Commerce, and a director of Jardine Matheson, held a seat. From 1971 to 1978, M.A.R. Young-Herries, managing director of Jardine Matheson, held a seat.

As an "unofficial," the seat holder had no vote, but access to information was complete, and influence could be brought to bear on the governor and on the Standing Finance Committee in private. Unofficial influence secured the withdrawal of bills even after their introduction into the Legislative Council. For example, the Commissions of Inquiry Bill of 1966 was withdrawn when the attorney general acknowledged the misgivings that had been expressed to him by the unofficial and by the Incorporated Law Society of Hong Kong since publication of the bill.

The "unofficials" represented a majority on the Standing Finance Committee and exerted the most influence there, where meetings were held in private and their proceedings were not published. Since most legislative and executives acts involved

Table 6.3
Jardine Matheson & Company Functional Boards, 1988 Example

Hong Kong Head Office (Local Issues)	Jardine Pacific Management Group (Trading Issues)	Asia Pacific Regional Board, (Regional Issues)	Jardine Matheson Holdings Board (Corporate Issues)
R.D.P. Michell, Director	G. J. Terry	M. G. Barrow	Simon Keswick, Chairman
R.J.O. Barton, Jardine Insurance Brokers	R. C. Sutton, Australia	Nigel Rich	Nigel Rich, Managing Director
W. M. Courtauld	D. Hon, Canada	R. J. Collins	P. J. Collins, Executive Director
D. A. Heenan, Theo Davies Hawaii	A.J.L. Nightingale, Hong Kong	R. S. Sutton, Australia	George Ho, OBE
R. G. Lee	H. Gunther, Indonesia	R.C. Kwok	Henry Keswick, Executive Director
	H. Yasuda, Japan	D. A. Heenan, Theo. Davies, Hawaii	R. C. Kwok
	P. Po, Beijing	R. E. Moore, head, Bermuda, Operations	C.G.R. Leach, head of Europe/UK
	K. C. Sitt, Shanghai	A. G. Morrison, Hongkong Land	R. E. Moore, head, Bermuda Operations
	M. Lo, Guangzhou	R.D.P. Michell	
	E.P.W. Weatherall, Philippines	A.J.L. Nightingale, Hong Kong	
	Y. C. Boon, Singapore	O. P. Howell-Price, Dairy Farm	
	C. C. Willis, Jr., South Korea	R. E. Riley, Mandarin Oriental	
	A. Mackinnon, Taiwan	A. H.Smith, Jardine Fleming	
	K. Sarasin, Thailand	G. J. Terry	
	D. A. Heenan, Theo. Davies, Hawaii	H. Yasuda, Japan	
	R. E. Moore, head, Bermuda OperationsC.G.R. Leach, Europe/UK	R.J.O. Barton, Jardine Insurance Brokers	
	R. B. Wilson, Middle East	Y. C. Boon, Singapore	
	R. H. Gunn, Netherlands		
	A. H. Smith, Jardine Fleming		
	O. P. Howell-Price, Dairy Farm		
	A. G. Morrison, Hongkong Land		
	R. E. Riley, Mandarin Oriental		
	R.J.O. Barton, Jardine Insurance Brokers		

finance, the Standing Finance Committee discussed most aspects of government policy, although discussions were limited to expenditures, not to revenue.

Because the strength of the British colonial government rested on the alliance between British officials and the Chinese business community, support to both sides was assured by the British business community, which collectively contributed in excess of 12% to the GDP of Hong Kong and formed a highly influential power bloc. It consisted of Jardine Matheson & Company; Butterfield and Swire, Hutchison International, the Dairy Farm Ice & Cold Storage Company; Wheelock Marden & Co.; and the Hong Kong & Shanghai Banking Corporation.

The meetings of the Standing Finance Committee were sometimes held at the Royal Hong Kong Jockey Club, whose stewards in 1969 included J.A.H. Saunders, chairman of the Jockey Club, member of the Executive Council, and chairman of the Hong Kong & Shanghai Banking Corporation; Sir Sik-nin Chau, chairman of Dairy Farm Ice & Cold Storage; J. L. Marden, member of the Executive Council and chairman of Wheelock Marden; J.D. Clague, director of Dairy Farm and member of the Executive Council; Fung Ping-fan, member of the Legislative Council; M.A.R. Young-Herries, chairman, Jardine Matheson & Company and member of the Legislative Council; and Djun J. Ruttonjee, formerly senior official in the Legislative Council. The exclusive club was immensely influential. The Jockey Club held a monopoly on legalized gambling in Hong Kong, and its stewards were responsible for making lavish charitable donations from gambling earnings. Representatives of Jardine Matheson also sat on specific committees of the Legislative and Executive Councils.

Board Membership—Hongkong & Shanghai Bank

From 1877 through 1996, members of Jardine Matheson sat on the Board of Directors and the London Advisory Council of the Hongkong & Shanghai Banking Corporation. (See Tables 6.4 and 6.5.) So did Jardine Matheson's major competitors or peers in Hong Kong. The dozen or so rivals included Swire, Wheelock, and Cheung Kong (Hutchison Whampoa), as well as local competitors such as Dodwell's and Gibb Livingston. Therefore, these seats were even more important to information access—and potential collaboration—than to influence and individual firm advantage.

Jardine Matheson & Company and the Hongkong & Shanghai Bank (HKSB) became partners in at least six Jardine-owned businesses: Central Registration—Hong Kong, 1973 (HKSB had 50% equity); East Point Reinsurance in 1979 (HKSB held 15% equity); Jardine Matheson Holdings (HKSB held 5% equity); British & Chinese Corp. (HKSB had 50% equity); Far Eastern Economic Review (HKSB held 50% equity); and South China Morning Post (HKSB held 40% equity).

The British & Chinese Corporation was a 20th century relic of the firm cofounded by Jardine Matheson and the Hongkong & Shanghai Bank to fund railroads in China. The collaboration continued deep into the 20th century, during

Table 6.4
Hongkong & Shanghai Banking Corporation—Board of Directors

Company	Subsidiary	Years Represented
Jardine Matheson		1877
		1962–1985
Swire Group	Butterfield & Swire	1914
		1962–1974
	John Swire & Sons	1974–1985
Inchcape (HK)	Gilman & Co.	1864
		1962–1985
	Dodwell & Co.	1895
		1962–1985
Mackinnon, Mackenzie		1929
		1962–1974
Imperial Chemical Industries		1946
		1962–1974
Caldbeck, Macgregor		1956
		1962–1965
Sir Elly Kadoorie & Sons		1957
		1962–1967
John D. Hutchison		1930
		1962–1976
Union Insurance Company of Canton		1966–1968
Hongkong Bank		1941
		1962–1985
Deacon & Co.		1969–1980
Wheelock Marden & Co.		1972–1985
World Wide Shipping		1972–1985
Central Development		1974–1985
Mass Transit Railway		1979–1985
Heng Seng Bank		1979–1985
Cheung Kong		1980–1985
Hong Kong Electric		1980–1985
Gibb, Livingston & Co.		1,869

Source: Frank H. H. King, *The History of the Hongkong and Shanghai Banking Corporation,* vols. 3, 4 (Cambridge: Cambridge University Press, 1988–1991).

Table 6.5

Jardine Matheson & Company—Executive Representation on the Board of Directors
and London Advisory Council, Hongkong & Shanghai Banking Corporation

Jardine Matheson Executive	Board of Directors	London Advisory Council
William Keswick	1877, Deputy Chairman 1879–1880; Chairman 1880–1881; Resigned 1886	
F. B. Johnson	1881–1886	
J. Bell-Irving	1886; Deputy Chairman 1887; Chairman 1888–1889, Resigned 1889; Returned 1893; Deputy Chairman 1897–1898; Chairman 1898–1899; Deputy Chairman 1902–1903	
J. J. Keswick	1890–1895; 1899–1900; Chairman 1901–1902	
H.D.M. Barton	Chairman 1962–1964	
J. H. Keswick		1962–1970
M.A.R. Young-Herries	1965–1970	1970–1975
H.S.I. Keswick	1971–1975	1975–Present
D. K. Newbigging	1975–1983	
S. L. Keswick	1984–Present	

Source: Frank H. H. King, *The History of the Hongkong and Shanghai Banking Corporation*, vols. 3, 4 (Cambridge: Cambridge University Press, 1988–1991).

the 1960s and 1970s, the period of Hong Kong's industrial development. As discussed earlier, Jardine Matheson & Company invested in every sector of Hong Kong business. At the same time, the Hongkong & Shanghai Bank made HK$976 million in loans and advances to local Hong Kong firms, often to companies that enjoyed a relationship with Jardine Matheson in the areas of manufacturing, textiles, electrical and electronics, transport, electricity and gas, building construction, and general commerce.

The record of actual loans and advances made by the Hongkong & Shanghai Bank understates the whole investment story. The bank assisted local manufacturers through a phenomenon called "packing credits," bills of credit drawn on the Hongkong & Shanghai Bank by manufacturers for purchase orders from firms such as Jardine Matheson; Gibb, Livingston; Dodwell's and Hutchison for the sale of merchandise. The packing credit provided an advance to the small manufacturer for the raw materials necessary to produce goods for shipment and sale. The packing credit is an example of the use of an unofficial, short-to-medium-term loan to facilitate trade, where one or more of the participants have low working capital. Jardine Matheson also made use of this convention in its relations with subsidiaries and customers.

THE EXTERNAL ORGANIZATION AND GROWTH

Chapter 6 has dealt explicitly with the role of Jardine Matheson's managers and directors in building, guiding, and managing the relationships between the parent firm and its subsidiaries and associated firms, on the one hand, and negotiating the parent firm's relationships with the outside world, on the other.

This section concludes the discussion by returning to two questions posed at the beginning of the chapter: What was the organizational structure of the firm that allowed for consistent business routines and promoted organizational learning? How did Jardine Matheson promote managerial initiative while curbing opportunism?

The External Organization of the Firm

Jardine Matheson's founders and subsequent managers developed an "architecture" or "administrative framework" for learning and collaboration. This framework included interorganizational linkages that were mutually beneficial to participants and important to Jardine Matheson for the development of capabilities, trustworthiness, and consistent patterns of behavior and effective forms of governance. Jardine Matheson's plan for interorganizational continuity and growth required the exposure of high-potential managers to a variety of geographic and functional assignments over time. This was accomplished without disruption to the business by a succession scheme under which junior managers would be groomed to replace senior managers who had been elevated to associate director and above.

Senior members of the staff mentored junior associates for a three-year trial period until juniors were put in charge of a profit center and given the chance to prove themselves. The culture was a close one. Jardine Matheson's managers on a fast track were expected to play a public role in the life of Hong Kong and the regions. As described in this chapter, this life might include membership on the Hong Kong Legislative Council or membership on the Hong Kong or London board of the Hongkong & Shanghai Bank. Participation in public life was not a competitive tactic. It *was* about information, getting a piece of the opportunity for Jardine, building a community in which Jardine Matheson was an influential player.

Jardine Matheson's knowledge-based culture was not at all above increasing efficiencies and keeping transaction costs low, although these were benefits. The environment of risk and uncertainty made collaboration essential to survival. This meant collaboration between headquarters and associated firms—as well as between and among Jardine Matheson's associated firms. The geographic spread of

Jardine Matheson's resources, embedded in associated and subsidiary firms, and their involvement in the value chain of diverse industries support the notion that this was a highly collaborative firm. The review boards, which were established by Jardine Matheson to assure that the potential for broader, geographic, and organizational impact was explored before a decision was rendered on a potential investment, are a further example of organizational commitment to learning and sharing. While there is little doubt that the Jardine Matheson's analysts saw cost reduction advantages to frictionless contracting among members of an external organization, the objective was collaboration, not merely cost reduction.

Encouraging Initiative While Curbing Opportunism

In the Penrosean firm, initiative or "enterprise" is rewarded and opportunism is more often depicted as opportunity—the opportunity to extend the firm's interorganizational linkages to include a new, but familiar, business partner with known and consistent business behaviors, making partners out of a competitors. In this section, the opportunism of competitors and associated firms is considered first, then managerial opportunism.

As in the early period, bringing potential competitors into their orbit—making collaborators of competitors, like the Swire Group or Hutchison Whampoa—served Jardine Matheson's interests very well. Collaboration opened new opportunities for shared investment and access to information from different markets and reduced the risk of commodity price and shipping rate fluctuations.[6]

In the 20th century, Jardine Matheson built a network of trade and minority equity-based relationships with associated Hong Kong and ASEAN firms. As the network builder, Jardine Matheson encouraged the initiative of local firms for which it served as a source of financial services, insurance, and shipping. Jardine Matheson's pattern of minority positions left the bulk of the fund-raising to local firms, achieving growth at the expense of control. But Jardine's influence surpassed its equity stake. In building this network or "external organization," Jardine Matheson made itself indispensable to manufacturers, retailers, and service establishments alike, who could expect credit terms of up to two years, as well as transportation, distribution, and marketing services from their Hong Kong partner.

The firm avoided the fate of many merchant intermediaries who could be locked out or eased out of business if their contractual agreements with manufacturers were not renewed. Network relationships were based on trust, not contract. The advantages derived from the ongoing relationship with Jardine Matheson were perceived by associated firms to be greater than the gains of opportunistic behavior.

The best managers needed to be compensated to remain with the firm to grow firm business. The key issue was incentive-compatibility. The distribution of knowledge in the firm (and among members of its external organization) might well provide opportunities for individuals to gain by concealing or misrepresenting their private information, while reducing overall efficiency. However, restoring efficiency allows for gains all around, and so "farsighted" contracting permits the design of incentive structures that ensure disclosure of private information, if necessary, by putting the owner of this private information in charge. Examples of this kind of incentive structure include the comprehensive education of Jardine Matheson's high-potential managers who were groomed for leadership or creation of a seat on the board of Jardine Matheson & Company for the head of the Hongkong Land Company after the mutual stock swap and takeover attempt in the 1980s.

Jardine Matheson was very aware of the potential for opportunism and used collaborative tactics—interorganizational linkages, cross-board holdings, equity accounting, multiboard reviews, and proactive government and bank relationships, among other inventions—to circumvent it.

NOTES

1. Jeremy Brown to Carol Connell, interview at Matheson & Company, London, May 1998.

2. Roy Hill, "Venerable Trading House Youth at the Helm," *International Management* (August 1975): 33.

3. Ibid., p. 34.

4. Ibid.

5. Jeremy Brown to Carol Connell, June 1998.

6. During the 1970s and 1980s, examples of investment partners included the Swire Group, a joint-venture partner in real estate; Mac Millan Bloedel in timber; Schindler in elevators; and Securicor in security services.

CHANGE AND LEARNING IN THE
HONG KONG TRADING INDUSTRY

The Hong Kong trading companies have gone through political upheaval and global and regional economic crises. They have survived and transformed themselves several times in the process. The argument is made here that learning derived from the special and changing business, social, and political environment into which the trading companies entered and the firms' concentration on building patterns of relationships within and outside the firm that fostered the flow of information, the knowledge with which to interpret it, the ability to influence others, and the reputation to attract and retain trading partners. The purpose of this chapter is to assess the ability of the Hong Kong trading company to respond to a changing environment and apply new learning to capture value, effectively transforming the company from within.

The chapter takes a historical-transformation approach to learning and knowledge in the Hong Kong trading industry across three break points, focusing on Jardine Matheson & Company as a special case:1977, at the height of the firm's aggressive acquisition strategy; 1996, after the sell-offs of the early 1980s, when the firm had refocused on its distinctive capabilities and before the Asian financial crisis; and 2002, after the Asian financial crisis and during the current economic downturn. At each break point, Jardine Matheson is compared with other firms in the industry.[1]

MEASURING LEARNING

This study of change and learning in the Hong Kong trading industry is about the ability of the firm to continuously acquire, integrate, and apply knowledge from a variety of sources, usually in response to perceived opportunities and threats in the external environment. Learning is depicted through:

- changes in the use and value of resources from one period to the next; for example, Jardine's change in strategy, with the sell-off of costly to maintain physical assets, like ships, and new focus on shipping services;

- the capabilities or organizational routines that have been the source of competitive advantage to the firm. The core competences of the firm, developed during the early period, are identified and compared with their use or extension during the later period;

- the internal and external organization of the firm, including how relationships developed and changed from the early to later period. Changes and use of management resources and organizational form and governance as well as relationships with buyers and suppliers are charted and analyzed;

- the firm's response or adaptation to its environment, including the major strategic groups, industry and market trends, regulatory environment, market served, value chain, and consumer demand, is identified and compared from one period to the next.

Through a comparison of their decisions over three break points, Jardine Matheson and peer firms can be seen to accumulate experiences, draw on past decisions, adjust their reactions to similar problems and add to their repertoire of responses to deal with novel situations. This chapter presents an argument for the relevance of adaptability and learning to the ongoing strategic management of the firm.

INDUSTRY ENVIRONMENT AND FIRM RESPONSE, 1977–1996–2002

The Industry Background

In 1977, the industry was largely, but not exclusively, commodities trading. There were at least two strategic groups, defined by security analysts of the period: traditional commodities specialists, focused on a single country, and single product or service; and commodities generalists, including the *sogo shosha* or general trading companies. Traditional commodities specialists included S&W Berisford, Booker McConnell, Daigety, and James Finlay. Generalists included Jardine Matheson, Gill & Duffus, Harrisons & Crosfield, S. Hoffnung, and also Mitsubishi, Mitsui, Marubeni, the latter, Japanese general trading companies. The principal trends in the industry were intertwined: the opening of China to trade made investment in Hong Kong, the financial capital of Asia, desirable on the part of both Hong Kong-based firms and North American and European firms looking to establish an office close to China. Members of the industry served as intermediaries or consultants, often on retainer to firms seeking an Asian presence.

By 1996, the industry had changed dramatically: firms located in Hong Kong had come to own very divergent businesses in Hong Kong, Asia, or worldwide. The largest members of the emerging multi-industry conglomerate sector were Swire Pacific (descended from Butterfield & Swire); Hutchison Whampoa; Wheelock (descended from Wheelock Marden, an early trading company), Jardine Matheson, First Pacific and the Chinese investment conglomerate, CITIC. The intermediary role to Asian trade is still vital to privileged franchise expansion, but the Pacific trade and distribution (or trade and marketing) segment of the conglomerate's business was but one spoke in the wheel of businesses, which might be very diverse, including telecommunications, infrastructure, aviation, banking, property, and development. Under the Takeover Code, Hong Kong would return to China in 1997. The business atmosphere was apprehensive.

Teetering on the edge of the Asian financial crisis and economic downturn, the leading Hong Kong conglomerates—CITIC, Hutchison Whampoa, Swire Pacific and Jardine Matheson—were more or less comfortably placed to withstand the impact of the crisis, given their financial strength, franchise quality and returns track record. Exposure to weakened currencies would require strong liquid cash assets or hedges to offset liabilities, manageable debt/equity ratios, and increasing debt maturity.

In terms of financial strength, at year end 1997, Swire Pacific (14.1%) and Jardine Matheson (19.8%) had the lowest debt/equity ratios; Hutchison (60%) and the China government sponsored CITIC (56.2%) had the highest. Jardine Matheson entered 1998 in the most comfortable position in terms of balance sheet currency exposure, with US$ and Sterling assets of $24M, and by 1998, had increased its cash assets by another US$318M.

With financial strength critical to investors and partners, the guarantee of extensive levels of debt by the conglomerate's head offices, especially in relation to property projects, was an area of concern. Two trends were emerging, namely, guarantees wrapped as off-balance sheet accounted joint ventures and the "ring fencing" of the debt of associated companies, that is, debt not guaranteed by the parent company. Hutchison raised debt guaranteed by specific operating units, like the development of its non-Asian port interests by West Ports, the holding vehicle for its three UK ports, and the port and airport complex in the Bahamas and Panama. Jardine Matheson guaranteed its property-related debt by specific buildings, not by Jardine's head office nor Hongkong Land's head office. Such conservatism was likely the product of management's folk memory of the Hongkong Land affair and the debt difficulties into which Jardine Matheson plunged in the early 1980s.

The issues that became important to the rest of the world only after Enron in 2001 had become important to East Asia as early as 1997. By 2002, loan guarantees and "ring fencing" were even more important to investors and business partners who were looking for verification that the relationships in which they had trusted were equipped to handle their debt but were not so desperately and wrongly engaged in off-balance sheet transactions that belief could not be verified by investigation.

Demand and Markets

In 1977, the trading company was selling on its own account and as an agent of foreign firms. Hong Kong was a supplier of manufactures, a major entrepôt for export, import, reexport, and a booming property market. Southeast Asia was a source market for materials, manufactures, engineering, and construction contracts. South Africa was a source market for raw materials, textiles, and leather. North America and Europe were a source of manufactures for sale to China,, and a demand market for Southeast Asian and South African raw materials.

Outside of Hong Kong, the industry was business-to-business in 1977. Commodities traders brokered everything sold to international business customers from Dunhill lighters to military aircraft. Business-to-business communications was largely through *Lloyds' List*, the respected publication of the commodities and shipping industries, the *Financial Times, South China Morning Post, Far East Asian Review*, and local advertising.

By 1996, Hong Kong was largely a container port and property market for the conglomerates. Northeast Asia had become a market for merchant banking, luxury autos, and business services. Australasia and Southeast Asia were markets for business services and franchises. China was a market for infrastructure investment, manufacturing and privileged franchises. North America and Europe were markets for merchant banking, insurance and property development. The conglomerates had bought the right to sell international brand names in Asia—luxury cars, hotels, restaurants. They owned basic services—transportation, electricity and telephone—or sophisticated business services, international brand names in merchant banking, insurance and aviation, and they owned privileged franchises. Extensive trade and brand advertising campaigns were launched to support their offerings.

Entering the crisis, the major Hongs were potentially exposed to credit crises, weakened demand and low pricing power. A significant amount of both their equity and profits came from the region. Contagion effects threatened to make future equity and profits more vulnerable.

Infrastructure projects and utilities accounted for 45% of CITIC Pacific's cash flow at year end 1997 and 17% of Hutchison Whampoa's. Container terminals accounted for 33% of Hutchison's cash flow, 11% of Swire Pacific's, and 1% of Jardine Matheson's. Telecommunications accounted for 13% of Hutchison Whampoa's cash flow and 5% of CITIC's. Property rental and property services accounted for 55% of Swire Pacific's cash flow, 23% of CITIC's, 18% of Jardine Matheson's, and 9% of Hutchison's. Property development and construction accounted for 14% of Swire Pacific's cash flow, 15% of CITIC's, 10% of Hutchison's and 4% of Jardine's. Consumer necessities accounted for 48% of Jardine Matheson's cash flow, and 11% of Swire Pacific's, while consumer discretionaries accounted for 19% of Jardine Matheson's cash flow, and 10% of CITIC's.

Four issues important to understanding both the Asian financial crisis and the economic downturn and underlying ability of the Hongs to withstand them were at play here: (1) exposure to property revaluation and the need to hedge against negative revaluations; (2) exposure to weakened demand, most evident in retail, particularly consumer discretionaries; (3) contract or license protections, most evident in private projects; (4) government regulation or policy shifts, most evident in major infrastructure and container projects.

The weakness of other Hongs and single-product firms might also throw up some opportunities to the better positioned leaders. At the outset of the crisis, Hutchison Whampoa had the highest level of cash resources to spend on asset fire sales, HK$47,364M; Jardine Matheson's debt was the lowest at HK$6,520. A measurement of available cash is times interest coverage, or the number of times a company can make its interest payments with earnings before interest and taxes (EBIT). Jardine Matheson had the highest cash interest cover—6x, compared with Swire Pacific at 4.5x and Hutchison at 4x.[2]

The franchises owned and managed by the leading hongs were in 1997 the top in Hong Kong, among the best in Asia and sometimes even the world. Among the number one franchises in Hong Kong were CITIC's luxury automobile dealership Dah Chong Kong and Hutchison's HK International Terminals; Jardine Lloyd Thompson in Insurance and Gammon/Jardine Schindler in engineering and construction. Watson's Convenience Stores and Watson's distilled water, managed by Hutchison; Dairy Farm (Wellcome), managed by Jardine Matheson; Swire Beverages, managed by Swire Pacific.

Among the top franchises in Asia, based on critical mass, brand equity, and reputation, were Jardine Fleming, owned by Jardine Matheson until 1998; the Mandarin Oriental; Gammon/Jardine Schindler; HongKong Land; Jardine Lloyd Thomspon, and Cycle and Carriage.

Hutchison's top franchises in Asia included Hutchison Telephone, AS Watson, Hutchison Port Holdings, HK Electric, and Proctor & Gamble Hutchison. Swire Pacific's top three in Asia included Swire Properties, Swire Beverages, Modern Terminals Ltd., and Cathay Pacific/Dragonair. CITIC's top Asian francichises included CLP Holdings and Cathay Pacific/Dragonair, its joint venture with Swire Pacific.

Among the top three global leaders were Jardine Matheson's Hongkong Land, Swire and CITIC's CPA/Dragonair and Hutchison's Portholdings.

Costs and Value

In 1977, commodities traders, like the early private traders, brokered the whole transaction. Using steel as an example, the trading firm would upload the raw product in its own vessel, transport it to a blast furnace or manufacturing site, and pick up the steel ingots or product of manufacture for transport by sea or road to an industrial client. Raw material prices might be impacted by unused capacity at the blast furnace or product mix issues. Freight transportation commission rates depended on ship capacity. By the time the industrial client accepted the goods and paid, perhaps two years had elapsed. For the trader, the credit terms he could extend to industrial clients on the one end of the value chain and raw materials producers at the other are a source of his advantage to this market. Firms able to profit from the arrangement included Jardine Matheson at 14%, Sime Darby at 10.6%, James Finlay at 9.3%, Inchcape at 6.1%, and Harrisons & Crosfield at 3.4%.

By 1996, the distribution value chain had changed. The conglomerate more often than not had no ships of its own. Its expertise on behalf of an industrial client might be supply chain management at a distance: arranging warehousing documentation, financing, and insurance for international IKEA brand furniture bound for Singapore; ship arranged through Safmarine & Rennies, South African shipowners. The furniture might be warehoused at a container freight station in Singapore, then carried by truck to IKEA outlets. The conglomerate might do all of the supply chain management for franchise business it has an equity stake in. At each stage of the value chain there were charges. There was a commission charged on the total volume to be shipped. There were interest rates on any financing and insurance provided. There were ship chartering feeds, warehousing fees and ground transportation fees—and a percent of each sale benefits the franchisee.

Looking at the largest conglomerates in 1996, Jardine Matheson's added value was 22.4%; Swire Pacific's and First Pacific's were both 22%; Hutchison's was 19%. CITIC achieved an added value of 55%, but only because it issued new shares in 1996. The industry and its ability to add value had undergone tremendous change since 1977, and many of the major players were entirely different.

Given the key franchises of these leaders in 2002 and the environment in which they were operating, competition sought to increase, while pricing power was constrained during the downturn. The advantage any one of them might enjoy was bounded by barriers to entry and oligopolistic/monopolistic positions in certain markets.

For example, of their key franchises, CITIC's Dah Chong Hong was the biggest motor distributor in Hong Kong. Pricing power was limited, driven by the economic cycle. But, CITIC enjoyed exclusive distribution rights for its brands. Similarly, Jardine Matheson's Jardine International Motors and Cycle & Carriage were the biggest distributors of luxury cars in Hong Kong and Singapore. While pricing power was limited by the economic cycle, both companies enjoyed exclusive distribution rights for their luxury brands.

Jardine Matheson's Wellcome supermarket chain and Hutchisons Park 'n Shop owned 70% of the market share between them. Hutchison Port Holdings, HK International Terminals was the biggest operator of container terminals in Hong Kong and China. Hutchison enjoyed the highest pricing in the world, given its duopoly market position. The other member of the duopoly was Modern Terminals Ltd, jointly owned by Swire Pacific and Wharf Holdings. Hutchison enjoys exclusive port deals in China. High capital requirements limited new entrants. A trigger mechanism restricted the supply of new port holdings.

The Swire Pacific/CITIC joint venture Dragonair was the number one carrier between Hong Kong and China. The franchise enjoyed premium pricing and high load factors versus competition. Barriers to new entrants included licensed route structure, slot ownership and high management and capital requirements.

Most of the Hongs' franchises were either the biggest operator in their key domestic market (Hong Kong) or the second largest operator. Further, most of the hongs enjoyed some advantage deriving from the Hong Kong regulatory environment:

- favorable regulatory schemes like Hutchison's Hongkong Electric and CITIC's CLP Holdings permitted a guaranteed level of return on capital committed;
- comfortable oligopolies where competition on pricing was limited, for example supermarkets or container terminal operations;
- areas where the government tolerated limits on supply, such as the container terminals' trigger mechanism, which ensured that new supply didn't come onstream until certain capacity utilization levels had been achieved;
- assets where the government guaranteed a certain level of return, CITIC's cross-harbor tunnels in Hong Kong, for example, and Hutchison's infrastructure projects in China. Jardine Matheson and Swire Pacific were far less protected here.

Some of the franchises were operating in a mature market where new entry was not attractive, given capital requirements were high and returns unappealing, for example, supermarkets, electricity provision or container terminal operation.

In 2002, the global economic downturn made return to profitability slow and expectations of recovery before 2003 diminished. The Hongs, like most corporations around the world, were reluctant to invest in highly visible new value creating initiatives before profitability returned.

Distinctive Capabilities and Competitive Advantage

In 1977, innovation was important; bringing new technology to bear on communications (cell phones, faxes) and logistics (EDI) would for a time provide an advantage to firms on the leading edge of the new technology. But the technology was not proprietary to the trading firm and was easily copied or purchased. Architecture was even more important in 1977, because a firm's international business customers were looking for everything they didn't have in Asia, from relationships and knowledge to impact and influence.

In 1977, the long-term experience in Asia of trading firms like Jardine Matheson, Harrisons & Crosfield, James Finlay and others was a powerful advantage in the eyes of firms looking for knowledgeable agents or strategic partners. Such prospective partners would be looking to long-term profitability and significant additions to retained earnings as an indication of sound financial management and sustainable competitive advantage. The Far Eastern Shipping Conferences, still in existence in 1977, erected barriers for new entrants into Asian shipping. Because there was considerable competition for Hong Kong government contracts and licenses, all of the old trading companies made sure they had representatives on the Legislative Council, on the board of the Hongkong & Shanghai Bank, and among the stewards of the Jockey Club, so they might maintain access to information and influence. The origin of strategic assets was incumbency and influence.

By 1996, the conglomerates were beginning to be held to the same measures and standards as modern businesses. Cash flow analysis, valuation modes, economic value added and discounted cash flow analysis were increasingly being used to determine the contribution of individual businesses in conglomerate hands, the strength of cash flows and the impact of the holding company or corporate center to add value. Innovative business routines and architecture were important capabilities in 1996.

Long-term experience became a double-edged sword in 1996, when an opium past was held against some of the old trading companies, now conglomerates, wishing to establish joint ventures in China. A strong relationship with China's government was seen as a better reputation to have, evidenced by the strong positions CITIC, Hutchison Whampoa, and Swire Pacific had been able to achieve. Some first-mover or privileged joint-venture contract advantages existed in China in 1996. Their origin was incumbency and willingness to invest in China's infrastructure.

Going into the Asian financial crisis and the economic downturn, reputation and a record of trust were critical, for both investors and customers: the ability to secure cash flows, manage debt, reengineer troubled businesses, and self-manage and control the operations of major subsidiaries was an important differentiator, determining their ability to sustain their margins and returns in the face of a downturn. Not surprisingly, the conglomerate franchises were doing far better than single-product firms at the outset of the crisis, as noted by their number one or number two market share positions and critical mass. However, another, equally important aspect was their ability to reengineer the franchises cost bases and utilize effectively their funding arrangements. At the outset of the crisis, Hutchison Whampoa and Jardine Matheson had been the most vigorous, divesting non-core assets and underperforming businesses.

Through 2002, when near-term opportunities were diminishing and the cost of capital was rising for Asian firms, the track record of the firm and its ability to create added value, through increasing reserves or retained earnings, became far more important. Strategic assets had increased value to the firm in this environment, where more than half of the franchises enjoyed some kind of protection, ranging from exclusive service contracts and distribution rights to government price protection.

Jardine Matheson Corporate Strategy, 1977–1996–2002

In 1977, Jardine Matheson & Company was engaged in an aggressive acquisition campaign that included investments in raw materials as well as manufacturing. Among Western firms trading in general commodities, like Harrisons & Crosfield, and Gill & Duffus, among others, the firm was unique, pursuing minority equity relationships with buyer and seller firms both upstream and downstream in the value chains for transportation, steel, textiles, and sugar. Jardine Matheson offered acquired firms investment, as well as financial, insurance, shipping, marketing, and distribution services at lower cost than would be available in the marketplace. Jardine Matheson had a reputation for financial management that was appealing to ASEAN firms low on working capital and the architecture necessary to secure buyers for their goods. In 1977 Jardine Matheson had 50,000 employees, 41,000 of whom were on the ground in Asia.

Strategic assets in 1977 included the firm's trading/shipping routes, protected by the Far East Shipping Conferences, a self-governing body. Jardine Matheson used its equity relationships to establish first-mover advantage in Singapore, Philippines, Malaysia, Australia, and Japan. In Hong Kong, Jardine Matheson represented 17% of the total capitalization of the Hong Kong stock exchange. The firm's contribution to Hong Kong GDP was 3.9%, higher than that of any competitor. The power and influence accruing to a firm that important to a national market, while based on distinctive capabilities and assets, are itself a strategic asset of the firm. The markets for Jardine Matheson's distinctive capabilities in 1977 included the home market, Hong Kong, where contribution to GDP, "unofficial" involvement of the Legislative Council and Board Membership in the Hong Kong & Shanghai Bank, gave Jardine Matheson the "ear" of the colonial government and access to government contracts. Jardine Matheson was also heavily involved in manufacturing, business services, and property development in Hong Kong. Other important markets were Southern Africa and Australasia, a source of primary goods and manufacturing sites in which Jardine Matheson invested, as well as North America and Europe, interested in buying and selling in Asia Pacific but lacking the local contacts. Jardine Matheson understood the value its architecture would have to firms seeking an Asian presence and advertised its consulting services on a $30,000/month retainer.

In 1977, the profit/equity contribution of the markets for Jardine Matheson's distinctive capabilities was Hong Kong at 57%/37%; Australasia at 7%/14%; N. America at 7%/8%; Europe at 7%/8%; Southern Africa at 5%/5%; and Middle East at 6%/6%. In addition, Southeast Asia, contributing 10% of the equity, but only 4% of the profit, and Northeast Asia, contributing 5% of the equity and 7% of the profit, were important markets for Jardine Matheson. Southeast Asia was a source of raw materials and manufacturing. Emulating a business model closer to the Japanese *sogo shosha* than to the conventional trading firm, Jardine Matheson created a broader and different presence for itself in Asia, based on architecture. Competitors like the Swire Group and Wheelock Marden were focused mainly on Hong Kong. Jardine Matheson brought innovation to its portfolio management scheme, giving associated firms 3 years to meet a hurdle rate of 25%, or divesting them. The year 1977 saw nearly as many divestitures as acquisitions, an extraordinary affirmation of a pipeline management strategy at play.

Compare Jardine Matheson's corporate strategy in 1996. The firm's reputation for financial strength and its financial performance had been weakened by the Hongkong Land affair and consequent debt accumulation. The market began giving Jardine Matheson bad grades for management and for building a defensive control mechanism in the center, Jardine Strategic, seen as getting in the way of the profitability of Jardine's businesses. It would appear that Jardine Matheson had lost the right to grow and was unable to convince the market that the company's businesses were sufficiently strong and well run to sustain the diversion of cash and management attention to growth initiatives. Far from ex-growth, the company continued to grow not by changing the industry structure through acquisitions and alliances, not by integrating vertically and not by expanding into new geographies but rather by taking new approaches to marketing and distributing to existing customers; applying its superior local knowledge to managing privileged franchises; and investing in the growth of existing subsidiaries and associates. The reputation the firm had gained for international brand marketing made Jardine Matheson the partner of choice for Chubb, IKEA, Taco Bell, and Moet-Hennessey, among others. The firm had built several of its own brands into substantial, stand-alone businesses, among them Jardine Fleming in finance, Dairy Farm in grocery, Mandarin Oriental in hotels, Jardine Lloyd Thompson in insurance. The firm's 1996 markets were largely confined to the Pacific region: Hong Kong and China representing 61% of the firm's profits; Northeast Asia 14%; Southeast Asia 12%; North America, Europe, and the Middle East collectively 11%; and Australasia for another 2%. Together they gave Jardine Matheson a worldwide reach and a base from which to launch into new businesses, should the need rise. Jardine Matheson's competitive advantage in 1996 derived from strong cash flows generated by its franchises and name brands.

At the outset of the downturn, Jardine Matheson was best positioned in terms of financial strength—including balance sheet currency exposure—to withstand the impact. At year end December 1997, Jardine had a financial asset cushion of US$24M. By the end of the first quarter of 1998, the firm had sold Simago and its stake in Somerfield supermarkets and raised an additional US$318M. Jardine's net financial liability position included some weakened currencies and a net liability position in Hong Kong. The only real blemish was a net financial asset position in Chinese currency. None of the other Hongs had quite such a comfortable position as Jardine Matheson nor gave as much concrete detail in their last stated accounts.

Knowing the attractiveness of its reputation for financial probity and long-term trust experience, Jardine Matheson pursued fuller disclosure than ever before in its public history. While Hutchison and Swire Pacific had aggressively raised foreign (largely U.S. dollar denominated) debt in recent years to finance their ASEAN and Korean expansion, raising concerns of a potential currency mismatch in the event of an Hong Kong dollar devaluation. Jardine Matheson had fully hedged its positions against possible government interventions.

Jardine Matheson had HK$11,008M going into the downturn, and HK$4,131M in short term and HK$12,887M in long-term debt, giving Jardine Matheson considerable cash to spare to fund investments should opportunities arise and a flexible response to the problem of rolling over debt in an increasingly tight credit market. A dual-edged sword in Jardine Matheson' risk management strategy was the guaranteeing of property debt by specific buildings, a conservative strategy but practiced at the expense of reducing funding costs. While at the beginning of the downturn, Jardine Matheson had a 9x interest cover, this would fall to 2x or less over the next five years.

Jardine Matheson could curtail its capital expenditures, given the localized, services-intense nature of its Hong Kong businesses, which required asset development activities that could be delayed if demand was weak without significant detriment to the property's long-term competitive position or asset value, and distribution businesses which require little recurrent capital expenditure. Additional capital expenditure, as it might be needed during the downturn, could be financed internally.

Jardine Matheson's cash flow was reasonably high, with relatively little (4%) dependence on property sales, but higher dependence on discretionary items (19%) than peer firms. At the outset, Jardine Matheson was sitting on significant cash reserves to spend on new opportunities that might arise as the crisis progressed.

Jardine Matheson's top franchises, namely, Jardine Lloyd Thompson, insurance; Gammon/Jardine Schindler, engineering and construction; Hongkong Land, property development; Dairy Farm (Welcome), supermarket; Jardine Fleming, investment management; Mandarin Oriental, hotels; Jardine International Motors and Cycle & Carriage, luxury motors were number one or number two in their markets. For the most part, these franchises were actively managed by Jardine; hence, in the absence of strategic assets, the firm could control the internal costs associated with them.

Looking at the franchises, only three relied on exclusive rights, Jardine Pacific's Jardine Schindler and Jardine Securicor, and Jardine International Motors/Cycle & Carriage. The others were capability-based: Jardine Pacific's Gammon, based on management capability and technical expertise, primarily engineering, and Jardine Pacific's Jardine Office Systems, the largest technology provider with critical mass and technology skills responsible for competitive advantage, not formal and contractual strategic controls. Daily Farm (Welcome) supermarkets enjoyed a duopoly in Hong Kong (with A. S.Watson). Dairy Farm's Woolworth in New Zealand was the biggest supermarket chain in New Zealand, but the market was mature and new entrants few. Mandarin Oriental hotel chain had significant brand equity: the product is among the most highly rated in the world. Hongkong Land has a competitive advantage based on sheer mass. Jardine Lloyd Thompson and Jardine Lloyd Fleming were market leaders, but the advantage was skill and management-based. Unlike competitors in the region, Jardine Matheson's market leaders were capabilities-based, not strategic asset-based.

In comparison, Swire Pacific enjoyed route licenses for its leading brands, Cathay Pacific Airlines and Dragonair. Returns on HACTL were regulated by the government and a trigger mechanism protected Modern Terminals Inc. from competition. Swire Beverage enjoyed privileged rights from the Coca-Cola company.

Hutchison also enjoyed more strategic assets, in the form of licenses for Hutchison Telephone and Organge, its telecommunications brands, and regulated and exclusive arrangements for Cheung Kong infrastructure, and trigger mechanisms that restricted new entrants to Hutichison Port Holdings.

Interestingly and more negatively, Jardine Matheson's elaborate governance structure of listed entities and shared ownership structures effectively resulted in the head office being less able to source dividends from its key associates and subsidiaries than was the case for peer firms. Neither of Jardine Matheson's two cash-generating businesses in 1997 were wholly or even directly owned, Dairy Farm and Jardine International Motors.

Jardine Matheson had made considerable, additional disvestments since 1996, selling off non-core assets at Jardine Pacific and Dairy Farm in 1996, 1997 and 1998. Going forward, the key assets that might potentially be divested, should the firm require cash to change its strategy or to cover losses in a prolonged downturn were Jardine Matheson's 34% minority stake in Jardine Lloyd Thompson, a medium-sized insurance broker in a consolidating industry, and Jardine Fleming, possible by selling the firm back to its parent, Robert Fleming, or other minority stakes divestments, which could amount to HK$6,500M if required.

At the outset of the crisis, Jardine Matheson held a sizable investment property portfolio. Jardine's balance sheet had been boosted by property revaluation reserves. As property values began to decline, Jardine's balance sheet shrank and its debt coverage eroded.

To the extent that markets are mature and industries are regulated, the competitive environment is stable. That said, pricing power is weak in the downturn economy, with Gammon engineering, Schindler Elevator, Jardine Wnes and Sprits, Jardine Office Systems, Jardine International Motors and Cycle &Carriage, Mandarin Oriental, Hongkong Land, Jardine Lloyd Thompson and Jardine Fleming had limited pricing power.

In comparison, Hutchison Port Terminals, AS Watson, A.S. Watson Distilled Water (which enjoyed a quasi monopoly), Hutchison Telephone, Cheung Kong Infrastructure and Proctor & Gamble Hutchison, were protected franchises which enjoyed far more price flexibility. In a downturn and in the midst of a financial crisis, oligopolies, monopolies, and strategic assets of all kinds protect businesses from the most negative effeccts of the environment.

In 2002, the firm continued to focus on retail operations in Hong Kong and ASEAN. By 2002, Jardine Matheson's franchises were experiencing strong growth. The contribution of Jardine Pacific had grown 9% year-on-year, with major contributions from HACTL (61% increase), Jardine Schindler (21%), and Gammon (14% growth).

Jardine International Motors, on the other hand, experienced a 27% decline in Hong Kong. Dairy Farm began to release substantial profit growth in Southeast Asia; Maxim grew 24% in Hong Kong. Hongkong Land growth was flat year-on-year, with a decline expected around 20%. Mandarin Oriental similarly was flat, with declines expected. Cycle & Carriage's Astra franchise was up 2.5 times in the first half of 2002, coming from a 19% increase in motor vehicle sales and a 72% increase in motorcycle sales.

In 2002, Jardine Matheson continued its stock repurchases, including a tender offer by Dairy Farm to repurchase 10% of its shares. The new arrangement gives Jardine Matheson 62% ownership of Dairy Farm, up from 55% in 1999 and 60% in 2000. The firm also increased its ownership of Jardine International Motors from 75% in 1999 to 100% in 2001 and going forward and Cycle & Carriage from 25% in 1999 to 29% in 2001, giving Jardine Matheson greater access to the returns and dividends generated by these cash-generating businesses.

Jardine Matheson's key franchises are leaders in their categories. During the downturn, the firm has reengineered Dairy Farm and Jardine Pacific and reorganized its governance structure to access more of the profits and dividends provided by Dairy Farm, Jardine International Motors and Cycle & Carriage. The sale of Jardine Fleming to Robert Fleming and thence to Chase Manhattan in 1998 released US$1B to Jardine Matheson for new opportunities.

Of its strategic group, Jardine Matheson has a significantly higher percent of its investments in cyclical businesses, with more exposure to weakened consumer demand and less protection from government protection.

CAN JARDINE MATHESON USE KNOWLEDGE AND LEARNING TO REINVENT ITS FUTURE?

The development of knowledge and skills, whether by individual managers or by the firm itself, depends and builds upon a network of existing capabilities and underlying resources, and internal and external relationships, as well as routines and rules for conceptualizing and resolving problems. This section identifies summarizes the conditions creating the impetus for change, followed by a discussion of the persistent baseline against which change and innovation occurred.

Conditions Creating the Impetus for Change; Jardine Matheson Response

Some of the major changes made by Jardine Matheson were induced by changes in the environment and industry or by the existence of a vacuum in strategic groups. In the midst of such change or in the absence of competitors Jardine Matheson was able to apply its market knowledge to capture greater value. In the firm's early history, from 1832 to 1885, value was moving from trade to investment, and strategic groups were changing (from trading companies to trading companies with associated freestanding investment houses) to capture it. In 1977, value was available at many stages of the supply chain, and upstream participating firms were too cashpoor or risk averse to caputure it for themselves. Jardine Matheson saw a vacuum in strategic groups that it sought to fill with a business model closer to that played by the Japanese *sogo shosha*, with its horizontal relationships linked through trade, equity and debt arrangements.

Jardine Matheson changed the industry through acquisitions, alliances, and vertical integration to capture more value in 1977 at many stages of the supply chain. By offering financing and insurance services to firms at upstream and downstream ends of the supply chain, Jardine Matheson & Company was testing a new business model, similar to that of the Japanese *sogo shosha*.

From 1977 to 1996, value was moving from manufacturing and raw materials to services and from commodities trading to international brand marketing. The strategic groups are increasingly multi-industry conglomerates with alliances with international brand owners for distribution and marketing of brands in Hong

Kong and China or in Asia. While the emphasis on outsourced architecture remains the same, the competitive focus is clearly on marketing skills.

Jardine Matheson was in a leadership position with finance, insurance, dairy, and liquor brand offerings under its own or subsidiary firm brand names. The firm has made Asian market leaders of Caterpillar, Dunhill, Sherwin Williams and Kodak, companies that have used Jardine Matheson as their floating representative office. A development of the 1990s is the international franchise business. By 1996, Jardine Matheson had franchise licenses with IKEA, Taco Bell, Seven Eleven, Kentucky Fried Chicken and Pizza Hut.

From 1996 to the present, value has moved from brand marketing and new business development to international brand franchises and business replication. Exclusive contracts, exclusive distribution rights, and trigger mechanisms are the strategic assets necessary to protect such franchises from competition, which, in an atmosphere of economic downturn, can make possession of such franchise rights unprofitable for the Hongs. Jardine Matheson's franchises are market leaders in Hong Kong, Asia, the world, but Jardine Matheson does not have the strategic asset protection of Hutchison, CITIC and Swire and is more vulnerable to competition and downturn.

Baseline Attributes: Capabilities and Resources

Throughout its history, the customer for Jardine Matheson's products and services was more often a business than a private individual and at a significant distance from the market for supply or demand. For example, the customer in 1832 was a Chinese merchant buying opium for distribution and London merchants buying silk, tea and other commodities. In 1885 the customer was an Asian or London merchant transporting, financing, and insuring goods carried by third-party ships. Investment in manufacturing plants, railways, and mines predominated; the investor sometimes a wealthy individual, more often a firm.

In 1977 Jardine Matheson's customer was usually an American or European firm seeking a market presence in Asia; Asian companies were looking for a partner to finance, insure, and broker the relationship with a buyer. By 1996, the customer was an international brand owner looking to establish Asian franchises. What makes the period 1996 to 2002 interesting is the extent to which Jardine Matheson has refocused its interests on the Asian consumer through retail selling, the mere beginning of which trend was evident in 1996, when Jardine Matheson began to take minority positions in retail clothing and opticals. In a downturn and at a time when Jardine Matheson's business customers are less likely to invest in customer intimacy experiments in Asian markets, Jardine Matheson is developing a relationship with the Asian consumer.

Jardine Matheson and its business customers have had a single goal. In 1832 it was to grow rich from trade; in 1885 it was to grow richer with less effort through investment. In 1977 it was to expand into new markets and in 1996 to continue expansion with less effort. In each year, and no less during the five years that followed the Asian financial crisis, it was of highest value to the business customer to achieve wealth while lowering risk through the agency services of a trusted partner, like Jardine Matheson.

The basis of trust was reputation, built on financial probity and the ability of the firm to absorb trading risk while profiting from the experience. To absorb the risk of others, Jardine Matheson itself required long-term internal and external relationships built on high trust and the avoidance of speculation in commodities (like indigo in the early period) or in other business interests (like Hongkong Landabout which information (in this case about individual investments and commitments) was incomplete.

While environmental change brought on by competition, globalization, change in the regulatory environmentand other aspects of the external environment make it unlikely that any capability will continue to remain valuable independent of the scenario in which a firm is operating, there has been great stability in the value of Jardine Matheson's capabilities and the resources underlying them.

The early resources underlying Jardine Matheson's distinctive capabilities are its trading relationships, market knowledge, and investment capital. The firm leveraged these intangible resources to become a risk broker and supply chain expert, the basis for its early strategic position. Through risk brokerage, the firm came to own the relationship between customer, agent, and supplier (i.e, the architecture) and to develop a reputation for financing and capital management. Managing risk and stretching capital required innovation, which further increased the firm's financial returns and freed up some of the company's financial capacity for further investments (added value). In its first century Jardine Matheson had applied its trading relationships, market knowledge, and (some limited) investment capital to the creation of a freestanding investment house, Matheson & Company. In 1885, while still engaged in the Pacific trade, the firm leveraged these resources to become an investment manager and financier. The firm earned a reputation for financial management, risk management, capital management, and deal structuring, competences that are transferable across many markets and businesses. The firm's reputation was a source of added value for continued growth.

But let's look what has happened from 1977 to 1996. The opportunity to capture greater value from trading relationships, market knowledge, and investment capital in 1977 created a new class of resources, namely, equity relationships, and these have required the engagement of Jardine Matheson's existing financial management, risk management, capital management and deal structuring skills as well as the short- and medium-term development of new competences, like acquisition and postmerger management skills and marketing skills. These skills added to Jardine Matheson's reputation and architecture, while requiring heavy investment capital (and reducing added value). Strategic divestment in 1977–1978 and again in 1981–1983 and 1996–1998 reduced the burden of equity relationships. By 1996 another class of resources had been added, privileged franchises, built on trading relationships and market knowledge. This class of resources put less drag on investment capital, used existing financial management and marketing skills, and

Figure 7.1
Jardine Matheson & Company Framework for Growth, 1977–2002

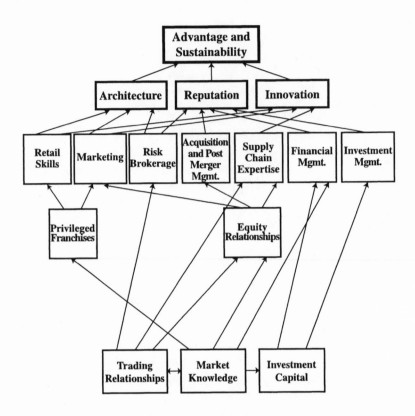

required the short-term development or acquisition of retailing skills. The relationship between resources, capabilities and competitive advantage is drawn in Figure 7.1. The ability to develop or acquire new skills or to put existing skills to new uses, has added to a third distinctive capability, namely, innovation in the areas of management practice and technology. In 2002, Jardine Matheson & Company continued to acquire significant added value for future growth.

NOTES

1. In this chapter, the data for market share, debt and debt servicing, and interest coverage are derived from independent stock market analyses available for the break point years 1977, 1996, and 2002.

2. A measurement of available cash is times interest coverage, or the number of times a company can make its interest payments with earnings before interest and taxes (EBIT).

8

A PENROSEAN THEORY OF THE HONG KONG TRADING COMPANY

Chapter 8 summarizes the findings of this research, reexamines the applicability of a Penrosean interpretation of strategic management in Jardine Matheson and the Hong Kong trading industry, and suggests directions for further research.

SUMMARY OF KEY FINDINGS AND INSIGHTS

Chapter 2 focused on the early private trade. The primary source for the early Jardine Matheson & Company was handwritten correspondence now housed in the Jardine Matheson Archives at Cambridge University. Individual histories of peer firms—like Inchcape, Harrison & Crosfields, Dodwells and Swire & Sons—rounded out the assessment of operations, capabilities, routines, and relationships. Even before Jardine Matheson was formally constituted in 1832, the firm already had long-term relationships with agents, suppliers, and customers—some 50 correspondents were noted in the pre-1832 letters. The relationships were the consequence of an unbroken chain of private partnerships from 1810 to 1832. Reputation and trust were essential to the China trade and led to very long-lived relationships.

The routine of frequent correspondence (letters dealing with management subjects not only with sales and remittances) between partners, agents, customers, and suppliers was well established. While the Jardine Matheson letters were modeled on the British East India Company prototypes, a Jardine Matheson innovation was the signature of an individual partner on some 3,000 letters in the Private Letter Books. These signed letters are distinctive in discussing the economics and politics of the trade, the firm's plans, and enlisting the correspondent's assistance.

The routines of the commission trade (the interest rates to be charged for shipping, insurance, banking, etc.) were well known and accepted by the emerging industry of private traders. A private trader could make 45 cents on every dollar from some 16 separate commissions called "agency services."

Little working capital was required to run a profitable business in the Far East. As James Matheson advised his nephew Hugh, with little investment, it was possible to grow very rich "in the snug way of the China trade."

Many private traders and agency houses went bankrupt engaging in speculation in commodities. Others like Jardine Matheson & Company, Swire & Sons, Harrisons & Crosfield prospered by setting rules for the conduct of their agents that prohibited speculation on their own account. The Jardine Matheson Archives reveal that the firm communicated its financial reporting and investment policies to its agents and monitored their performance, often sending junior partners to work alongside intractable agents.

Jardine Matheson was both the inheritor of a reputation for financial management and the builder of such a reputation. The firm sought to shape, and did shape, its political and economic environment, campaigning for government intervention in trade and later for the Treaty Port System. James Matheson's *Prospects of the British Trade with China*, published by Smith Elder, was based on a speech Matheson had made to Parliament, urging government intervention and drawing on the principles of natural law. James Matheson, William Jardine, and their successors sat on the Select Committees for Trade in London, and both founders played an active role in the founding of Hong Kong and later the Treaty Port System.

Jardine Matheson, Butterfield & Swire, and other trading companies saw advantage in partnering with government in railway, mining, and quarrying projects and sought investment capital abroad to finance these projects, adapting to the trend toward free-standing investment houses associated with trading firms. They invested in warehouses, textile, sugar, and silk manufactures in Japan and China, when the Chinese and Japanese governments began to allow joint manufacturing ventures.

Jardine Matheson partnered with Dent & Company on insurance and with Butterfield & Swire on shipping and later on investment projects with the Chinese government as a partner. Such collaboration reduced risk and allowed firms to participate more broadly in investment opportunities than they would using only their own capital.

Chapter 3 dealt with the interwar period, when globalization was constrained by the tariffs and rising transportation costs. Jardine Matheson and peer firms reduced their business lines and concentrated on host country opportunities. The period saw the emergence of the Japanese *sogo shosha* as a competitor for raw materials and customers in Southeast Asia.

Chapter 4 focused on Jardine Matheson's expansion, 1961–1996, a period when Jardine Matheson increased its market diversity by leveraging its reputation for sound finance, insurance, trading, and shipping—that is, for agency services—throughout Asia.

The period of the firm's greatest expansion and diversification occurred when the firm was a shipowner and may initially have been a response to excess physical capacity on board Jardine Matheson's 35 vessels, as well as access to opportunities through the commodities trade.

During 1972–1977, the firm diversified forward and backward into shipping services and made horizontal acquisitions in a number of raw materials, natural resources manufacturing, building an external organization to share knowledge and capture value at every stage of the value chain for transportation, steel, oil, sugar, coconut and other businesses.

Jardine Matheson corrected the course of its growth trajectory several times during the period, selling off unprofitable assets in 1978–1979 and again in 1981–1983, while giving acquired firms some three years to meet an established hurdle rate. Even when the firm appeared to forego growth after the Hong Kong Land-Jardine Matheson mutual stock swap, related diversification continued at the level of the firm's subsidiary and associated companies.

To even out the spread of profits and reduce risks, Jardine Matheson created a novel governance form—the holding company reporting to a holding company parent (Jardine Strategic) and paying a fixed return to the parent (Jardine Matheson Holdings Inc.). Jardine Strategic reduced the risk in Jardine Matheson's portfolio. It was further found that Jardine Matheson's use of Jardine Strategic to manage its high-risk subsidiaries—indeed, the use of holding companies for this purpose—actually added financial value to the firm without additional governance cost and provided subsidiaries the opportunity to raise their own equity for further development and expansion.

Chapter 5 focused on the nature, the "industrial logic," of Jardine Matheson's acquisitions and divestitures from 1972 to 1996 and the skills required by acquired businesses. During 1972 to 1996, Jardine Matheson made half as many divestitures as acquisitions, 375 of which were in broadly horizontal businesses and 575 in vertical businesses. Finance, insurance, and real estate (major category 60–67) accounted for 198 of the vertical businesses. There was a significant increase in divestiture activity during the Harvest and Divest period 1978–1984, but divestment was integral to firm strategy throughout the study period.

Jardine Matheson's trading and financial services core businesses put a high demand on top management, marketing, and financial management skills that were transferable across the firm's newly acquired businesses. The firm's manufacturing acquisitions relied on low-cost labor available in the ASEAN between 1972 and 1977. When the firm divested these holdings, exit was easy. Jardine Matheson's expansion into new retail and grocery industries required investment in industry-specific skills.

The overall shape of Jardine Matheson's acquisition pattern was similar to that of trading and financial firms studied by analysts of mergers and acquisitions like R. S. Khemani, that is, broadly horizontal at the outset (for Jardine Matheson, this occurred five years earlier, 1972–1977, not 1978–1979) with increasing contraction through 1988–1989. Overall, some 75% of Jardine Matheson's acquisitions were made in Asia, including 40% in Hong Kong or China and 25% in Southeast Asia. Jardine Matheson's services acquisitions mirrored those of the Japanese conglomerates studied by Rugman and Waverman, in contrast with European Community and American mergers and acquisitions in the same period.

Chapter 6 focused on Jardine Matheson's architecture, that is, the relationships developed by the firm's managers with associated and subsidiary firms, government, and banking/investment institutions. Senior management at Jardine Matheson enjoyed long tenure. How much senior managers know about custom, language, and doing business in a geography as well as functional knowledge is very important to Jardine Matheson; hence, the firm moved senior executives around from one function to another and from one geography to another. The firm published the names of senior executives down to the level of regional or country office head in its Annual Report. It was obviously important to the firm's customers to know that their Jardine Matheson representative had authority and recognition.

Jardine Matheson's senior executives were expected to play a role on the boards of subsidiary firms, including monitoring performance, advising on investments, and sharing their functional or company knowledge. Jardine Matheson's senior executives were expected to serve on the external boards of highly visible and influential government and banking/investment bodies, like the Hong Kong Legislative Council and the Hongkong & Shanghai Bank.

Jardine Matheson held very widely dispersed resources. That meant that the firm could supply its full range of services anywhere in the world, adding to the firm's competitive advantage. It also meant that relations between headquarters and subsidiaries were interdependent, suggesting a transnational management system.

When compared with the Japanese *sogo shosha*, Jardine Matheson also emerges as a quasi-insurance agent, providing trading and production credits to customer and supplier firms and deriving competitive advantage from a hybrid governance arrangement that was neither internalization (vertical integration) nor market governance (commodities purchase in the open market. Like the *sogo shosha*, Jardine Matheson's architecture was based on dense interfirm relationships that contributed to the competitive advantage of the firm and to the national economies in which the firm operated.

Chapter 7 audited the environment, the industry, and the firm to contrast Jardine Matheson and the Hong Kong trading industry at the height of the Exploit and Develop Period, 1977 with the retrenchment characteristic of the Focus on Distinctive Capabilities Period, 1996–2002.

From its origin, the trading company's customer through 1996 was more often a business than a private individual and at a significant distance from the market for supply or demand, for example:

- 1832—Chinese merchants buying opium for distribution; London merchants buying silk, tea;
- 1885—Asian and London merchants transporting, financing, and insuring goods carried by third-party ships. Investment in manufacturing plants, railways, mines; the investor sometimes a wealthy individual, more often a firm;

- 1977—International firms seeking a market presence in Asia; Asian companies looking for a partner to finance, insure, and broker the relationship with a buyer;
- 1996—International brand owners looking to establish Asian franchises;
- 2002—Trading companies distinguished themselves by choosing to continue the long business-to-business tradition (Hutchison Whampoa, Swire Pacific) or take a new business-to-consumer route, like Jardine Matheson.

At each of these break points Jardine Matheson belonged to a different strategic group within a different industry with different kinds of competitors and collaborators. Industry changes over the four break points can be attributed to new opportunities to capture value.

By 1977 the existing industry of generalists and specialist commodities traders was inadequate to capture the value possible from new raw material markets and manufactures. Jardine Matheson changed the industry through acquisitions, alliances, and vertical integration to capture more value in 1977 at many stages of the supply chain. Offering financing and insurance services to firms at upstream and downstream ends of the supply chain, Jardine Matheson & Company was testing a new business model, similar to that of the Japanese *sogo shosha*.

From 1977 to 1996 two major changes took place: the worldwide growth in services businesses and the migration of value from commodities trading to international brand marketing. Jardine Matheson began a sell-off of manufacturing and other fixed assets, concentrating on business services, including marketing services to international clients like Dunhill, and Moet-Hennessey, among others.

By 1996, the strategic groups were increasingly multi-industry conglomerates with alliances with international brand owners for distribution and marketing of brands in Hong Kong and China or in Asia. In 1996 value was moving from new businesses to replication and franchise, from business-to-business to business-to-consumer. Jardine Matheson traded reputation, financial acumen, and property for privileged franchises like Taco Bell, IKEA, 7 Eleven and others. The firm invests heavily in retail establishments—chain restaurants, computer hardware and software, clothing, and optical store chains—under the aegis of its subsidiaries.

Of consistent value to the market were Jardine Matheson's distinctive capabilities, specifically, the firm's external organization or "architecture" of customers, suppliers, partners, and government; distribution network; and its reputation, based on architecture, but also on financing, capital management, and risk management skills. In 1977 and after, the firm added acquisition and postmerger management and brand management skills; the ability to anticipate change and "innovate" organizational routine, develop new skills, and bundle skills to meet changing customer needs.

Jardine Matheson's distinctive capabilities have remained important to the market largely because the firm's international business customers prefer to concentrate on their strengths and to "outsource" architecture, relying on an "outsource" partner with long-lived experience and reputation in the region.

EDITH PENROSE AND THE HONG KONG TRADING COMPANY

While Edith Penrose never studied the Hong Kong trading industry, her *Theory of the Growth of the Firm* and study of the Hercules Power Company provide insight into firms as innovators, as coordinators of the capabilities of their managers, who recombine resources—and learn from mistakes time and again—to provide distinctive and creative products and services that are valuable to the firm's markets. In the Penrosean firm, managers are responsible for the growth of the firm and for whatever limits there may be to the rate of growth.

Questions about managerial strategic choice have been raised throughout this study, about the initial resources/services choices of firms, explanation of failure, organizational structure, environmental factors, managerial initiative versus opportunism, and the fund-raising activities of the Hong Kong trading company. In the special case of Jardine Matheson & Company, how and why did Jardine Matheson's founders and managers develop particular resources and services? What internal (including the firm and its agents) and external (including competition, new entrants, buyers, and suppliers) factors were responsible for their choices? At the firm's origin—and again after World War II and the Korean War—there were as yet no markets in Asia, in the sense of market institutions. What role did the firm play in the development of markets? What was the organizational structure of the firm, including both internal and external, that allowed for consistent business routines and promoted organizational learning? The firm's choices met with some notable successes—and some notable failures. How are the firm's failures explained? How did Jardine Matheson promote managerial initiative while curbing opportunism? How did Jardine Matheson raise funds for growth, given managerial initiative/opportunism and governance issues?

What follows is a summary discussion of these questions in light of Jardine Matheson's distinctive capabilities and critical uncertainties.

Strategic Choices

Overall, the research findings support a Penrosean interpretation in which firm growth is based on initial resources and capabilities and strategy evolves to take advantage of manager-perceived opportunities to capture value. "Manager perception" includes entrepreneurial vision and innovation as well as fallible conjecture. The resource and services choices made by Jardine Matheson were necessitated by the trade, the distance, the risk, the cultural divide between Chinese and Indian and private English participants, as well as the piratical practices that prevailed on the high seas and coastal waters. Chapter 2 looked at the demand for security among private traders and their clientele, in the midst of high risk and political volatility endemic to trade and particularly to the burgeoning private trade. Trading credit loans and insurance on every facet of the trade reduced risk for buyers and sellers; hence, financial management, insurance, banking, shipping and trading became the cluster of capabilities known as "agency services."

The security of buyers and sellers depended largely on the financial probity of the agency house, intangible, hence ascertainable largely through reputation. The pursuit of security was an overweening concern of Jardine Matheson and Company, exemplified in the firm's abjuring speculation at all costs and disciplining agents who speculated on their own account and jeopardized the reputation of the firm. The contrast was made early with the vicarious experiments by competitors like Dent & Company and Palmer's, among many other trading firms, that engaged in speculation in commodities like indigo and lost everything.

Opportunity was everywhere, but risks, too, were everywhere. Collaboration, rather than competition, was the preferred survival tactic. Notable examples were the development of an external organization to reduce risk in the shipping and insurance businesses (specifically, the Canton Insurance Company, led in alternate years by Jardine Matheson & Company and Dent & Company, and the Shipping Conferences of the 1880s, founded by Butterfield & Swire to which the major houses like Jardine Matheson belonged). A second example is the "free-standing" investment house, which sought to spread business risk among private investors.

The private traders preferred the "snug way of the China trade" because their lack of working capital was not a disadvantage in a business built on commissions, reducing the cost of production through vertical integration. While British rule of law might have provided an advantage close to ownership, it was a pipe dream of the private trade until the creation of the Treaty Port System, which regularized the trade and the system of tariffs and duties for all competitors.

In the 20th century, Jardine Matheson attempted to put its reputation and architecture to use in response to perceived opportunity and environmental requirements, as the company understood them. The assessment of Henry Keswick, that the firm sought to infuse its own methods into—but not to strip the assets of—acquired companies, provides some insight into firm thinking.

From 1961 to 1971, the firm sought to deepen its involvement in Hong Kong, diversifying into growing textile and electronics businesses while building its core financial services, shipping, insurance and trading businesses in the colony. Jardines also sought to export its core businesses into new markets, like Australia, Japan, South Africa, and Singapore, through joint ventures and acquisitions.

In the 1970s, the firm's diversification into raw materials, natural resources, and manufactures was an innovative, if risky, solution to the problem of excess physical capability—and the opportunity to provide access to markets to producers of raw materials, natural resources, and manufactures in the ASEAN. These firms required shipment from one location to another as primary goods and manufactures were transformed into end-user goods, marketed, and distributed. Such goods could fill existing Jardine ships at several value chain stages—and the firm, its customers, and its joint-venture partners could realize savings from Jardine Matheson's integrated end-to-end shipping services. By making the appropriate investments, Jardine's managers sought to capture more of the value available from upstream and downstream stages of the value chain.

As noted in Chapter 4, Jardine Matheson & Company emerged from World War II with few of its assets intact. The firm's decision to become a publicly traded company in 1961—like the decision in 1885 to create a "freestanding" investment house—can be explained as a desire to grow but at less risk. Jardine Matheson's development of an extensive external organization across the Pacific, cemented by minority equity positions and trade credits, can be explained as the pursuit of opportunity and value and the absorption of risk for organization members who would not have found markets for their products without access to Jardine Matheson's capabilities. From 1977 to 1996, Jardine Matheson's strategic moves have focused on selling off physical assets and concentrating on franchises and business services, providing to its customers the value of its architecture and reputation.

Internal and External Factors Responsible for Strategic Choices

A central theme of this study has been the Penrosean view that development of a pattern of relationships within and outside the business would foster the flow of information, the knowledge with which to interpret it, the ability to influence others, and the reputation to attract and retain trading partners. In the early period, as explained in Chapter 2, an environment of high risk and uncertainty made partnerships and alliances both necessary and attractive to Jardine Matheson. Clearly, an early advantage to the firm was the 50 agents inherited from the previous partnership of Magniac & Jardine. Jardine Matheson went on to build a network of 150 agents. Among the first steps the firm took to create community among the European traders and their suppliers and customers was the publication of the *Canton Register* and the firm's practice of corresponding with its constituents on issues of market conditions and social and political developments, as well as routine news of impending shipments. When Jardine Matheson needed support for its appeal to Parliament to protect the trade, the trading community that James Matheson built signed a petition that Matheson read in the House of Commons.

While working capital requirements were low, the more prosperous trading firms like Jardine Matheson and Swire's sought to own their own ships. Given the capital-intensive nature of shipping, it was a costly endeavor to expand market penetration. Forging substantive strategic partnerships or alliances was attractive to Jardine Matheson because it allowed the firm to accomplish market expansion with less risk and cost. Jardine Matheson & Company joined John Samuel Swire's Shipping Conference, which, even to the present, sets shipping routes and discourages participants from engaging in a competitive fight to the finish.

Jardine Matheson's range and flexibility increased dramatically when partnerships were created that linked Hong Kong and Calcutta, Hong Kong and Singapore, Hong Kong and London. As noted earlier, relationships with American and British manufacturers increased the firm's access to capital and investments. The political risks of war and blockade became more manageable because cargoes could be diverted to other ports, like Manila in the case of James Matheson and the opium blockade. Even when the Chinese government forced British traders out of

Canton, Jardine Matheson & Company continued its trade using competitive American firms as intermediaries. The captains or supercargoes of foreign merchant ships were useful partners, strengthening shipping interests, increasing international contracts, and introducing into the firm associates who knew another aspect of the import-export trade.

During the early period, collaboration with competitors was also a means of survival in the insurance business. Jardine Matheson and Dent & Company shared management responsibility for the Canton Insurance Company and pooled their resources to manage the risks of piracy, storms at sea, and spoilage, among other potential hazards to which they and their customers were exposed.

In the latter decades of the 19th century, the Treaty Port System had an extraordinary effect on trade and development in Asia, making trade more predictable and opening new markets to trade and development. During this time, Jardine Matheson and Butterfield & Swire were frequent investment partners in China. Jardine Matheson found investors and partners for its manufacturing, mining, and other ventures through Matheson & Company, its freestanding investment house.

As detailed in Chapter 4, Jardine Matheson & Company invested heavily in Hong Kong, southern China and the ASEAN during the mid-20th century, building an external organization through minority equity positions and joint ventures with local entrepreneurs, government, and cooperating competitors. This was the period when Hong Kong experienced dramatic changes in its industrial structure and economic development. Manufacturing industries came to the forefront. Jardine Matheson & Company and the Hongkong & Shanghai Bank offered packing credits to Hong Kong firms—or bought minority holdings in these firms.

Jardine Matheson and its partners exerted pressure on the government in Hong Kong as "unofficial" (a formal term), but highly influential, members. Under their influence, the Hong Kong government pursued a general laissez-faire approach, offering various liberal, fiscal, and monetary measures such as tax incentives and free capital mobility to stimulate industrial and economic development.

In the 1980s, when the future of Hong Kong became uncertain, Jardine Matheson's relocation of its holding company to Bermuda in 1984 was significant. The conflicting pursuit of China opportunity in the midst of political uncertainty in China is reflected in Jardine Matheson's investments during the 1990s. Some 80% or more of the firm's capital base derives from Hong Kong and China.

The Role of Jardine Matheson & Company in Creating Market Institutions

A Penrosean interpretation acknowledges the role of individual firms in creating market institutions, making a strong case for the challenge and opportunity Jardine Matheson shared with other private firms operating in the shadow of the East India Company in 1832—and again recovering from the shocks of World War II and the Korean War in 1961.

While the East India Company had held a monopoly on trade in the East, Jardine Matheson and peer firms lacked the Royal Charter, the self-perpetuating institutions of minting money, and raising a militia. Out of the East India Company came a rich heritage of management letters. From 1810 to 1906, Jardine Matheson & Company added its own letters to that history, generating some 200,000 letters to its constituents and agents, framing business arrangements, making payment and insurance promises, and disciplining agents.

Without the East India Company's Royal Charter, firms needed to rely on their own capabilities, reputation, relationships, and innovation to build consumer confidence and secure the trade. Jardine Matheson sought to build its reputation on financial wisdom and a network of relationships that its constituents could rely upon. The firm had to absorb the trading risk of its constituents by basing its own bills on trustworthy financiers in Britain and the United States. Essential to financial wisdom was the firm's avoidance of speculation, which had brought down many agency houses.

In the early period, private traders were more often collaborators in the development of market institutions—setting and agreeing to interest rate commissions on agency services, pooling resources for paying insurance claims, and establishing shipping routes. As explained in Chapter 2, Jardine Matheson & Company, Dent & Company, and others in the private trade committed themselves to live by a set of rates for agency services. The price of the commodities they traded was communicated broadly in "The Price Current," a bimonthly insert in the *Canton Register*, the first English-language newspaper in China, published by Jardine Matheson & Company.

The personal efforts of William Jardine and James Matheson to secure the trade resulted in the ceding of Hong Kong to Britain and the creation of the Treaty Port System, which provided for the first time a level of regularity to trade and predictability to the costs of trade with China, Singapore, Malaysia, Philippines, South Africa and Japan that lasted until World War II.

The creation of Matheson & Company, a freestanding investment house, provided shared benefits and limited risks among institutional and private investors, using Jardine Matheson's superior market knowledge to identify new prospects for funding. The outcome for Jardine Matheson & Company was indeed enhanced wealth, but competitors (like Butterfield & Swire) were welcome. Jardine Matheson & Company and Butterfield & Swire were collaborators on railway and other projects, with government as a public partner, well into the 20th century.

In the late 19th and early 20th centuries, Jardine Matheson & Company was one of the first Hong Kong firms to provide foreign direct investment to growth in the ASEAN. The firm's development of an external organization linked by minority equity holdings throughout the ASEAN was an adaptation of the Japanese general trading company or network organization model and allowed participating firms with limited working capital—and little if any access to markets—to benefit from Jardine Matheson's market knowledge and financing, insurance, and shipping and distribution services.

The Internal and External Organization of the Firm for Knowledge and Learning

Jardine Matheson's founders and subsequent managers developed an "architecture" or "administrative framework" for learning and collaboration. This framework included interorganizational linkages for risk reduction and learning important for developing capabilities, trustworthiness, and consistent patterns of behavior and effective forms of governance. It was part of interorganizational succession planning that managers could be moved from one geography to another, one function to another, with enhanced effectiveness and without disruption of the business. The environment made collaboration essential to survival. This meant collaboration between headquarters and associated firms—as well as between and among Jardine Matheson's associated firms. The description in Chapter 5 of the geographic spread of Jardine Matheson's resources, distributed among associated and subsidiary firms and their involvement in the value chains of diverse industries, supports the notion that this was a highly collaborative firm. In Chapter 6, the review boards established by Jardine Matheson assure that the potential for broader, geographic, and organizational impact was explored before a go/no-go decision was rendered on a potential investment, a further example of organizational commitment to learning and sharing.

Historically, Jardine Matheson's management team has included business builders and entrepreneurs, comfortable with ambiguity and change, top-line focused, sharp decision makers, free to act with autonomy and mandated to create and build businesses. Chapter 7 demonstrated that Jardine's rising star business leaders held multiple cross-geography and cross-function appointments and were charged with contributing to firm influence and reputation by playing active roles of legislative, bank and other external councils as well as occupying cross-board positions on the boards of subsidiary companies. (The appointment of Percy Weatherall, head of Hongkong Land, to replace Jardine Matheson senior managing director Alasdair Morrison in 1999 confirms a tradition of choosing leaders with long experience at Jardine and a large stake in the firm.)

Explanation of Failure

According to a Penrosean interpretation, Jardine Matheson's strategic choices were based on the firm's interpretation of the opportunity present to which its distinctive capabilities might be put. When the firm's strategy failed, that failure could be attributed to the firm's misunderstanding of its current capabilities or the capabilities needed in a new market.

In the early period, Jardine Matheson considered its decision to avoid speculation to be a reason for its financial stability and the basis for the firm's reputation and sustainability. Avoiding speculation was tantamount to limiting risk by focusing on what a firm's agents did or could know about a market through local communications and sharing knowledge among agents, firm partners, suppliers, and

customers. Jardine Matheson sought to instruct, discipline, send representation if
necessary (in the case of Otadui & Company), and penalize associated agents who
speculated on their own behalf. Into the early 20th century, the firm would close
offices if necessary: for example, Jardine Matheson's New York office was closed in
the early 1930s because the associates speculated in dog fur.

There was a natural tension between the type of personality attracted to trading—and the safekeeping (or risk-averse) personality required to protect the assets
of customers and the reputation of the company. Jardine Matheson sought to develop an entrepreneurial culture that was based on accumulating and sharing local
market knowledge, on the basis of which sound judgments were made. That the
firm was successful in this aim is demonstrated by its ability to survive the credit
crises that bankrupted firms like Palmers and Dents.

In the mid-20th century, Jardine Matheson confronted its first experience of
failure as a public company. During the late 1970s and early 1980s, to support its
capital-intensive shipping and oil servicing businesses, Jardine borrowed from, or
increasingly frequently sold property to, the Hongkong Land Company, of which
it was a 12% owner. When, in the early 1980s, the Hong Kong property market began a swift and steady decline, Jardine Matheson lost significantly, both as an investor and as a seller. However, it was Jardine's reputation for financial
management that took a beating with the press and the firm's investors. Jardine's
real estate sell-offs (using Hongkong Land as a bank) were seen by entrepreneurs
like Li Kashing as a sign of management weakness, and the Keswick family's 10%
ownership—which was low-enough to stimulate investment by other firms—also
made Jardine Matheson a possible takeover target. Li Kashing made a bid for
Hongkong Land. Jardine fought to protect itself by buying 40% of Hongkong
Land's attending shares. The Land Company retaliated by buying 40% of Jardine
Matheson. The mutual hostage-taking moves were protective—and very costly.
They were made to protect the Keswick family's interest in Jardine Matheson. To
protect these interests in the longer term, Jardine Matheson adopted a more aggressive management stance: more stringent controls on investment projects
through governance structures like Jardine Strategic; the public sacking of executives who had worked in property, oil, and shipping (when the areas they represented were divested); the reorganization of Hongkong Land; and the removal of
corporate headquarters from Hong Kong to Bermuda, to ensure the firm would be
under British law and under a different takeover code.

In its public acknowledgment of the failure, Jardine Matheson blamed its ignorance of the extent of the contracts Hongkong Land held for highly speculative real
estate development projects. (Hongkong Land did not operate on equity accounting convention; hence, its investments were not transparent to Jardine Matheson.)
The "judgment" of former Jardine Matheson taipan David Newbigging was called
into question, and Newbigging was fired. The failure in Jardine Matheson's view
was lack of information, or failure to pursue information, necessary to make sound
financial judgments. Unlike episodes in the prepublic history of the firm, this failure of the public company had a significant impact on Jardine Matheson's reputa-

tion and the reputation of the firm's owner, the Keswick family—who perceived the reputation of family and firm to be one and the same.

Encouraging Initiative While Curbing Opportunism

In the Penrosean view, initiative or "enterprise" is rewarded, and opportunism is more often depicted as opportunity—the opportunity to extend the firm's interorganizational linkages to include a new, but familiar, business partner with known and consistent business behaviors, making partners out of a competitors. Bringing potential competitors into their orbit—making collaborators of competitors, like Dent and Russell and Butterfield & Swire—served Jardine Matheson's interests very well. Collaboration opened new opportunities for shared investment and access to information from different markets and reduced the risk of price and shipping rate fluctuations.

In the 20th century, Jardine Matheson built a network of trade and equity-based relationships with associated Hong Kong and ASEAN firms. As the network builder, Jardine Matheson encouraged the initiative of local firms that it served as a single source for financial services, insurance, and shipping. In building this network or "external organization," Jardine Matheson made itself indispensable to manufacturers, retailers, and service establishments alike, who could expect credit terms of up to two years. The advantages derived from the ongoing relationship were perceived by its members to be greater than the gains of opportunistic behavior. Another source of managerial initiative and potential opportunism was Jardine Matheson's cadre of agents in the field and managers at headquarters and in the branch offices.

Jardine Matheson's early taipans were attentive to the training and disciplining of those who would be the keepers and brokers of the firm's reputation. Instruction in company routines and desired behavior was conducted via frequent management letter and, whenever possible, in person. Agents were strongly discouraged from speculating on their own behalf. They would be reprimanded or, like John Shilaber and E. de Otadui, might be visited by a Jardine associate with a mandate to set the business straight.

In the early 20th century, representative offices might be closed if the firm could not control its associates from speculating on their own behalf, losing the company's money, and endangering its reputation. Nevertheless, entrepreneurship was strongly encouraged, as in the story of David Newbigging and the cadet-run profit centers told in Chapter 6. Associates with high potential were groomed for senior management and given cross-functional and cross-geographic experience to round out their knowledge and understanding of Jardine Matheson's businesses and build social capital that would make them effective directors and, eventually, members of the board. The average term of employment with Jardine Matheson was 20 years or more; the average length of time to a board seat from associate director was 4 years; the average length of time on the board was 12 years. Employment with Jardine Matheson is another example of a long-term relationship built on trust, where the advantages outweighed the potential rewards of opportunism.

Penrosean theory recognizes that the best managers need to be compensated to remain with the firm to grow firm business. The key issue is incentive-compatibility. The distribution of knowledge in the firm (and among members of its external organization) may provide opportunities for individuals to gain by concealing or misrepresenting their private information, while reducing overall efficiency. However, restoring efficiency allows for gains all around, and so "farsighted" contracting permits the design of incentive structures that ensure disclosure of private information, if necessary, by putting the owner of this private information in charge. Examples of this behavior include the comprehensive education of Jardine Matheson's high-potential managers who were groomed for leadership, or creation of a board seat on the board of Jardine Matheson & Company for the head of the Hongkong Land Company after the mutual stock swap and takeover attempt in the 1980s.

How Jardine Matheson Raised Funds for New Investments

In the Penrosean view, raising funds, when necessary, is part of the managerial or entrepreneurial task. This task might be accomplished through an "external organization" in which the raising of funds is relatively easy—or through intrafirm boards that review and approve fund-raising projects.

From 1885 to 1961 Matheson & Company, the firm's freestanding investment house, raised funds from European and American investors to finance new projects, like the silk and textile mills in China and Japan and mining expeditions in Africa, Spain, and Korea. The "freestanding" investment house handled investments in other companies, as well as all investments in projects discovered by, or operated by, Jardine Matheson & Company.

From 1961 to 1972, all of Jardine Matheson's investment was internally financed. During the Exploit and Develop period, 1972–1977, the firm borrowed to support growth. Jardine Matheson established aggressive hurdle rates for acquired firms and sold nonperforming investments within three years, returning the proceeds of asset sales to reserves for future growth.

From 1980 and through 1996, Jardine Matheson redesigned its corporate structure a dozen times, as discussed in Chapter 4, to reduce risk and contain costs as well as to allow subsidiary and associated firms to continue to fund-raise outside the Jardine Matheson orbit.

In 1987, to even out the spread of profits and reduce risk, Jardine Matheson created a novel governance form—the holding company reporting to a holding company parent and paying a fixed return to the parent. Jardine Strategic reduced the risk in Jardine Matheson's portfolio. It was further found that Jardine Matheson's use of Jardine strategic to manage its high-risk subsidiaries—indeed, the use of holding companies for this purpose—actually added financial value to the firm without additional governance cost and provided subsidiaries the opportunity to raise their own equity.

CONTRIBUTION OF THIS STUDY TO THE HISTORY OF ECONOMICS AND SUGGESTIONS FOR FUTURE RESEARCH

This study has used the Penrosean view to interpret the historical development of a major company, explaining that firm's sustainability and the consistency of its strategic practices, policy, and management. The choice of a trading firm underlines the importance of this category to the development of the international services business.

The multinational trading company is also a worthy target of study because of its contribution to foreign direct investment and the GDP of the nations in which it owns assets, employs agents, and intermediates trade.

Recently, researchers like Casson and Roehl and Hennart have applied transaction cost theory to an analysis of trading companies, identifying information asymmetry and opportunism as important considerations for diversification into nontrading activities. The trading company has had greater coverage among business historians, from the previously mentioned Mira Wilkins and Stanley Chapman and Geoffrey Jones.

What makes the early trading firm an interesting candidate for a Penrosean interpretation is, first and foremost, the lack of working capital needed to get into business (the nonexistence of entry barriers), the perception of productive opportunity (managerial enterprise) independent of licenses and exclusivity contracts and physical assets (no ownership advantage), and the development by private traders, like Jardine Matheson, of simple decision rules for profit and growth in highly uncertain times (the existence of strategic management). These rules were to avoid speculation and use other people's money.

The decision rule "avoid speculation" was critical to the development of reputation, immensely important to customers at a vast distance from the goods to be bought or sold on their behalf. What was speculation and what was wise investment was often a fine line to draw, the difference between the two being history, experience, the shared knowledge of peer firms, and the counsel of partners in the firm. This decision rule was the basis of Jardine Matheson's sustainability through the credit crises of the early period and the dismemberment of the Hongkong Land Company after the stock swap and takeover attempt of the 1980s. Jardine Strategic was created in 1986 to control the speculative behavior of the firm's high-growth businesses, the Hongkong Land Company and its formerly associated businesses, the Mandarin Oriental chain and Dairy Farm.

The decision rule to seek external investment capital was critical to growth and sustainability. Tying up your own money in a single venture meant that it was unavailable to pursue other opportunities as they came along, that your fortunes rose and fell with a single "stock." Pursuing this decision rule made Jardine Matheson a collaborator, a risk-sharer, more often than a competitor in the ASEAN. This decision rule was the basis of the development of an external organization based on long-term trading relationships and minority equity holdings.

The use of Penrosean theory as an interpretive framework for strategic management in Jardine Matheson & Company does not diminish the importance of uncertainty and risk. Since the necessary conditions for Penrosean theory are highly imperfect knowledge and cognitive limitations, any intentionally comprehensive strategy must include more than the development and application of capabilities; it requires the management of uncertainty, which is a question both of productive and marketing capabilities and of governance. The simple decision rules discussed earlier were intended to manage uncertainty, while building the firm's knowledge-based capabilities. There is an unavoidable tension between uncertainty and knowledge. Jardine Matheson's decision rules were created to make the firm the best negotiator of this tension on behalf of its customers, partners, and investors. Penrosean theory views the constraints on governance to be (1) the perception of productive opportunities, which depends on entrepreneurial skills operating on developing capabilities, and (2) the receding managerial limit. In Penrose's theory, raising funds is part of the managerial/entrepreneurial task and essential both to the pursuit of opportunities and the reduction of the managerial limit to expansion. In Jardine Matheson, the managerial fund-raising task was expanded by the creation of an 'external organization' in which the raising of funds was relatively easy, "using other people's money." In the early period, this took the form of Matheson & Company, a freestanding investment house. In the mid-1970s, this was accomplished through minority equity holdings in hundreds of firms in a cluster of industries in Hong Kong and the ASEAN. While the relationship with Jardine Matheson was advantageous, providing services and favorable credit terms, each of the associated firms was forced to fund-raise on its own behalf. In 1980s and 1990s, the creation of a new governance model, Jardine Strategic, imposed on managed firms the obligation to seek funding outside the Jardine Matheson orbit. In each of these cases this external organization was the result of strategic choice.

Unlike Farjoun, Palepu, Montgomery and others cited in this study who looked at physical relatedness and skills relatedness of acquired business for an explanation of the acquirer's growth and profitability, I am convinced that the quantification (in the sense of who buys what from whom, let us say) of the patterns of relationships built by Jardine Matheson & Company would add support to the argument of conscious strategic choice. An increase or decrease in the value of relationships to Jardine Matheson would result in a change in strategy—and possibly the emergence of a new network builder from the existing network, or outside it. More than the interrelatedness of resources and capabilities, the external organization through which these resources and capabilities are deployed is the real differentiator and source of new growth opportunities and the sustainability of the firm.

In 1998, I asked former managing director Jeremy Brown, how e-business would change the asset intensity of Jardine Matheson's Asian business operations. He responded that the relationship with China required continued high levels of physical asset ownership, if not investment. But, in fact, in the last three years, Jardine Matheson has been extending its architecture and creating "virtual networks" for supply chain, customer relationship management, and financial services—services that have been the firm's historic source of wealth and the basis of its reputation.

Based on the preceding discussion of external organization—and the worldwide growth of e-business—it is not surprising that Jardine Matheson, through the computer services division of Jardine Pacific (JardineOneSolution), has partnered with CommerceOne Bank to provide internet-based supply chain and procurement services to trading partners like Swire Pacific in Hong Kong and China through a virtual trading company e-marketplace called Asia2B, a new virtual market institution for putting business service providers and customers together at low risk. Founded in March 2001, Asia2B is a joint venture comprising SUN Microsystems eVision, the Swire Group, New World China Enterprises, Beijing Enterprises Holdings, and CommerceOne. The partnership provides collaborative commerce, procurement, and fulfillment services, using the Internet to correct the inefficiencies in the traditional supply chain. The trading portal comprises many industries including aviation, automotive supply chain, building materials, computers and components, fixed and wireless telecommunications, hotels, medical and health-care products, retail, shipping, and logistics.

JardineOneSolution is the largest IT hardware, software and services provider in Hong Kong at $500M US/annually. Jardine OneSolution (JOS) has also formed of a joint venture with TELUS International Inc., a wholly owned subsidiary of TELUS Enterprise Solutions Inc., one of Canada's leading IT consulting and outsourcing services providers to provide information technology (IT)-related consulting, customer relationship management (CRM) and enterprise resource planning (ERP) and e-Procurement outsourcing to Hong Kong and China. The Jardine/Tellus joint venture is 75% owned by Jardine OneSolution and 25% by TELUS International. The joint venture has an initial focus on the Hong Kong market and will expand into the nearby region after establishing itself in Hong.

In 1997, Jardine Matheson sold its financial services company Jardine Fleming to Chase Bank for US$1.2 billion. In 2002, Jardine Matheson is rebuilding its financial services business, under the leadership of David Keenan, recently of UBS Warburg. Jardine's new financial hub provides secure Internet banking and mortgage banking services to consumers and businesses globally.

Using its historic capabilities—including architecture and reputation—and competences—including financial management, risk brokerage, and retail—Jardine Matheson continues to grow and to innovate, linking its business customers to each other and to end users in an increasingly virtual marketplace. Cementing these relationships are Jardine Matheson's historic "agency services," financing, insurance, and distribution services. The firm is living example of the Penrosean view: making decisions that build on historic capabilities and exploit opportunities in the marketplace, learning from failure, creating new market institutions, relying on an internal and external organization to deliver business value and manage uncertainty, fund-raising for growth and encouraging continued innovation.

In 2003, Jardine Matheson was an Asian multinational, with a range of activities encompassing financial services, including insurance, transportation services, distribution and marketing, property, motor trading, hotels and retail grocery and drug—and continuing to absorb business risk for its network of suppliers and buyers. The Jardine Matheson of 2003 was not the powerhouse of strategic intent it was in the 1970s but a resilient firm with a sustainable business model committed to building the wealth of its managers, member network, and large investors.

For Jardine Matheson, the recent Asian financial crisis and economic downturn were externalities, like many in the firm's history, that might be ignored, managed, require the investigation of multiple scenarios—or, at worst, require a change in strategy. In fact, the crisis impacted Jardine Matheson both indirectly and directly: indirectly by necessitating the imposition of stricter credit restrictions on the firm's East Asian suppliers and buyers and potentially changing the configuration of its value net, its network of external relationships through which the firm provides value to its customers; directly reducing the demand for Pacific trade, travel, property and hotel—major industries in which the firm competes—and forcing a recomposition of Jardine Matheson's investment portfolio, and, again, directly, through changes to the international accounting standards to which even firms domiciled in Bermuda like Jardine, Matheson are subject.

This case of the evolution of a 19th century-trading and investment firm into a 20th-century conglomerate demonstrates the close relationship between the various kinds of resources with which the firm worked and the development of the ideas, experience, and knowledge of its managers and founders. Over time, their changing experience and knowledge affected not only the productive services available from the firm's original "agency" services, namely, banking and financial services, marine insurance and shipping, but also the perceived "demand" for these services relevant to its 20th-century investments in the development of manufacturing and service economies of Hong Kong and the ASEAN.

The story of Jardine Matheson's 20th-century growth supports a Penrosean view in which expansion must draw the productive services, including entrepreneurial services, of the firm's existing management; consequently, the services available from such management set a fundamental limit to the amount of expansion that can be either planned or executed even if all other resources are obtainable in the market.

Jardine Matheson's failures (most notably, the asset sales and house cleaning after the Hongkong Land affair of the mid-1980s) and performance disappointments during the later period are explained by the uncertainty and incomplete knowledge that underlie managerial decision making in the Penrosean firm. Managers make fallible conjectures, and, knowing that they may not have complete information, must make the best decisions they can. Uncertainty will limit expansion only to the extent that managerial resources are limited. Each new activity undertaken by the firm requires an increased input of managerial services, not only to obtain sufficient information but to develop sufficiently well worked out plans to reduce risk. Jardine Matheson's long-lived reputation for risk management contributes to its reputation, to its value as a trading partner, and hence to a distinctive capability that remains of critical importance to the market, but it also constrains the firm's managerial resources and, therefore, the firm's expansion plans. The greater the risk or uncertainty, the greater is the managerial task. Hence, the expansion plans of a firm are necessarily restricted by the capacity of management.

What began as a dense network of affiliative and cooperative relationships in the 19th century, held together through written communication, were seamed in the 1970s by minority investments that provided a balance of administrative control and autonomy for associated firms. Failure in the mid-1980s engrossed the firm's managerial resources in the development of more stringent risk management programs, including review boards and control mechanisms, like the cross-board shareholding scheme that is Jardine Strategic, to preserve the firm's distinctive capability, its reputation for financial management. This capability is both a source of sustainable advantage to the firm and a constraint on managerial resources.

Selected Bibliography

ARCHIVAL SOURCES

Canton Register, 1827–1843. Microfilm, Library of Congress, Washington, DC.
East India Company Archives, India Office Records. British Library Oriental and India Office Collection.
Jardine Matheson Archives, Private Letter Books and Unbound Correspondence, Cambridge University Library.
Jardine Matheson Annual Reports 1961–2002.

BOOKS AND JOURNAL ARTICLES

Amit, R. and J. Livnat. "Diversification Strategies, Business Cycles and Economic Performance." *Strategic Management Journal* 9 (2): 99–110.
Bergh, Donald D. and Gordon F. Holbein. "Assessment and Redirection of Longitudinal Analysis:
Demonstration with a Study of the Diversification and Divestiture Relationship." *Strategic Management Journal* 18 (7): 557–571.
Barney, Jay. "Strategic Factor Markets: Expectation, Luck and Business Strategy." *Management Science* 32 (1986): 1231–1241.
Blake, Robert. *Jardine Matheson: Traders of the Far East.* London: Weidenfeld & Nicholson, 1999.
Casson, Mark C. (1982). "Transaction Costs and the Theory of Multinational Enterprise." In Alan M. Rugman, ed., *New Theories of the Multinational Enterprise.* London: Croom Helm, 1982: 10–28.
Chandler, Alfred D. *Scale and Scope.* Cambridge: Belknap Press, 1990.
Chapman, Stanley D. "The International Houses: The Continental Contribution to British Commerce 1800–1860." *The Journal of European Economic History* 6 (Spring 1977): 5–48.

——. "British-based Investment Groups before 1914." *Economic History Review* 38 (1980): 230–251.

——. *Merchant Enterprise in Britain: From the Industrial Revolution to World War 1.* Cambridge: Cambridge University Press, 1992.

Chatterjee, Sayan and Birgir Wernerfelt. "The Link between Resources and Type of Diversification: Theory and Evidence." *Strategic Management Journal* 12 (1991): 33–48.

Chen, Edward K. Y. "Hong Kong's Role in Asian and Pacific Economic Development." *Asian Development Review* 7 (1989): 26–47.

——. "Changing Patterns of Financial Flows in the Asia-Pacific Region and Policy Responses." *Asian Development Review* 10 (1992): 46–85.

——. "Economic Restructuring and Industrial Development in the Asia-Pacific: Competition or Complementarily?" *Business and the Contemporary World* (Spring 1993a): 67–88.

——. "Foreign Direct Investment in East Asia." *Asian Development Review* 11 (1993b): 24–59.

Davis, R. and I. M. Duhaime. "Diversification, Industry Analysis and Vertical Integration: New Perspectives and Measurement." *Strategic Management Journal* 13 (1993): 511–524.

Demaree, Allen T. "The Old China Hands Who Know How to Live with the New Asia." *Fortune* (November 1971): 133–135.

D'Cruz, Joseph and Alan Rugman. "A Theory of Business Networks." In L. Eden, ed., *Multinationals in North America.* Calgary: University of Calgary Press, 1994.

Dunning, John H., ed. *Governments, Globalization and International Business.* New York: Oxford University Press, 1997.

Dunning, John H. and Rajneesh Narula. *Foreign Direct Investment and Governments.* London: Routledge, 1996.

Farjoun, Moshe. "Beyond Industry Boundaries: Human Expertise, Diversification and Resource-related Industry Groups." *Organization Science* 5 (1994): 185–199.

——. "The Skill and Physical Bases of Relatedness." *Strategic Management Journal* 19 (1998): 611–630.

Gerlach, Michael L. *Alliance Capitalism: The Social Organization of Japanese Business.* Berkeley: University of California Press, 1992.

Goldberg, Walter H. *Ailing Steel: The Transoceanic Quarrel.* New York: St. Martin's Press, 1986.

Gomes-Casseres, B. "Group versus Group: How Alliance Networks Compete." *Harvard Business Review* (July–August 1994).

Greenberg, Michael. *British Trade and the Opening of China, 1800–1842.* Cambridge: Cambridge University Press, 1951.

Gulati, Ranjay, Nitin Nohria, and Akbar Zaheer. "Strategic Networks." *Strategic Management Journal* 21(2000): 203–215.

Gull, E. M. *British Economic Interests in the Far East.* New York: Institute of Pacific Relations, 1943.

Harvey, Charles E. *The Rio Tinto Company.* Cornwall: Allison Hodge, 1981.

Hiroshi, Shimizu. "Evolution of the Japanese Commercial Community in the Netherlands Indies in the Pre-War Period (from Karayuki-san to Sogo Shosha)." *Japan Forum* 3 (April 1991): 9–56.

Hoskisson, Robert E., Richard A. Johnson, and Douglas D. Moesel. "Corporate Divestiture Intensity in Restructuring Firms: Effects of Governance, Strategy and Performance." *Academy of Management Journal* 37 (1994): 1207–1251.

Hsiao Liang-lin. *China's Foreign Trade Statistics, 1864–1949.* Cambridge: Harvard University Press, 1974.

Jones, Geoffrey. *British Multinational Banking, 1830–1990.* Oxford, UK: Clarendon Press, 1993.

——. *Merchants to Multinationals.* Oxford: Oxford University Press, 2000.

Jones, Geoffrey and Judith Wale. "Merchants as Business Groups: British Trading Companies in Asia before 1945." *Business History Review* 72 (1998): 357–408.

Kay, John. *Foundations of Corporate Success.* London: Oxford University Press, 1993.

Keswick, Maggie, ed. *The Thistle and the Jade.* Hong Kong: Octopus Books, 1982.

King, Frank H. H. *The History of the Hongkong and Shanghai Banking Corporation.* Vol. 1: *The Hongkong Bank in Late Imperial China, 1864–1902.* Cambridge: Cambridge University Press, 1988.

——. Vol. 3: *The Hongkong Bank between the Wars and the Bank Interned, 1919–1945.* Cambridge, UK: Cambridge University Press, 1988.

——. Vol. 4: *The Hong Kong Bank in the Period of Development and Nationalism, 1941–1984.* Cambridge: Cambridge University Press, 1991.

Knight, Frank H. *Risk, Uncertainty and Profit.* Boston: Houghton Mifflin, 1921.

Lazonick, William. "Innovative Enterprise and Historical Transformation." *Enterprise & Society* 3 (2002): 3–47.

Lefevour, Edward. *Western Enterprise in Late Ch'ing China.* Cambridge: Harvard University Press, 1968.

Lifson, Thomas. "A Theoretical Model of Japan's Sogo Shosha (General Trading Firms)." *Proceedings of the Academy of Management* (August 2–5, 1981): 69–73.

Loasby, Brian J. "Edith T. Penrose's Place in the Filiation of Economic Ideas." *Oeconomia* 29 (1999a): 103–121.

——. "The Significance of Penrose's Theory for the Development of Economics." *Contributions to Political Economy* 18 (1999b): 31–45.

——. "Market Institutions and Economic Evolution." *Journal of Evolutionary Economics* 10 (2000b).

——. "Organizations as Interpretive Systems." *Revue d'Economie Industrielle* 97 (4th Quarter, 2001): 17–34.

——. "The Evolution of Knowledge," DRUID Conference, Denmark, May 11, 2001.

Marshall, Alfred. *Principles of Economics.* London: Macmillan, 1920.

Matheson, James. *Present Position and Prospects of the British Trade with China.* London: Smith, Elder, 1836.

Napier, Christopher. llies or Subsidiaries. *Business History* 39 (1997): 69 3.

Palepu, Krishna. "Diversification Strategy, Profit Performance and the Entropy Measure." *Strategic Management Journal* 6 (1985): 239–255.

Penrose, Edith T. "The Growth of the Firm—a Case Study: The Hercules Powder Company." *Business History Review* 34 (1960).

——. *The Theory of the Growth of the Firm.* New York: John Wiley & Co., 1995.

Pitelis, Christos, ed. *The Growth of the Firm: The Legacy of Edith Penrose.* Oxford, UK, 2002.

Richardson, George B. "The Organization of Industry." *Economic Journal* 82 (September 1972): 883–896.

Sheard, Paul. "The Japanese General Trading Company as an Aspect of Interfirm Risk-Sharing." *Journal of the Japanese and International Economies* 3 (1989): 308–322.

Sugiyama, Shinya and Milagros C. Guerrero. *International Commercial Rivalry in Southeast Asia in the Interwar Period.* Monograph 39, Yale Southeast Asia Studies. New Haven, CT: Yale University Press, 1994.

Waverman, Leonard, ed. *Corporate Globalization through Mergers and Acquisitions.* Calgary: University of Calgary Press, 1991.

Wernerfelt, Birger. "A Resource-based View of the Firm." *Strategic Management Journal* 5 (1984): 171–180.

Wilkins, Mira. "The Free-standing Company, 1870–1914: An Important Type of British Direct Foreign Investment." *Economic History Review*, 2nd ser., 41 (1988): 259–282.

Williamson, Oliver F. *The Economic Institutions of Capitalism: Firms, Markets, Relational Contracting.* New York: Free Press, 1985.

Wray, William D. *Mitsubishi and the N.Y.K., 1870–1914.* Cambridge: Harvard University Press, 1984.

Yashuda, Michael. *The International Politics of the Asia Pacific.* London: Routledge, 1996.

Yeung, Henry Wai-Chung. *Transnational Corporations and Business Networks.* London: Routledge, 1998.

Yonekawa, Shin'ichi. *General Trading Companies: A Comparative and Historical Study.* Tokyo: United Nations University Press, 1990.

Yoshino, M. Y. and Thomas B. Lifson. *The Invisible Link: Japan's Sogo Shosha and the Organization of Trade.* Cambridge: MIT Press, 1986.

Yu, Tony Fu-Lai. *Entrepreneurship and Economic Development in Hong Kong: The Key to China's Open Door Policy.* London: Routledge, 1997

Yun-Wing Sung. *The China-Hong Kong Connection: The Key to China's Open Door Policy.* Cambridge: Cambridge University Press, 1991.

ONLINE SOURCES

CIA. *World Factbook 2003.* "China." http://www.cia.gov/cia/publications/factbook/geos/ch.html

CIA. *World Factbook 2003.* "Malaysia." http://www.cia.gov/cia/publications/factbook/geos/my.html.

Index

ABOUT THE AUTHOR

CAROL MATHESON CONNELL is Senior Strategy Consultant for IBM and a descendant of James Matheson, co-founder with William Jardine of Jardine Matheson & Company.